A17000 112301

Other books by Geoffrey Skelton

WAGNER AT BAYREUTH: EXPERIMENT AND TRADITION

WIELAND WAGNER: THE POSITIVE SCEPTIC

Editor (with Robert L. Jacobs): WAGNER WRITES FROM PARIS . . .

CONTENTS

Acknowledgements   9

Introduction   11

PART ONE: THE GERMAN ROOTS

  1 1895–1913: Origins and Early Years   25
  2 1914–18: A Musician in Wartime   40
  3 1919–22: The Breakthrough   56
  4 1922–27: Early Mastery   70
  5 1927–32: Music to Sing and Play   85

PART TWO: SEMI-EXILE

  1 1933–34: A Trial of Strength   105
  2 1935–37: The Unintentional Ambassador   125
  3 The Craft of Musical Composition   142
  4 1937–40: Good Music and a Clean Conscience   154

PART THREE: LAND OF LIMITED IMPOSSIBILITIES

  1 1940: Settling In   173
  2 The Teacher and his American Students   189
  3 1941–45: Musical Activities in America   201
  4 1945–47: Harmless New Englander   215

PART FOUR: DUAL NATIONALITY

  1 1947–53: A Visitor to Europe   231
  2 A Composer's World   246
  3 1953–57: A New Career as Conductor   261
  4 1958–62: Discord and Reconciliation   277
  5 1963: The Final Year   288

Bibliography   297

Chronological list of works   299

Gramophone recordings made by Hindemith   308

Index   311

PAUL HINDEMITH

THE MAN BEHIND THE MUSIC

A Biography

by

GEOFFREY SKELTON

LONDON
VICTOR GOLLANCZ LTD
1975

ISBN 0 575 01988 3

VVH 584.
Sk 26p

Printed in Great Britain by
The Camelot Press Ltd, Southampton

LIST OF ILLUSTRATIONS

All photographs acknowledged P-H-I are reproduced by kind permission of the Paul-Hindemith-Institut, Frankfurt/M.

facing page

Paul Hindemith with his parents and sister Toni (*P-H-I*)   64

Paul Hindemith with members of the summer orchestra in Heiden, Switzerland, 1914 (*P-H-I*)   65

Paul Hindemith as a soldier in the First World War, 1918 (*P-H-I*)   65

Paul Hindemith's musical handwriting: (*a*) from his sketchbooks: passage from unpublished Piano Sonata, Opus 17 (1920); (*b*) clean copy: passage from *Nobilissima Visione* (Troubadour's Song) in his own arrangement for piano (1938) (*both P-H-I*)   96

Paul and Gertrud Hindemith in 1924, the year of their marriage (*photo: E. Hoenisch, Leipzig, P-H-I*)   97

Paul Hindemith at Boston on his first visit to the United States, 1937 (*Egone Photo, Boston, P-H-I*)   97

Paul and Gertrud Hindemith in Minneapolis, 1945 (*photo: Minneapolis Star, P-H-I*)   160

Paul Hindemith with pupils Sam Bonaventura and Yehudi Wyner at the Yale School of Music, 1953 (*photo: C. T. Alburtus, Yale University Hindemith Collection*)   160

Mural painted by Hindemith in May 1953 for farewell party in his New Haven home (*photo: C. T. Alburtus, Yale University Hindemith Collection*)   161

Christmas and New Year greetings card, 1950 (*P-H-I*)   161

Hindemith's handwriting: passages from letter to Dame Edith Sitwell (*courtesy British Museum, London*)   192

Hindemith conducting, Munich, 1957 (*photo: Rudolf Betz, Munich, P-H-I*)   193

Paul and Gertrud Hindemith, 1958 (*photo: Anton Fischer, Waldhofen, P-H-I*)   193

ACKNOWLEDGEMENTS

IN GATHERING MATERIAL for this book, I am much indebted to the following: the Hindemith Institute in Frankfurt (Director: Dr Dieter Rexroth) and the firm of Schott in Mainz; the Hindemith Collection at Yale University (Director: Professor Luther Noss); and the Osborne Collection in the Bienicke Library, New Haven—all of whom allowed me unrestricted access to the documents in their possession. The British Broadcasting Corporation has kindly permitted the use of interviews made by me in 1968 for a radio feature on Hindemith.

My thanks are also due to the following individual persons with whom I have either spoken or corresponded (listed in alphabetical order): Mrs Phyllis Bauer, Professor Howard Boatwright, Dr Arnold Cooke, Mrs Gabriele Flesch, Dr Max Flesch-Thebesius, Mr Lukas Foss, Mr Walter Legge, Mrs Margret Lowe, the late M. Darius Milhaud, Mr Carl S. Miller, Professor Luther Noss, Mrs Osea Noss, Dr Dieter Rexroth, the late Mr Franz Reizenstein, Herr Günther Schneider-Schott, Professor Bruce Simonds, Mr Kurt Stone, Mr Peter Ustinov, Dr Arno Volk, Sir William Walton, Mr Thornton Wilder, Dr Emanuel Winternitz.

I have also made grateful use of already published reminiscences by individuals who knew Hindemith personally. Some are printed in book form, some in periodicals and some recorded on tapes preserved in the Hindemith Collection at Yale University. In all these cases the source is indicated in the text of my book or in the bibliography at the end.

And finally I wish to thank the Phoenix Trust for financial aid enabling me to carry out my researches.

G. S.

INTRODUCTION

PAUL HINDEMITH IS one of the dominant musical figures of
the twentieth century. A vastly prolific composer, his works
ranging from little pieces for children up to operas of imposing
proportions, he was also a practising musician, both as violist
and as orchestral conductor, an influential teacher in both
Europe and America, and a writer whose books, whether
educational or literary, are among the most revealing written
on the subject of music.

It is possible, perhaps, to be all these things without being of
much interest as a human being—possible, but not very likely.
The purpose of this book is to portray the human being, and in
setting that as my aim I am conscious that I am defying the
wish of Paul Hindemith himself. He was more than reticent
about his private life: he was downright secretive. To all who
suggested a biography of him he invariably returned the
answer: "Anyone who wishes to know about me should look at
my works." But it was he himself, in a lecture on Johann
Sebastian Bach, who observed: "About his human qualities
his musical works are quite naturally a poor source of
information."

He appeared to regret this fact. "What we get from biographies of Bach too readily fosters our inclination to take the
statue for the living being," he observed. "He became that
banal figure which meets our eyes every day: a man in a full-
skirted coat, with a wig he never lays by. . . ." So I have felt
justified in trying to do for him what nobody did for Bach
during his lifetime or shortly after his death: to provide an
account of the man while memories of him are still alive.

However, this will be no book of mere reminiscences. I myself
did not know Hindemith personally, but I have talked with
many people who did. If I were to confine myself to their
anecdotes alone (of real assistance to me though these have
been) I should probably produce a figure as banal as the accepted view of Bach. No full-skirted coat and wig would emerge,
but a stocky, bald-headed man of boundless energy, for ever
joking, with or without a musical instrument in his hand.
Hindemith did indeed possess immense humour, which in the
circumstances of his life was just as well, but he did tend, both

in his social and in his professional activities, to use it as a protective device to conceal his deeper feelings.

Beneath the sturdy façade there was a contemplative, profoundly serious artist. That is no new discovery, since it is evident in so many of his works (the song cycle *Das Marienleben* for instance, and the two largest operas *Mathis der Maler* and *Die Harmonie der Welt*). To that extent Hindemith was right in directing our attention to his music as a guide to his essential self. However, music is not good at conveying facts, and for more concrete evidence of this hidden self I have had to seek more explicit sources. I have found them in his own writings—his books, his opera librettos, his lectures and his correspondence—though with regard to this last I must point out that much of it, including the letters to his wife Gertrud, is not yet accessible. He was a good letter writer, and with two of his friends in particular—his German publisher Willy Strecker and his American lawyer Oscar Cox—he often let the mask of facetiousness fall and revealed the sensitive character beneath.

What has become evident to me through a study of all these sources is the extent to which Hindemith's being was dominated and regulated by music. He lived and breathed music as naturally and involuntarily as all of us breathe air. For him music was not only a part of living, as it may have been even for some of the greatest composers, it was the whole of life. He seems to have had neither time nor inclination for non-musical distractions of any but the most ephemeral kind, and consequently there are no scandals in his life (unless he kept them very well concealed) on which a biographer can seize to enliven his pages. On the other hand, he was anything but a dry and silent figure, sitting at a desk unconcernedly turning out music as the world went by.

The reason he was not, lay in his conception of what music is: a divine gift, of course, but one as necessary to mankind as the very food we eat. In his view it was the social duty of the musician, as of any good farmer, to make his products not only as good as possible, but accessible—even (if I may dare use such a dangerous word in this context) palatable. This does not mean making concessions to those of lesser intelligence for the sake of fame or financial reward; it means expressing oneself as clearly as one can in order to make oneself understandable. And to express oneself clearly one needs skill. Hence Hindemith's lifelong insistence on the need for technique and the constant desire to increase his skill.

His teaching was the instrument with which he achieved this object. He believed that a part of the artist's social duty lay in passing on his discoveries to younger generations. But there was profit in teaching for himself too, for it gave him a group of guinea-pigs on whom to try out his experiments. It also had its creative uses. In an interview made at the time he was lecturing at Harvard University, he was asked whether he considered teaching to be detrimental to composition. He replied (according to the *Harvard Crimson* of 29 November 1949): "Myself, I cannot compose all the time. I don't get ideas just sitting around waiting for them. They come from somewhere, and I get them teaching."

He was a remarkable teacher, but also, for all but the strongest, a dangerous one. Even a cursory glance through his educational books will reveal his talent for explaining things clearly and interestingly, mainly by the use of apt and striking metaphors. His pupils, both in Europe and in America, bear witness to the invigorating effect of his classes, to his unrelenting insistence on sheer hard work made bearable by his high spirits, and his interest in and involvement with each one of them individually. The danger lay in the fact that his personality was so forceful and his style of writing so very much his own that his pupils were tempted into copying him. All young American composers, Aaron Copland complained at the time Hindemith was teaching at Yale University, seemed to be writing Hindemithian music.

Yet, as he constantly protested, this was not his intention at all. He advocated no particular style of composition. His fundamental belief was that in music tonality was a physical law as inescapable as the force of gravity. What he set out to do, as a teacher, was to free the notes of the existing musical scale from their traditional associations and, by examining their acoustical relationships, discover a coherent pattern which would enable a composer to use them in a different, but consciously controlled, way. The manner in which the composer then manipulated these notes lay entirely in his own hands.

Hindemith's ideas on the materials of music will of course be dealt with in greater detail later in my book. The point to establish here is that these ideas were the product of his own practical nature and of his conception of the artist as a person who had at one and the same time to be the master of his tools, but the servant of his art.

If this point is understood, it is easier to assess his own musical development. He was born into the very end of the Romantic era, and was certainly not alone among the composers of his day in feeling the need for a new approach to music. There were Schönberg and Stravinsky and Bartók, to mention only the names which, together with his, were most in the forefront in the first half of the twentieth century. Popular opinion lumped them all together and called them atonalists, which really meant nothing more than that they all made use of sounds and progressions which were unfamiliar—not intermittently (which even the accepted composers did), but all the time. Atonality is of course a meaningless term: all music, as Hindemith asserted, is constructed of tones and must therefore logically be tonal. Where his doubts lay was whether, all the old traditional laws having been overthrown, the music thereafter produced possessed a tonality consciously willed by the composer or whether, in the intoxication of his new-found freedom, he was merely running wild. In other words, did he really know what he was doing?

He himself, even in his earliest compositions, claimed to know at least what he intended to do, though he was not so sure of his technical ability to do it. His first guide was his ear alone. Later, through his teaching and with the help of his pupils, he set about analysing what he and others of his contemporaries had done, seeking to find an ordered basis for it which would act as a yardstick, both for himself and others. The discoveries expounded in the first volume of his book *The Craft of Musical Composition* were only the beginning of this process. He continued it throughout his life and died without completing it: inevitably, of course, for the road he was treading had no ending, as he knew. But he was always going forward: he cannot accurately be described as the youthful iconoclast who turned with advancing age into a comfortable reactionary. The differences between his first significant compositions and his last, apart from the expected traces of youthful high spirits and elderly sobriety, are the differences of technical skill and increased refinement in the use of it.

His own style is unmistakable, as is that of any great composer. But his range is wide, not only in terms of form, but also in content. He was not rhythmically adventurous: what Stravinsky once called his "setting-up exercises" and other critics his "motorised" rhythms are conspicuous in the sonatas and concertos and even in some of the larger works such as the comic opera *Neues vom Tage*. But they are much less obtrusive in works such as *Das Marienleben*, *Mathis der Maler* and the *Ludus Tonalis* for piano, which are just as characteristic of him. Nor will they be found in the slow movements of any of his instrumental works, from the earliest to the latest. In these the mood is inward-looking and the feeling profound, yet always rigidly controlled.

The same restraint that governed his relations with his fellow men—another word for it would be pride—is at work in his music. He did not wear his emotions on his sleeve. And, however far he may have ranged in his harmonic journeys, he always came back with the concluding notes of a piece to a simple tonic chord, depositing the listener after a flight into imaginative realms back on firm ground. This was not a mannerism, nor a secret capitulation to traditional ideas, but the confirmation of an artistic conviction. As he expressed it in *The Craft of Musical Composition*: "Music, as long as it exists, will always take its departure from the major triad and return to it. The musician cannot escape it any more than the painter his primary colours or the architect his three dimensions. In composition, the triad or its direct extensions can never be avoided for more than a short time without completely confusing the listener."

These last words provide an important clue both to Hindemith's conception of what music is and to his manner of writing it. It was the musician's task, as he saw it, to communicate, and this could not be done by solitarily pursuing sounds into unfamiliar regions with no thought for the difficulties of those struggling to follow on behind. These must be given both the ability and the will to join in the spiritual adventure. He diagnosed two forms of musical isolationism: music which, because of the obscurity of its language, one could not grasp; and music which, because of its technical difficulty, one could not play. He detested them both.

His own music is never too difficult to sing or play. It may often demand a high measure of technical ability, but it is never made (or made to sound) deliberately difficult just in order to excite the admiration of the listener for the performer. The reason for this is that Hindemith saw music as an *active* social occupation. He wanted people to make music: merely to listen to it was not enough.

Out of this belief arose what has come to be known as *Gebrauchsmusik*, a word Hindemith himself heartily disliked and one which, as he justifiably complains in *A Composer's World*, has led to a great deal of confusion and misunderstanding of his intentions. He once used the word which, as he observes, is "in German . . . as hideous as its English equivalents, workaday music, music for use, utility music, and similar verbal beauties", in a discussion with some German choral conductors. In warning them of "the danger of an esoteric isolationism in music", he stressed the need for new works in a contemporary style which children and beginners could use to familiarise themselves with new styles of composition and thus come nearer to understanding them. Practical as always, he himself set about composing suitable simple vocal and instrumental pieces which were published, together with pieces by other composers (including Milhaud) under the title *Das neue Werk* (New Work). And, indefatigable as he also was, he soon found himself composing the lion's share of this music, both within and outside the framework of *Das neue Werk*. He called these works for children and amateurs (written between the years 1927 and 1932) *Sing- und Spielmusik* (English title: *Music to Sing and Play*), and they range from simple violin pieces in the first position to more ambitious choral and instrumental works. The two best-known compositions in this series are the musical play for children *Wir bauen eine Stadt* (English title: *Let's Build a Town*) and *Lehrstück* (English title: *Lesson on Consent*), the latter to a text by Bertolt Brecht.

All these works were written, as one would expect, in Hindemith's usual musical style, still clearly recognisable however much simplified. The trouble arose when the word *Gebrauchsmusik*, adopted by others, was extended to describe the *style* rather than the function of these pieces. It was then, because of the similarities of style, superficially applied to virtually the whole of his music, arousing the impression—in those who were unable or unwilling to look for themselves—that Hindemith's aim in life was to provide a sort of practical "workaday" music, good enough for a background, but not to be listened to with any degree of concentration. This is manifestly unjust not only to his works as a whole, but also to the pieces written for children and amateurs themselves, which contain a high proportion of fine and deeply-felt music.

Hindemith wrote a lot of music, as did both Bach and Mozart, the two composers with whom he would probably most wish to be compared. In the output of all three there is much that is mere routine (though in saying that I am not forgetting that the routine works of the great might well be more rewarding than the masterpieces of the lesser fry). There are other resemblances: both Bach and Mozart were practising musicians: they played instruments in public, and they composed a lot of works for particular occasions. The idea of the composer living in isolation, patiently or impatiently awaiting inspiration, was a product of the Romantic era. Hindemith, rebelling against that idea, deliberately went back, for his interpretation of a musician's function, to the eighteenth century and earlier, when the task of a composer was to create and play music for present use (and to pass on his example to the young). If in the course of his daily work inspiration chose to visit him, that was a matter for strictly private rejoicing.

The eighteenth century and earlier also shaped Hindemith's musical style, once he had tired of the undisciplined freedom of his earliest composing years. It is polyphonic and contrapuntal, but it is never mere imitation. He regarded singing as "the most natural of musical utterances" and at all stages of his life wrote a lot for the voice, seeing in this the most direct way to persuade people to *make* music, not just to listen to it.

Readers who are interested in a detailed analysis and assessment of the music itself are directed to biographies other than mine: to Heinrich Strobel and Andres Briner in German and to Ian Kemp in English (they will find details in the bibliography at the end of this book). I do not ignore the music (how could I when writing about a man whose whole life *was* music?), but I have deliberately refrained from examining it in isolation, preferring to concentrate my and the reader's attention on the man as he wrote it. I have devoted a chapter each to the two main literary works, *The Craft of Musical Composition* and *A Composer's World*, since they contain so much direct evidence of the man behind the music, and I have not neglected the librettos, written by himself, of the two major operas *Mathis der Maler* and *Die Harmonie der Welt*, both of them dealing with the dilemma of the individual in times of social disturbance. Each has strong autobiographical traces. There can surely be no doubt that the words Hindemith puts into Mathis's mouth, stressing that a man's duty is above all to remain true to himself, are a reflection of his own innermost convictions:

> Dem Kreis, der uns geboren hat, können wir nicht
>   entrinnen,
> Auf allen Wegen schreiten wir stets in ihm hinein.
> Über uns zeigt sich ein weiterer Kreis:
> Die Kraft, die uns aufrecht erhält.
> Was wir auch beginnen, sollen wir uns echt bewähren,
> Muss unser Tun nach beiden Mitten weisen.
> Lasst uns dem Boden danken.
> Lasst uns den Himmel preisen.

("We cannot escape the sphere into which we are born: on all our paths we tread within it. Above us can be seen another sphere: the strength that holds us upright. In whatever we begin we must keep our integrity, directing our acts to both centres. Let us thank the earth. Let us praise heaven.")

Like his two operatic heroes, Matthias Grünewald the painter and Johannes Kepler the astronomer, both historical figures, Hindemith was born into a time when social unrest made the arts seem of no immediate relevance. Had the artist, as an individual, any significant contribution to make with his art? Was it not his duty to join his fellow mortals in direct battle rather than to seek to stand aside in isolation, committed to none? In the First World War his country turned him into a soldier but, as he later said, it gave him no pride to wear the Kaiser's uniform. He was never a patriot, yet he was deeply attached to his German roots, and the true test came when his country was taken over by a totalitarian regime which he thoroughly disliked. He tried hard to arrange a *modus vivendi* with the Nazis—not for material reasons, but because he was a German and could not willingly sever himself from his German roots. He was defeated because he was unable to bring himself to grovel. His pride was fierce.

The full story of his struggles with the Nazis is told in the second part of this book, and it presents a picture that differs in many ways from the version hitherto accepted. He was not a voluntary exile, yet the fact that he at last decided to sever his ties with Germany was not due to the fact that his wife was half-Jewish. This consideration does not in fact seem to have played any part in his decision. It was financial necessity, not political conviction, that drove him in 1940 to emigrate to the United States.

The four parts into which I have divided my book reflect what I have come to see as the central spiritual problem of his life: a man's inability, as he expressed it in Mathis's words, to escape the sphere into which he was born. His physical being was rooted in the German soil that had produced Bach and Beethoven as well as Grünewald and Kepler, yet his spiritual self, like theirs, was striving to speak to all humanity across the meaningless barrier of national boundaries. Art was the uniting force which could raise mankind above its petty temporal considerations and bring it closer to the universal harmony of which it is an infinitesimal part. Hindemith believed, religiously, in the presence of an eternal order (his music is a clear expression of that belief), but he was aware of the human limitations that made it so difficult to acknowledge and so impossible to understand.

He expressed the predicament of the mortal being confronting the mystery of life in his opera *Die Harmonie der Welt*. These are the words of Kepler, his astronomer hero, as he lies dying:

Was trieb mich, von meiner Liebsten Abschied
Zu nehmen, wegzuschweifen mehr und mehr,
Schuldeinzug, Forschung, Staatswohl als Vorwand?
Und war doch nur, das reine klare Lied
Irdischen Wohlklangs einmal zu hören.
In meiner Seele hab ich's nie gekannt.
So trieb mich's, dort es aufzustören,
Wo es nicht war, und ungläubig zu fliehn,
Wo es im engsten, bei den Meinen
Vertraut sich mir zu bieten schien.
Gross sollt es erklingen, nicht im Kleinen,
Und ich half selbst dem Hochverrat dafür.
Ungenügsam sucht ich, mit Neugier

Zu sehn, ob die geahnte Harmonie
Zur Tat gebracht, zur Regel werden könnt,
Was ich zeitlebens nie
An mir erfuhr, Erbarmen hätte,
Sich unterwürfe.
Und muss sehn am End:
Die grosse Harmonie, das ist der Tod.
Absterben ist, sie zu bewirken, nicht.
Im Leben hat sie keine Stätte.

("What drove me to take leave of my beloved, to wander further and further abroad, with debts, research, state business my excuse? It was only to hear for once the pure clear song of earthly euphony. In my soul I never knew it. So I was driven to seek it where it was not, and in unbelief to flee from where, among my own, it seemed familiarly to beckon. Large it should sound, not in little things, and I myself helped to betray it. Unsatisfied, I sought curiously to see—yet never could— whether the harmony I sensed could be translated into deeds, defined in rules, could take pity, could submit. And at the end I see: the great harmony is death. To effect it, we must die. In life it has no place.")

We need not take this too directly as autobiographical. It is a tragic formulation, to fit the operatic story, of the basic human dilemma. Hindemith himself was not a tragic figure. The practical side of his nature and his abundant humour enabled him to deal positively with the situations into which circumstances forced him. As a soldier in the First World War he did not fight, but played quartets to his colonel; ostracised by Nazi Germany, he went off to Turkey to organise a music school; exiled to the United States, he settled down cheerfully to train its young composers; back in Europe after the Second World War he eventually overcame his sense of rootlessness by exploiting the advantages of his dual nationality. In all this there were of course moments of strain and uncertainty, but finally his ability to take an interest in what he was currently doing came to the rescue.

He enjoyed life. Always open to its influences, he could accept what it placed in his way and additionally find the means of putting it to the service of his art. One can find in all his creative work a reflection of this process of mutual exchange. The little *avant garde* musical societies in Germany before which he mainly appeared during the Twenties produced a succession of chamber works and orchestral works for small combinations; the festivals at Donaueschingen and Baden-Baden brought experiments with mechanical instruments; his connection with the German Youth Movement, vocal and instrumental works for children and amateurs; his years in America, large orchestral works suitable for a land dominated by crack symphony orchestras and star conductors; and so on. If his life had taken a different course, some of these works might not have been written. In place of them there would have been others, which would no doubt have expressed the different circumstances. One can be sure, however, that these hypothetical compositions would—as all the existing ones do—have borne the unmistakable stamp of his personality, to which he always, whatever the circumstances, remained true.

His works are a reflection of that inner integrity which only those who are unsympathetic to it would call obstinacy. His inability, for instance, to see any merit in Schönberg's twelve-tone system does suggest a certain narrowness of mind, though —in view of the strength of his own musical beliefs—one can hardly be surprised by it. He lived to see the younger generation following Schönberg rather than himself, and this, it has been suggested, embittered his final years. But in his final lecture, delivered in Bonn in the year of his death, the tone was not bitter. On the contrary, it was defiant, and full of hope. One day, he clearly stated, composers would acknowledge that the language of music had its limits as surely as the language of literature, and learn to live with the fact. They need not fear: its physical limitations had never hindered, nor need they ever prevent the artist from expressing new things. "The inexhaustibility of artistic creators is the inexhaustibility of human thought itself, and if a musician has received the gift of presenting his fellow mortals with an image of this inexhaustibility in his own way (and subject to the limitations of his time and material) and with each work conjures up for them a small universe, then he has fulfilled his artistic task. But not if he hides himself behind aurally incomprehensible formulae and contents himself, for his own pleasure, with the mere technical solution of sound problems."

This is a purely factual statement to which no one need take exception. The most one might do would be to agree to differ with Hindemith about the point at which experimentation ceases to be legitimate. But he himself had no need to feel bitter just because some composers (and by no means all) chose to ignore the laws of tonality he had gone to such pains to bring up to date both in his books and in his music. If those who devotedly copied his style in the belief that they were adopting his ideas failed to make an impact, that did not prove him wrong or in any way reduce his own significance. The important thing is that his ideas were valid for himself and enabled him, in a long line of works, to express himself in a way that commands attention. The works still command attention and will continue to do so. And composers will continue to go to them, whether they acknowledge it or not, to find out how he did it, to learn from him and to try to improve on him.

In doing so they will be following his own example. He himself spoke in *The Craft of Musical Composition* of "that inner strife whose aim is the perfection of one's own work". He was a man who, born into a transitional time of more than usual turbulence, clung with courage, humour, pride and boundless energy to an artistic ideal and, by remaining true to himself and his ideas, came through. He is thus, I think, in addition to being a significant musical figure, a remarkably resilient example of a twentieth-century man.

PART ONE

THE GERMAN ROOTS

Chapter 1

1895–1913:

ORIGINS AND EARLY YEARS

THE NAME HINDEMITH is an unusual one. Among the first things his publishers wanted to know, on accepting his earliest compositions, was whether it was a real or an assumed name. Paul Hindemith did not reply to the question. His brief biography for Schott's publicity department gave merely the date and place of his birth and a few details of his musical education and career. Yet to obtain information about his origins, one does not need to go far—only indeed as far as his own personal papers.

It is surprising that Hindemith, reticent to the point of neurosis about his private life, should have spent time and money in working out his family tree. His researches had nothing to do with the Nazis (who, as we know, used to insist on proof of their more prominent citizens' "Aryan" origins), for they preceded Hitler's rise to power by nine years. Hindemith began them in 1924 with a letter of enquiry to the mayor of Naumburg—not the famous old town on the river Saale, but a smaller market town in Silesia on the river Queis to the north-east of Breslau. Here, he told the mayor, he had spent some of his childhood years, in the home of his grandfather.

In that year (1924) Hindemith married Gertrud Rottenberg, who came of a family of higher social standing than his own. Her maternal grandfather, named Adickes, had been a mayor of Frankfurt, and an earlier Adickes was a member of the Diet in the post-Napoleonic years, when the city was the seat of the German Confederation. Hindemith, conscious of the plebeian origins of his own parents, might have been tempted to go in search of something in his more distant pedigree to match the distinction of his wife's.

By 1930, when he seems to have lost interest in the subject, he had traced his ancestry back as far as the sixteenth century, an unbroken line of male Hindemiths, all of whom had lived and worked in one small corner of Silesia. There they had

married their neighbours' daughters and followed their trades
as carpenters, saddlers, butchers, undaunted by the political
upheavals which have always plagued this part of Europe,
intermittently Austrian and German, and now Polish. The
Hindemiths were quite prolific, yet the family name has remained confined virtually to this one small area, giving the
impression that they were a solid, respectable but unambitious
clan, not much troubled by imagination.

And this is indeed what Paul Hindemith's grandfather
appears, from the only known reminiscence we have of him, to
have been. The evidence is contained in a letter written by one
Franz Kalkmann to the composer in 1948. Kalkmann was a
childhood friend of Paul Hindemith's step-uncle Karl, and his
letter was simply that of a person who was proud of having once
had a slight connection with a famous man and wanted him to
know it. Hindemith had no sympathy or patience with acquaintances of this sort, and his usual reaction was simply to write
scoffing comments on their letters before filing them away un-
answered. There are no such comments on Kalkmann's, so one
can perhaps assume that Hindemith felt his reminiscences to be
reasonably accurate.

In his references to the composer's grandfather, Carl Wilhelm
Paul Hindemith, Kalkmann provides a picture of a quiet and
respected elder citizen, a merchant who had lived all his life in
the little pottery town of Naumburg, and had been rewarded
towards the end of it with the position of *Amtmann*, or senior
councillor. He was a staunch Protestant, and his youngest son
Karl played the violin in church. So did Karl's friend, Franz
Kalkmann, and after rehearsals they went to the *Amtmann*'s
house, where his kind and comfortable wife fed them with home-
made cakes. Above the front-door there was a glass panel
bearing the words *Grüss Gott, tritt ein, bring Glück herein!* (God be
with you, come in and bring happiness). These words had been
painted there by Karl's older brother Robert Rudolph, whom
Kalkmann described as "a talented artist". Robert Rudolph
was Paul Hindemith's father.

Paul Hindemith's only marginal comment on Kalkmann's
account is a large exclamation mark pencilled beside the words
inscribed on the glass panel, and this gives the impression that
the composer's reluctance to talk or write about his early childhood was in some way connected with the character of his

father. Robert Rudolph Emil Hindemith, born on 15 May 1870, was the third surviving son of Carl Wilhelm Paul's first marriage, and his mother was a Catholic. The *Amtmann*'s wife mentioned by Kalkmann was Robert Rudolph's step-mother.

Beside his talent for painting (for which there is no evidence beyond Kalkmann's account), Robert Rudolph had a great love of music, and he played the zither. His artistic gifts were, however, insufficient to get him anywhere. He left home as a young man and went to complete his education in the province of Hessen. There, having achieved no more than the status of a certificated housepainter, he met and married Marie Sophie Warnecke, who was two years older than himself. Sophie came of a long line of sheep farmers and was born in Stammen on 29 January 1868. She, like her husband, was a Protestant. The couple settled in Hanau, where on 16 November 1895 their first child, Paul Hindemith, was born.

Hanau, before its almost total destruction in the last months of the Second World War, was a pleasant little industrial town on the river Main a few miles east of Frankfurt, with a castle and an elegant eighteenth-century town hall. Its main claim to artistic fame is that it was the birthplace of the brothers Grimm, the writers of fairy tales, and later of Paul Hindemith. To Robert Rudolph Hindemith, however, it was no more than a temporary place of work. Not long after Paul's birth, his parents moved to the nearby village of Niederrodenburg, where, on 20 February 1898, his sister Toni was born. Another move two years later, to Mühlheim on the river Main between Hanau and Frankfurt, coincided with the birth, on 9 January 1900, of their third and last child, Rudolf.

There is a discrepancy in the records at this point of time. According to *Paul Hindemith: Zeugnis in Bildern* (Testimony in Pictures), a biographical volume issued in 1955 by his publishers Schott with the composer's consent, the move to Mühlheim took place in 1901 following a year spent in Naumburg. It is of course possible that Paul had been sent at this time (as at later periods) to be taken care of by his grandparents, and rejoined his parents after they were established in Mühlheim. According to the same source, the family moved from Mühlheim to Frankfurt in 1902, but an end-of-term report from the local school in Mühlheim shows that both Paul and his sister Toni were still pupils there in 1905, and a news-paper account asserts that Paul received his first music lessons from a teacher in Mühlheim named Eugen Reinhardt. What-ever the place (and Frankfurt and Mühlheim are after all close enough to permit children living in one to attend lessons in the other) all sources appear to agree that Paul began to receive regular music lessons in 1904, when he was in his ninth year.

Less important anyway than the actual places is the picture that emerges of Robert Rudolph Hindemith, still a young man and probably restless by nature, moving to wherever work was to be found in or around Frankfurt in an effort to provide for his wife and growing family. The photographs of that period still in existence betray no outward signs of poverty, but they are obviously studio portraits, all participants being dressed in their best clothes and photographer's props brought in to heighten the effect of respectability. Beneath the beard and the more copious hair of the father one can detect something of the determination and doggedness, perhaps even the high spirits, that characterised his son at a similar age, while his mother's plain features suggest a reserved and level-headed nature. The economics of life might often have been very difficult for the couple, but there is nothing to give the impression that their difficulties were due to fecklessness. On the contrary, they were both in their different ways proud people. A biographical sketch marked "strictly confidential" in the Schott files (it appears to have been drafted as evidence for the Nazis of Hindemith's humble but "truly German" upbringing) reveals that on one occasion when Robert Rudolph was out of work, friends and neighbours made a collection to enable his children to continue their musical education. He returned the money untouched. His family's upkeep was his responsibility, he declared, and where necessary the boys would help themselves.

Possibly Robert Rudolph's pride and spirit of independence may have led him to place a greater burden of duty on his three children than was good for them at a very early age. And his own frustrated longings as a musician may have induced him to force their musical talents, of which all three children showed early signs. Kalkmann in his letter recalls seeing Paul Hindemith for the first time (unfortunately he gives no date) when he gave a performance in Naumburg together with his sister and brother. They were billed as the *Frankfurter Kindertrio* (Frankfurt Children's Trio): Paul and his sister Toni played violins, Rudolf the cello, and they were accompanied on the zither by their father. Kalkmann, like other members of the audience, bought a postcard of the trio (one presumes in place of an admittance fee), but later lost it, and no further copies of this interesting piece of evidence have yet come to light.

Further evidence of Robert Rudolph's grim determination to make musicians of his children is provided by Eberhard Preussner, a Viennese musicologist who in 1952 was invited by Schott's to write a monograph of the composer. Preussner's first chapter, submitted to Hindemith for his approval, was enough to revive all his old reluctance to disclose the secrets of his early family life, and he vetoed it. "Of the biographical details he should take only the essential and inevitable facts," he wrote to the publishers, "and otherwise restrict himself to what he knows himself about my life and work. That is enough."

It is hardly surprising that Preussner, thus constrained, abandoned his monograph altogether, and nothing remains of it but a bare synopsis and a typescript of the first chapter. This may have been rejected by its subject, but one is entitled to assume that the facts contained in it were not invented by Preussner, but were told to him, if not by Hindemith himself, then by his wife at second hand. Preussner's account of the childhood period confirms the story as so far told—the poverty and the insecurity of the house-painter and his wife against the respectable and idyllic family background of Naumburg. Robert Rudolph is described as a man "full of internal conflict, bordering on the tragic", his wife Sophie as "the point of rest". She was of a happy disposition, self-assured and self-possessed, whereas he was harder and stricter. But it was he who, for all the lack of money, occasionally took the children to the Frankfurt Opera, walking a large part of the way to save on fares. He told them in detail about the works they were going to see and on the way home would question them closely to find out how much they had understood. If their answers were stupid or dense he would punish them with slaps.

If this is so, one must conclude that Robert Rudolph, for all his good intentions, committed the sin against his children of turning what should at their age have been a pleasure into a grim duty. His sons must indeed have been deeply musical to have eventually adopted the life of musicians instead of throwing it to the winds at the first opportunity. Their sister Toni, described by Preussner as a good pianist (and, since Kalkmann described her as a violinist, she must have shared to some extent her brother Paul's versatility), was the only one to drop her music in adult years. The children no doubt found some comfort with their mother, to whom they remained devoted to the end of her long life, but she was by all accounts an undemonstrative person, and she does not seem to have been actively opposed to the spartan conditions of her children's upbringing.

There is later evidence, of an indirect but quite valid sort, showing what effect this joyless childhood had on the outlook and character of Paul Hindemith himself. In the year 1913, when he was in his late teens, he began to write short plays, which were performed by himself and his friends in private during the summer holidays. All the plays are burlesques of one sort or another, and they have no real literary merit—in fact, one could describe them even as immature for their author's age. What is, however, remarkable about them is the ever-recurring theme of the pressure of duty, illustrated usually by reluctant young people being forced to practise on musical instruments. One of the plays, entitled *Das Leben dringt in die Zelle* (Life Invades the Cell), is about a monk who is instructed to write a song for a religious ceremony. Having no ideas, he offers to sell his soul to the devil in return for a melody. In the course of the play he reveals that he entered the monastery in order to escape from music, and in particular from a father who throughout his childhood had interpreted all his actions, good or bad, as proof of his remarkable musicality. Another play is based, as the author notes on his manuscript, on actual happenings, and it reveals a rough and rather turbulent domestic life dominated by music and the constant exhortation to practise.

The whole series of plays, written over a period of about seven years and described facetiously by their author on the title page of the manuscripts as *Dramatische Meisterwerke* (Dramatic Masterpieces), culminates in a longer piece in verse entitled *Das Bratschenfimmel* (The Viola Craze). In this an unhappy young bank clerk resolves to kill his hated boss by playing the viola in his presence until he can stand it no more. At the time he wrote this piece Hindemith was already twenty-five, and he had now learned a few things about dramatic techniques, especially Expressionist ones. To accomplish his aim, the bank clerk goes around collecting violas by fair means or foul. During the operation a number of people perish, but the boss remains obstinately alive. In the end the bank clerk is reduced to despair and commits suicide by putting his head into a lavatory pan and pulling the chain on himself.

There are obvious psychological defence mechanisms at work here, and all the high spirits cannot hide the basic suffering and the loneliness which the play betrays. The underlying message seems to be that life is harsh, and the only way to deal with it effectively is to protect vulnerable emotions by concealing them or, better still, laughing at them.

This attempt to pry into the carefully guarded secrets of Hindemith's childhood has led me far beyond childhood years, leaving so far untouched those aspects which he regarded as the only ones of any significance—the facts of his musical education. He began regular violin lessons, as we have already noted, in 1904 with a teacher in Mühlheim. After that—in either 1906 or 1907 (Hindemith himself seems to have been uncertain)—he went on to study with Anna Hegner in Frankfurt. Anna Hegner, whose older brother Otto was a well-known concert pianist, was herself a very capable violinist and led a string quartet of her own in Basle, her native city. Successful while still only in her twenties, she almost certainly accepted Paul as a pupil on account of his talent and not because of the fees, which would presumably have been beyond Robert Rudolph's shaky resources in any case. She has left no known reminiscences, but it is clear from the fact that in his adult years Hindemith frequently visited her at her home in Switzerland that the relationship between teacher and pupil was a harmonious one. It lasted less than two years when, on leaving Frankfurt, she introduced the boy, still no more than twelve, to Adolf Rebner who, besides being a teacher at the Hoch Conservatorium, was concertmaster of the Opera and a member of the Museumsquartett in Frankfurt.

Unlike Anna Hegner, Rebner did later write down some reminiscences, which can be read in the *Hindemith-Jahrbuch I* of 1971. At his first audition in 1907, he tells us, Paul played one

of the Kreutzer studies and the Cavatina by Raff. "I immediately recognised the boy's remarkable talent. He was a quiet
but very attentive pupil, and his progress was so amazing that
in a comparatively short time he was able to make his mark at
concerts in the Frankfurt Conservatorium with performances of
such works as the Bach Chaconne and the Beethoven Violin
Concerto."

This rather startling assertion is no more than a slight
stretching of the truth. As Peter Cahn in his detailed study of
Hindemith's early years in Frankfurt (*Hindemith-Jahrbuch II*,
1972) has established, Hindemith did play both works, but not
until the years 1914–16, by which time his study at the Conservatorium was drawing to its close. But his earlier appearances
at the school concerts are impressive enough, including as they
did trio sonatas by Handel and Corelli in 1909, a Tartini sonata
in 1910 and the first movement of Mozart's D Major Violin
Concerto in 1911. At first he studied privately with Rebner,
since he had still to complete his ordinary education at the
elementary school at Mühlheim. He left that school at the age
of thirteen and, with the help of a scholarship, joined Rebner's
violin class at the Conservatorium in the winter of 1908. A
photograph of the class taken in the following year and reproduced in *Paul Hindemith: Zeugnis in Bildern* shows a frail-looking
boy in a sailor-suit, flanked by five buxom young ladies, a few
maturer male students behind. Rebner revealed in a letter
written after Hindemith's death that the sailor-suit was a gift
of his own to his penurious young pupil.

Dr Hoch's Conservatorium, to give it the name that was
inscribed across its flat classical façade, owed its name to the
benefactor who endowed it. Although not the oldest music
school in Frankfurt, it had assumed a leading position from the
year it first opened in 1878 under the directorship of Joachim
Raff. That prolific composer, of whose music little is still
remembered except the Cavatina which Paul played to Rebner
at his first audition, had assembled a distinguished group of
teachers, among them Clara Schumann and Humperdinck.
The same high standards were maintained by Raff's successor
Bernhard Scholz, even if, during his long period as director
(1882 to 1908), his methods and his outlook became increasingly
conservative. On his retirement the directorship was taken
over by Ivan Knorr, who had been professor of theory at the

Conservatorium since 1883. Knorr, a composer of operas as well as the author of musical textbooks, was a man of a more progressive frame of mind. Among the reforms he introduced (and of which Paul Hindemith, entering the school in the same year —1908—was to feel the benefit) were the establishment of a good school orchestra, a class for conductors and instruction in instrumentation techniques and musical analysis. Living composers of whom his predecessor would have disapproved, such as Debussy, Max Reger and Richard Strauss, were both studied and played.

Rebner, though appointed to the Conservatorium during the Scholz era, was both a practising musician and still a young man in his early thirties when Paul joined his class. His somewhat soulful and romantic attitude to music may later have irritated his pupil and led to a break between them, but in the years of study their relationship was one of affection and trust. During his first two years at the Conservatorium Paul studied only violin-playing, though the course included harmony as well as active participation in the orchestra and chamber music groups. Nevertheless, he had already started to compose, and the list of works he produced before beginning to study composition officially is imposing: it included a string quartet, two piano trios, three sonatas for violin and piano as well as extended works for cello (no doubt with his younger brother in mind) and for piano. Most of these compositions no longer exist, but the final page of one of the piano trios is reproduced in the volume *Paul Hindemith: Zeugnis in Bildern*. Harmonically unadventurous, it is inscribed at the bottom of the page with the date of completion (1.2.10) and beside it the relieved remark: *Endlich!* (At last!).

Outside the family circle Paul was intensely shy about his compositions. Preussner, in the uncompleted monograph which I have already cited, tells us that he would go from shop to shop in Frankfurt, buying a small amount of music paper at each, for fear that people might suspect that he imagined himself to be a composer (he also helped himself out of both this dilemma and the expense of buying paper by writing on staves ruled by hand, as the manuscript of the piano trio shows).

Rebner only gradually became aware that his pupil was interested in composing. He gave himself away by "for instance asking me to explain certain technical problems not directly

B

connected with the 'teaching material', or by beginning involuntarily to embellish on the violin a melody he had just played, to change its harmonies or to improvise on it". Rebner continues: "I encouraged him to show me his compositions, which he tended to conceal among his violin scores. In spite of his usual confidence in me, it appeared to be by no means easy for him to overcome his reserve; and so he was all the more pleased when I advised him to write a piece for violin, which he could then play himself at the Conservatorium's end-of-term concert."

Rebner as usual gives no dates, so it is impossible to know whether his encouragement in that instance produced definite results. Cahn's researches reveal that the first piece by Hindemith to be performed in a school concert was written for piano, not violin. It was a set of variations and was performed on 5 July 1913 by a fellow student, Heinrich Knettel. By that date, however, Paul was already studying composition officially.

His teacher was Arnold Mendelssohn, whose father had been a cousin of Felix Mendelssohn-Bartholdy. He must have joined the staff of the Hoch Conservatorium in a temporary capacity, for his main work was done in Darmstadt, where he was in the service of the Grand Duke of Hesse. He came to the Hoch Conservatorium in 1912 and in 1913 was already gone. All the same, he left an undying impression on his young pupil, both in relation to the technical doors he opened and to the awe-inspiring nature of his outward appearance. Now approaching his middle fifties, he was a large and imposing figure with a walrus moustache and fierce eyes under bushy grey eyebrows. He was always dressed in a formal black suit, and across the wide expanse of his chest hung a gold watch-chain. The Grand Duke is reported to have said that Mendelssohn was the only man he knew whose mere presence could reduce him to bashfulness.

The mixed feelings which Mendelssohn inspired in young Paul can best be illustrated by quoting a letter which Hindemith wrote to his former teacher on the occasion of Mendelssohn's seventy-fifth birthday in 1930. By that time Hindemith was himself a professor and, at the age of thirty-five, a composer with an international reputation. But his letter seems in the choice of words to suggest the persisting influence of those defence mechanisms which always tempted him to hide emotional feelings under a facetious barrier:

"I often think of you and look back with much pleasure and a little nostalgia to the times when I was privileged, so to speak, to suckle at your breast. You perhaps do not realise how important that short year under your guidance was for me—and why should you, for you had other things to do beyond treating one small pupil as a great occasion. And if I were to tell you, I should find myself perilously close to a confession of love: such things are hardly fitting for men of serious mind."

After Mendelssohn's departure from Frankfurt, Hindemith studied composition with Bernhard Sekles. The differing impact of the two men on their young pupil has been interestingly analysed in the *Hindemith-Jahrbuch II* by Peter Cahn (to whom I owe a great debt in this account of Hindemith's college career). Mendelssohn concentrated primarily on musical forms, and was content to allow his pupils to write in whatever style they chose. Of Hindemith he is reported to have said: "Once this turbulent must has cleared, it will produce a wonderful wine." Sekles took a stricter line. He was of the opinion that free composition should be discouraged until the technical means had been mastered, and he insisted that all his pupils' exercises, which included fugues and chorales in strict four-part counterpoint, should be written in the style of named classical composers. Though Hindemith chafed under this discipline (as his sarcastic note—"Long live sequences!"—on the manuscript of a string quartet movement in the manner of Felix Mendelssohn-Bartholdy reveals), it is significant that, when he himself came to teach, he followed Sekles's method rather than Mendelssohn's: one of the constantly recurring complaints of his pupils, both in Europe and America, was that Hindemith would never allow them to write in their own style.

Sekles, born in 1872 and thus of the generation of composers which includes Debussy and Richard Strauss, was himself a product of the Hoch Conservatorium, where he had been teaching since 1896, and of which he in 1923 became director. The somewhat military expression of his clean-cut face, combined with the more informal and modern cut of his clothing, suggests (in the photograph reproduced in *Zeugnis in Bildern*) a personality outwardly less formidable than Mendelssohn, but for that reason perhaps less susceptible to youthful charm. In their relationship of mutual respect there seems to have been none of the emotional undertones which characterised the student's feelings towards Mendelssohn and Rebner.

The fourth professor with whom Paul studied at the Conservatorium was Fritz Bassermann, who was in charge of all orchestral and chamber music rehearsals and also took classes in violin, viola and conducting. The oldest of them all, being already in his sixties, he was nevertheless the one with whom Paul felt most at ease, probably because he was always the practical musician, spoke in broad dialect and had a robust sense of humour. He was in fact that type of honest, down-to-earth musical craftsman that Hindemith himself later became (at least as far as his own more complicated nature permitted).

At Bassermann's rehearsals Paul was joined by his brother Rudolf, who had been admitted to the Conservatorium at the early age of ten to study cello-playing. Once there, he quickly won a reputation—even greater than his brother's—as an outstandingly accomplished instrumentalist. However, Paul had an elder brother's responsibilities, which he exercised in the manner which appears to have been common in the Hindemith household: with blows. It is recorded that, after one orchestral rehearsal in college in which Rudolf had behaved disrespectfully towards Bassermann, Paul grabbed him and administered physical punishment on the spot. However, there is no need to read any significance into this isolated instance of big-brotherly behaviour. The two were close companions and played a lot together, both outside the Conservatorium and within it. In 1911 (when Paul was fifteen years old and Rudolf eleven) they took part, as violinist and cellist respectively, in performances of a string quartet and a piano quartet by Mozart.

Of their fellow students at the Hoch Conservatorium only one later achieved wide fame as a composer: Ernst Toch. He was eight years Paul's senior, and he studied composition not with Sekles, but with Knorr. There was thus little personal contact between them, beyond the fact that Paul took part in a performance of Toch's Trio for Three Violins at a college concert in 1913. Another pupil at the time was Hans Rosbaud, who later developed into a distinguished conductor—one of the very few, incidentally, of whom Hindemith seems to have approved. In his student days Rosbaud was a composer as well as a very accomplished pianist, and he played the piano part in a college performance of his own Piano Trio in 1915, together with Paul and Rudolf Hindemith.

Paul Hindemith's youthful years do not fall into tidy patterns: his activities overlap in a way that defies any attempt to impose on them a neat chronological order. Throughout the years of their study at the Hoch Conservatorium both Paul and his brother were, outside it, professionally active as musicians, playing in taverns and in cinemas to earn money, out of which they bought their instruments and kept them in usable condition. One can perhaps assume that they spent as much time as possible away from their poverty-stricken home. Twice between the years 1909–13 their parents moved house as Robert Rudolph went in search of work to provide for their family, striving to the best of his ability to maintain respectable standards. A scribbled note, possibly in the handwriting of Paul's sister Toni, records the bare addresses and reveals that Paul was confirmed in 1911 at the Friedenskirche (a Protestant church in Frankfurt).

The brothers' social contacts outside the family home arose through their connections at the Conservatorium. Rebner, for instance, tells us that both boys were frequent visitors at his house. "I often encountered them in my children's play-room where, among other things, they had constructed a highly original marionette theatre, complete with hand-painted decorations, lighting, dolls and even some home-made Hindemith plays." One of these plays, contained in the second volume of the hand-written "Dramatic Masterpieces of Paul Hindemith", paints a faintly satirical portrait of the Rebner household, dominated as it was by quartet rehearsals at all times of day.

Another friend, who offered occasional escape from the city (and the chance of good meals) to the poor student, was a professor of philology, Karl Schmidt. He lived in Friedberg, about twenty-five miles north of Frankfurt, and was not only a good pianist, but a keen promoter of concerts of the most startling ambitiousness. The first of these at which Paul is known to have taken part was given in the little town of Lich, not far from Friedberg. The concert consisted entirely of works by Richard Strauss, and it began and ended with a performance of *Ein Heldenleben*, played on two pianos, a violin and a harmonium. The pieces in between, played by the two pianists, were *Till Eulenspiegel* and the closing scene from *Elektra*. This was of course the period at which Strauss's position as Germany's leading living composer was at its height, and one can presume that the little country town of Lich, in those pre-radio days, was glad of a chance to hear his works even in this scanty instrumentation. Paul had probably heard the works in their original form at the Museum concerts in Frankfurt, of which the Dutch conductor Willem Mengelberg was at that time in charge, and at the Frankfurt Opera, whose musical director, Ludwig Rottenberg, was a devoted Strauss supporter.

In his later American years Hindemith told a pupil that at one time he had considered *Ein Heldenleben* the greatest piece of music ever written. His instinct to hide his feelings by poking fun at what he loved seems to have been operative, however, even then. In the play *Das Leben dringt in die Zelle*, which he wrote somewhere in the years between 1913 and 1915, he introduced the character of Cravalla, a composer who believes that even such mundane things as sandwich wrappings (*Butterbrotpapiere*) can be used as instruments of artistic expression. It is interesting to note that the monk-hero of this play, based on Hindemith himself, rejects the arguments of Cravalla, who is patently derived from the Richard Strauss of the *Sinfonia Domestica*.

The first of the plays, dated 1913, was written for performance at Aarau in Switzerland, where Paul was spending a summer holiday at the home of Dr Gustav Weber, who was a great music-lover as well as being the local doctor. The play, entitled *Die Tragödie im Kino* (Tragedy in the Cinema), consists of a multitude of tiny scenes with a huge cast list ranging from Frankfurt workers speaking in broad dialect to a visiting minister. The author's sympathies—as far as any are discernible—lie nearer to the workers than to the higher classes, who are shown as either pompous or pretentious, and one feels that the poor young musician, however much he enjoyed the hospitality of comfortable Frankfurt families, retained a critical eye for their human frailties. But the writing is without real malice. If, as his later silence about his childhood suggests, there was a deep sense of repugnance, it seems to have been directed more against circumstances than against people (with the possible exception of his father). Its effect was not debilitating: the humour and the high spirits with which he had been born proved sturdy supports, and above all he had the knowledge of his creative talent.

His work, both literary and musical, was as yet derivative in style, and he had no clearly defined sense of artistic direction. The third of his plays, a skit on German opera entitled *Der verschleierte Raub* (The Veiled Robbery), contains, beside its otherwise unbroken succession of completely orthodox harmonies, only one monstrous chord, consisting of all the notes of the piano keyboard, spread across the double stave and extended by several leger lines above and below. This, he directs, is to be played by sitting on the keys. Still, however earnestly one analyses it, one can hardly read into it more than a gleeful recognition on the part of a budding composer of the infinite possibilities of musical expression.

Chapter 2

1914–18:

A MUSICIAN IN WARTIME

IN THE SUMMER of 1913 Paul received his first fully professional engagement: as first violinist in a small orchestra formed to entertain holiday-makers on the Bürgenstock in Switzerland, above the Vierwaldstättersee. In the following summer he took a similar post in Heiden, a summer resort on the Swiss side of Lake Constance. A photograph reproduced here (facing p. 65) shows a round-headed, clean-shaven eighteen-year-old surrounded by eleven middle-aged men with waxed moustaches and winged collars—his fellow players. While he was there, war broke out and he had hastily to cross the border back into Germany.

Whether it was patriotism or a desire to escape from the frustrations of his daily life that induced Robert Rudolph Hindemith at the age of forty-five to volunteer for the German army cannot be established. To the rare glimpses of him as a living person we can add only a couple more before he vanishes without trace. On the eve of his departure from Frankfurt he called on Rebner and thanked him for all he had done for "Paule"; and from France he sent on 9 July 1915 a note (now preserved in the Frankfurt city archives) authorising his son Paul, though not yet of legal age, to sign contracts on his own behalf. Very shortly afterwards (the exact date is not recorded) he was killed in Flanders.

Paul's acceptance of an engagement as first violinist in the orchestra of the Frankfurt Opera was certainly connected with the need to contribute to the support of his family during his father's absence, for his contract is dated 24 June 1915, a few days before Robert Rudolph's departure for France. The engagement meant that Paul had to give up the scholarship which had been granted him so that he could complete his studies at the Hoch Conservatorium. He did in fact continue to study there until 1917, playing in the opera orchestra at the same time. His initial earnings of 100 marks a month could have done little to improve the living standards of his family but, when his contract was confirmed in September and his position raised to that of *Konzertmeister* (leader of the orchestra), they were at least assured of security for the next two years.

He supplemented his income with private teaching, and he also played second violin in Rebner's string quartet, which gave concerts in Frankfurt and neighbouring towns. As a leader of the orchestra (or concertmaster) he took part in the series of symphony concerts in Frankfurt, known as the Museum Concerts, of which Willem Mengelberg was the permanent conductor. And at the Conservatorium, where his studies were now concentrated on composition (with Sekles) and conducting (with Bassermann), he was in 1916 awarded a prize for a string quartet (Opus 2, unpublished) which was worth 750 marks— more than half his yearly salary at the Frankfurt Opera.

The busy young man gives a vivid picture of his daily life at this time in a letter written in May 1917 to a friend, Emmy Ronnefeldt:

"Reading in your letter about ducks and geese and other menagerie beasts brings farmhouse memories from Basle and Oberhessen back to haunt me, the smell of stables and manure-heaps (begging your pardon!) crawls pleasantly up my nose and I can taste milk—real milk in huge masses! I have visions of all the remarkable activities that one lives through and shares in the country, such as grain-loading, milking, calves being born and other nice things of that sort. I get green with envy that I can't be there now too. Fields, woods, trees, brooks, villages, chickens, cows—God, how lovely it all is! And here I have to remain sitting in this miserable dump in all this wonderful weather! Terrrrible!! All day long nothing but music, snatching between whiles an hour or two of sleep when I can hardly keep my eyelids open any longer. It really is too bad! Lange (the principal leader) has been off sick for two weeks, so I am constantly in the theatre, trying to whip up enthusiasm evening after evening for works I know almost backwards. A constant succession of grand operas, and then on top of it the *Ring*. In addition to that, concerts on Fridays and Sundays and also the evenings with the Cäcilienverein [a choral society]. And all those endless rehearsals! Not to speak of that revolting red Dutchman [Mengelberg]. I really had my fill of this beastly musical hack last week! When I see this creature carving up splendid masterpieces into a collection of bowings, fingerings

and such-like instructions, with no other thought in his mind
than to show how clever he is, puffing himself up as the great
musical god looking down from his throne on all us other
earnestly striving mortals, when the music he makes is so often
unbearable—my blood begins to boil, and I frequently have to
hold myself back from dropping a dose of poison in his drink.
Not that he treats me badly—at least no worse than the others—
but that's enough to convince me what a nasty inconsiderate
person he is, and how passionately I loathe him. Last Friday we
did the Brahms D Major Symphony. I'm no great Brahms
admirer—but anything more un-Brahmslike it's impossible to
imagine: first movement brutal or sentimental, without any
feeling, the splendid second movement distorted and robbed of
all its swing, the third just empty notes and the coda of the
finale a timpani concerto with orchestral accompaniment.
Horrible! The *Titus* overture mauled, poor thing. The best was
the big *Leonore*, but that is so resilient that it always sounds
wonderful, however unmusically played. Hoffmann-Onegin
sang some Strauss songs, and in one of them I played the solo
violin part. The Sunday concert included Tchaikovsky's
Pathétique. I can imagine it done better, though this sort of
exalted music does suit Willem best. Then some Liszt songs,
sung by Mysz-Gmeiner, and again I played one of them (the
3 Zigeuner).

"Yesterday was the Cäcilienverein concert with 4 Bach
cantatas. The chorus of course was first-rate, but on the whole
I agree with the opinion of a member of the audience I heard
talking afterwards: 'It was terribly loud!'—I had three solos
that evening, and they went very well—even my enemy W.M.
couldn't help admitting it. So much for the Museum, the most
inartistic musical set-up you can imagine—next year I shall
refuse to take part in it.

"Now a bit about something more enjoyable: Rebner's and
Rottenberg's Mozart series are over. That was real music—
though I must admit I didn't care for R[ebner] at all. Frau Dr
L. calls him a café violinist in the noblest sense, and she's right.
But the Herr Doktor [Rottenberg]—there's a real musician—
when the mood is on him. He does mess about—plays things
one way, then the next time differently—but there's always
spirit in it. At least he's always musical. If only he weren't often
so pitifully helpless as a conductor!

"Irene H. comes over from Mainz every few days and visits us when she has nothing better to do. Recently I was with her in Mainz for a change, and we played piano duets of Russian music (Borodin, Glasunov, etc.) all day long together—it was great fun. We did a Schubert evening in Mainz too, which went brilliantly. Rudolf was there as well. The first movement of the B flat major Trio, the whole of the E flat major Trio and the brilliant Rondo in B minor. The reviews very good. Shortly before that we (she and I) had a long music session here (ten hours)—various old and new violin concertos, Beethoven sonatas, Tartini and other old fogeys, Schubert, etc., etc. Wouldn't you have liked to turn the pages for us? She also plays my compositions with great enthusiasm. She now does the Waltzes [for piano duet, Opus 6, unpublished] very well, we played them recently no less than seven times straight off in a row. She has also learned the Quintet [for piano and string quartet, Opus 7, destroyed] splendidly, and a short while ago we played it at Rebner's. This piece gives me tremendous joy, and I am longing to hear it properly, but at the moment I just don't feel like working on my things. All I have perpetrated in the past two weeks has been an arrangement (working out an unfigured bass) of an aria from a passion-oratorio by Keiser (16 . . to 16 . .) for Dr Schmidt in Friedberg, who has rewarded me with a letter full of praise. Yesterday he sent me yet another old score to arrange, he's having them all published.

"My cello pieces have been with Breitkopf & Härtel since last Saturday, maybe they'll be able to do something with them."

I have quoted this letter at length, for it is the first time we are able to hear the authentic voice of the young Hindemith, untouched by the later concealments and editings that make (and were designed to make) it difficult to convey the human being that lay behind the musician. Much in the letter—the slangy humorous tone, tending to facetiousness when true emotions are involved, the complete dedication to music, the nervous impatience, the energy—confirms the picture we have so far gained of him, but there is another quality that has not yet emerged in the memories recalled by his elders. Modest and shy they called him, yet his letter to Emmy Ronnefeldt shows how much this façade concealed a veritable volcano of opinions, convictions and feelings, together with a sovereign contempt for public reputations. Here, writing to a friend of his own generation and freed from the need for circumspection, he perhaps exaggerated a little. Later events, particularly with regard to the conductor Mengelberg, certainly suggest that his condemnations were not on reflection as wholesale as they here appear. But no one reading that letter could fail to recognise a personality of formidable purpose and drive.

Emmy Ronnefeldt was the daughter of a well-to-do Frankfurt family with strong musical interests. In an introduction to the letters, which have been published in the *Hindemith Jahrbuch II* (1972), she writes: "We first got to know Paul Hindemith in 1914 after the war started. . . . His father [before leaving for France] . . . visited my mother and asked whether his elder son Paul might now and again visit us as his younger son Rudolf, who took part in my piano class, was already doing." Her mother consented, and very soon both Paul and Rudolf were accepted into the Ronnefeldt family as they had previously been accepted into the Rebner family, sharing the same pastimes of theatricals and music-making. A whole notebook containing the words of parts in marionette plays, preserved in the collection of the Hindemith Institute in Frankfurt, shows with what enthusiasm the Ronnefeldt children and the Hindemith brothers pursued their hobby in their homemade *Theater zum lustigen Schlippy*. Her mother (writes Emmy in her introduction) "listened with great patience and much interest to Paul's youthful compositions, although she did not know much about music".

The names of the musicians with whom he was now playing in public show (whatever his opinion of their merits) that Paul Hindemith was, at the age of twenty, accepted as a fully-fledged violinist, beyond the stage of a promising student. The singers for whom he played solo parts—Lilli Hoffmann-Onegin (later better known as Sigrid Onegin) and Lula Mysz-Gmeiner, a Rumanian contralto, were both at the top of their profession, and the conductors, Willem Mengelberg and Ludwig Rottenberg, were, as musical directors of the Museum Concerts and the Opera respectively, the leading lights in a city which, if musically not quite in the same category as Berlin or Munich or Vienna, stood in reputation very high.

Mengelberg, at that time in his forties, combined his Frankfurt appointments with the directorship of the Amsterdam

Concertgebouw Orchestra, through which he is chiefly remembered. Rottenberg had been musical director at the Frankfurt Opera since 1892, owing his appointment, at the age of twenty-eight, to the recommendations of Hans von Bülow and Brahms, who in a letter to Clara Schumann (still in 1892 teaching at the Hoch Conservatorium in Frankfurt) described him as "a nice and sensitive soul, musically very accomplished and a very talented conductor". Born of Jewish parents in that part of the Austrian Empire known then as Bukovina (and now divided up between Soviet Russia and Rumania), he began his conducting career in Vienna. Hindemith's reference to his "occasional helplessness" on the rostrum seems all the more surprising since he not only enjoyed the respect of his orchestra, but even earned the praise of Gustav Mahler who, coming to Frankfurt in 1907 to conduct his Fourth Symphony, wrote from there to his wife: "Rottenberg did the early rehearsals and remains the same good comrade he always was." In that same year Rottenberg conducted the first performance in Germany of Debussy's *Pélleas et Mélisande*, and he was regularly given the privilege of launching the operas of Franz Schreker, then regarded as second in importance as an operatic composer only to Richard Strauss (another composer for whom Rottenberg was a dedicated protagonist). There seems no reason why, if he had wanted to, he could not have had a distinguished international career—he did in fact in 1913 appear in London at Covent Garden as conductor of Hermann Waltershausen's opera *Oberst Chabert*, which he had first brought out in Frankfurt the previous year. But in character he was a retiring sort of man who preferred to pursue his art in his own quiet way, and he remained all his life in Frankfurt, to which he became bound by family ties.

At this stage of his life Paul Hindemith does not appear to have had any social connection with Rottenberg and his wife, whose younger daughter he eventually married. His letter to Emmy Ronnefeldt does, however, introduce in passing another name which became of increasing importance in his later career. "Frau Dr L." was the wife of Dr Fried Lübbecke, a Frankfurt art historian, and under her professional name of Emma Lübbecke-Job she figured as solo pianist in many of the first concerts of Hindemith's works. He owed his acquaintance with the Lübbeckes to Rebner: they came together for the first time on 8 December 1915 at a combined lecture and music evening in Frankfurt. The Rebner Quartet played Beethoven, and Dr Lübbecke gave a lantern lecture on German art, during which, as he claims in his book *Der Muschelsaal* to have noticed, the Quartet's young second violinist showed particular interest in his slides depicting the Isenheim altar of Matthias Grünewald.

Perhaps this is no more than a product of Dr Lübbecke's imagination in the light of later events but, until we know more about the workings of the subconscious, it can be accepted at the very least as an intriguing sidelight on the origin of Hindemith's operatic masterpiece *Mathis der Maler*. His general education had been of the most limited kind, so that his knowledge of German pictorial art at the time of Lübbecke's lecture was likely to have been nil (his first visit to a picture gallery, according to the evidence of a later friend, Mrs Margret Lowe, did not on his own admission take place until several years later). Except as far as music was concerned, he was in his young years unquestionably ignorant (and therefore impressionable), and even his musical knowledge was probably restricted to the purely practical aspects. If musical history had been among his accomplishments, he would have known that Keiser, one of whose works he was arranging for Dr Schmidt in Friedberg, was an eighteenth-century rather than a seventeenth-century composer (1674–1739). However, that is perhaps being too pedantic: probably when he wrote to Emmy Ronnefeldt he just happened not to have a musical encyclopaedia beside him. . . .

The three pieces for cello and piano mentioned in his letter were first performed in May 1917 in Frankfurt by Maurits Frank, his colleague in the Rebner Quartet, and a pianist named Reuner. Hindemith's letter offering them to the publishers Breitkopf & Härtel, dated 21 March 1917, seems to be attempting to give the impression of a worldly man-to-man approach:

"I was thinking anyway of shortly going out in search of a publisher. I have been long enough working in seclusion for myself alone. Now I feel quite confident that I have long outgrown my compositional baby socks and am quite inclined on the whole to venture my first leap into the famous 'limelight'. I well know that the chance of taking that first leap is not so easy for a young and unknown musician, but I will trust to my luck, which has been kind to me for quite a while now, and keep both fingers crossed."

However, when Breitkopf & Härtel accepted his pieces and sent him the printed proofs in the summer of 1917, he was as thrilled as any other young artist in a similar position. "I was thoroughly proud," he wrote to Emmy Ronnefeldt on 16 September. "The 'Hindemith' on the title page looks colossally imposing. Just think, it might just as well have been 'Beethoven'!"

In that same year—1917—Hindemith's contract with the Frankfurt Opera came up for renewal, and the fact that he was now in his twenty-second year and could expect to be called up for military service at any time must have caused him some anxiety. However, he had the wholehearted support of his chief conductor, Ludwig Rottenberg, who wrote him a glowing testimonial: "Paul Hindemith is an unusually talented musician —I know a number of truly remarkable compositions by him— and an excellent violinist. Much can be expected of him in the future." On the strength of this his contract was renewed for a further four years at a substantially increased salary.

Within a few weeks of receiving it he was indeed called up. His army record card, dated 13 August 1917, describes him as of slim build, height 1 m. 65 cm. (equivalent to 5 ft. 5 ins.). He was sent to a barracks in Frankfurt, and from there he wrote on 6 September to Frau Ronnefeldt:

"I have acquired so much Prussian laziness that I could pass for a corporal at least. But all the same I am still only a very ordinary rookie, and as such hop around in the circus arena (alias the drill square), describing the most fantastic arcs. . . . I believe that in time I may become a quite presentable soldier. In the first week, when I found it terribly hard to get used to all this pyramidal loafing, I slept here in the barracks and made the interesting discovery that bedbugs—of which there are masses around—do not go for me. . . . But now I sleep at home, and consequently am able to enjoy two breakfasts and two suppers. . . .

"I work in the theatre as usual (but without rehearsals, thank goodness), and in that way am preserved from mental atrophy. . . . Yesterday I was on the point of being sent to

France, but objected on the grounds that I had been here only three weeks. But I won't be here much longer—I reckon another three or four weeks. I shall try in the meantime to get myself transferred to a military band in the field. I'm sure it would be much pleasanter than in the trenches."

His career as a soldier bears little resemblance to life in the German army as commonly depicted by writers on both sides. While still in Frankfurt, he could make life easy for himself by distributing free tickets to his superiors for the operas and concerts in which he was playing. Even when he was at last sent off to France at the beginning of 1918, the special position he had won for himself in the regiment continued to pay dividends. He managed to get himself a place in the military band. "I play the big drum," he wrote to Emmy Ronnefeldt on 9 February 1918, "and I am told that never before has this instrument been handled here with such rhythmic precision." He also played in a string quartet. "My fellow players," he continued in his letter, "are not exactly of the first rank, but they take tremendous trouble, so that—what with the many rehearsals I have with them—we produce quite tolerable music. Our commanding officer [Graf von Keilmannsegg], to whom we always play, is delighted. He is extremely nice to me. The day before yesterday he took me with him to Mülhausen, and throughout the journey we carried on a wonderful conversation. He is a really splendid person. In Mülhausen he presented me with a volume of Nietzsche, and also invited me to Weimar when he goes on leave."

This aristocratic colonel who (as Hindemith wrote in another letter to the Ronnefeldt family) "treats me like a friend and never parades his superiority", did more than just make his army career a tolerably pleasant one. A great lover of literature as well as of music, he doubtless filled in many gaps in the young man's education. Hindemith was a reluctant soldier. In later years he said that he had "worn the Kaiser's uniform without pride", but nevertheless his letters from France show that certain aspects of military life—the comradeship, the improvisation, the basic lack of responsibility—appealed to one side of his nature. This, however, did not go very deep: it was rather the result of his happy knack, preserved throughout his life, of being able to make the best of prevailing circumstances and to extract pleasure from whatever situation he happened to find himself in. His basic repugnance to war—which had nothing to do with fear, for he was never near enough to the front line to have been in any real danger—is revealed in the only war reminiscence to which he gave expression in later years. This anecdote, printed in *Paul Hindemith: Zeugnis in Bildern*, also involves his admired colonel, Graf von Keilmannsegg, though he is not mentioned by name:

"During my time as a soldier in the First World War I was a member of a string quartet which served our commanding officer as a means of escape from the miseries of war. He was a great music-lover and a connoisseur and admirer of French art. It was no wonder, then, that his dearest wish was to hear Debussy's String Quartet. We rehearsed the work and played it to him with much feeling at a private concert. Just after we had finished the slow movement the signals officer burst in and reported in great consternation that the news of Debussy's death [on 25 March 1918] had just come through on the radio. We did not continue our performance. It was as if the spirit had been removed from our playing. But now we felt for the first time how much more music is than just style, technique and an expression of personal feeling. Here music transcended all political barriers, national hatred and the horrors of war. Never before or since have I felt so clearly in which direction music must be made to go."

His service in the army, removing him as it necessarily did from the familiar surroundings of his earlier years, affected Hindemith in more ways than only this. Both in his compositions of the time and in the remarks he made, mainly in his letters to the Ronnefeldt family, about them, a very perceptible change can be seen. From his silence concerning it, one can perhaps assume that the Concerto for Cello and Orchestra, Opus 3, first performed by Maurits Frank at a concert at the Hoch Conservatorium in 1917, was an unproblematical, traditional work. The manuscript was destroyed in an air-raid which damaged the Hindemith house in Frankfurt during the Second World War. The same fate was unfortunately met by the Quintet for Piano and Strings which, to judge by the composer's references to it, was the first work in which he consciously tried to follow a definite path of his own. It is not the path that he later—and with greater conviction—took. In a letter written from France, probably before the first performance of the Quintet given privately for the Ronnefeldts at the beginning of 1918, he seems to be stressing its rhapsodical character when he tells the pianist, Emma Lübbecke-Job:

"The listener must never be given a chance to rest. Even the few quiet passages must have a threatening sense of thunder in the air. Above all, the piece must never sound like an orthodox quintet with first and second themes. It should always give the impression of a colourful improvisation. Spectres and dragons, landslides, battles, blood, trees, woods, sun and summer—all must be in it."

It was the coolness of his Conservatorium teachers Sekles and Rebner towards this work that strengthened Hindemith's resolve "always to write as necessary, never to give way, to make no concessions". In his letter of 21 March 1918 to Frau Ronnefeldt, he said plainly that he knew the path he had chosen was a difficult one which would lose him many friends. "But never mind—they don't matter, as long as a few of the faithful stay on till the end."

His growing repugnance for the safe and traditionally orientated line of his teachers is drastically expressed in an earlier letter (May 1917) to Emmy Ronnefeldt. In it he expressed disgust with Sekles for his criticism of the work on which he was then engaged, the Three Songs for Soprano and Orchestra, Opus 9:

"Do you know what worried him? That the songs are too free in form and bear absolutely no resemblance to 'usual' *Lieder*! And these are our modern musicians! Something written from the depths of one's soul, with no thought of *Lieder* forms or such-like rubbish, something a little bit unusual—this makes them nervous! I want to write *music*, not song and sonata forms!! Of course, if I write logically and my thoughts just happen to come out in an 'old' form, that's all right. But in God's name I'm not *bound* to keep on thinking in these old patterns! I see it's high time I shook myself free of all this conservatory nonsense. What ties me to these people, after all? Tradition, and nothing else. When I really want to know something, there's nobody who can help me, nobody to whom I can talk seriously about music, because none of them has any ideals left: their whole art has turned into mere handicraft. . . . One tries to pin down on humble paper the sweetest kisses of Frau Musica and—

when one thinks one has conjured up a vision of eternal bliss—
what do these blockheads hear? Not music, but just notes, bars,
dynamics, forms and such-like trivialities. The trouble with our
music is that it lacks music! And all I want to do is to make
music. I don't care a damn if people like it or not—as long as
it's genuine and true."

In her reply Emmy apparently remonstrated with him for
his attack on orthodox musicianship and reminded him that he
ought really to consider his audiences too. He was not to be
persuaded. If compelled to choose, he declared, between
the ignorant public, which could weep its eyes out over sentimental rubbish as well as over masterpieces, and "experts" who
cared only for questions of form and harmony, he would certainly prefer the latter, but on the whole there was nothing to
be gained by considering other people. "I write exactly as I
choose, and I don't care in the least whether people like it or
not."

Even more significant than this accurate description of his
lifelong attitude towards audiences is the definition of his feelings towards craftsmanship, a word which, used scornfully by
him to describe his teachers at the Conservatorium, has since
been used with equal scorn by his critics to define his own
musical character. Craftsmanship, he told Emmy, should not be
confused with technique. "All art needs technique. Without it,
no art. And that, for better or worse (mostly worse!) one has to
learn. But that is not the same thing as rules. . . . There is an
aesthetic rightness which is not bound by rules. And until one
learns enough technique to write what one really feels, a lot of
water will flow down the Main."

From remarks such as this it is possible to see how Hindemith,
at the age of twenty-one, was hovering on the edge of his
musical identity without being quite clear in which direction to
develop it. He was basically still a romantic both in his belief in
the validity of inspiration and in his imagery. To the dragons
and forests of his quintet he now added a picture of violence and
revolution in the last of the Three Songs for Soprano and
Orchestra, to which he had at last managed to win over his
teacher Sekles—a triumphant vindication of his self-reliance.
"At the end the solo voice has to scream continuously," he wrote
to Emmy. "Terrific, isn't it? Nothing for musical people. Tough
constitutions required!! A soprano with two sets of lungs."

But at the same time that he was giving free rein to a chaotic romantic imagination, he was emerging from his veneration of Richard Strauss. At a concert in Frankfurt he had played in a performance of the *Alpensymphonie*. "That's a real piece of hocus-pocus," he wrote to Emmy on 14 November 1917. "The man has let himself down terribly. Better to hang oneself than ever to write music like that." His new interest was Expressionism, which he had encountered for the first time in a new periodical called *Das Kunstblatt*. He was unsure, he wrote to Emmy, whether he yet really grasped what it was about, but it was perhaps the direction in which he himself would eventually go. The *Kunstblatt* of October 1917, it is interesting to note, was devoted to the paintings and writings of Oskar Kokoschka and contained a reference to the one-act play *Mörder, Hoffnung der Frauen*. A few years later Hindemith set this play to music.

In composition he was now exploring a totally different path —that of the compact miniature. "I have finished the third of the piano pieces," he wrote to Emmy on 28 November 1917. "It sounds thoroughly degenerate; has no rhythm, key or harmony of any recognisable sort. If I go on in this vein I shall come to a territory beyond good or evil where it will be impossible to know whether I have written a higher sort of music or just a substitute for music. But the things give me great joy. One of the pieces is nine bars long. My great ambition now is to write one of only three bars—theme, development, coda. . . ."

It is not always possible to tell for sure when Hindemith is being serious or is merely joking. One cannot be in much doubt, however, when he tells her that a piece still to be written will contain an instruction to the pianist to slam down the lid "always precisely at the point when an unclouded major chord manages to slip in unseen". All the same, the experiment in musical concentration which these piano pieces represented was clearly a serious technical exercise. They are nevertheless not mentioned in his own list of both published and unpublished works.

During his military service in France Hindemith's composing activities were necessarily restricted, though they were still more than most mortals would have achieved. The most substantial work was the String Quartet No. 1 in F minor, Opus 10, the romanticism of which was an expression of feeling for rather than a concession to the couple to whom he dedicated it, Herr and Frau Ronnefeldt. His affection for Frau Ronnefeldt, who did for him what his own mother could or would not do—sending him, among other things, a parcel of apples to the front ("I fell on them like a tiger," he told her)—was implicit in every word he wrote her, even when he was telling her that it was always better not to talk about feelings—"then they grow more easily". Breaking his own vow, he wrote to her and her husband on 15 February 1918 from France about their approaching silver wedding:

"On that day I intend to go up to the attic here with my violin and my Bach and there, where I shall be alone, play something lovely for you, the Chaconne or something else you like. . . . I wish I could send you a really nice present, but out here I'm as poor as a church mouse. I've got nothing but a head full of music and ideas—and you can't do much with those. However, if you would be content with a rough print of my ideas, I have written almost two movements of a string quartet, and when the whole piece is ready I should like to offer it to you as a small token of my love and gratitude."

Sending them the completed work three months later through his brother Rudolf, he again stressed the personal connection of this composition with the Ronnefeldts:

"My dearest wish is to give you and Herr R. real pleasure with it. Not just with the dedication—which is after all just something one writes on the title page. You can rest assured that the very first note of it was written for you, and everything that is in it now is yours entirely. If you enjoy listening to it, as I hope, the work will have fulfilled its purpose."

The first signs of a recognisable musical style of his own coincided with the first stirrings of an idea which was to persist throughout his life. In a letter to Emmy Ronnefeldt dated 28 September 1918 he wrote:

"The day before yesterday I completed the first movement of a sonatina for violin and piano. The last movement I am working on now, but I haven't yet got the middle movement. The piece will sound very al fresco, with great thick and widely sweeping brush strokes. . . . I want to compose a whole series of such sonatinas—or rather small sonatas, since they are too expansive for sonatinas. Each of them is to be completely different from the preceding ones—also in form. I want to see whether I can't, in a whole series of such pieces, increase the expressive potentialities (which are not very great in this type of music and this combination) and extend the horizon. It will take me quite a number of years to finish the job, if I ever do, but I feel it's an interesting task."

This was the beginning of Opus 11—not only the first of Hindemith's works to show an individual style, but also the first batch in the large output of instrumental sonatas which form so important a part of his life's work. As originally described to Emmy Ronnefeldt, the whole series was to be written for violin and piano, but in Opus 11 alone (written in the years 1918–19) there are sonatas too for both viola and cello. In later years he widened the series to include practically every instrument capable of sustaining a solo role, including the double-bass and the tuba.

To take up the story of Hindemith's army life again at the point at which we left it, we must go back a little, to the summer months of 1918, in which his commanding officer, Graf von Keilmannsegg, was killed in battle. Mixed with his personal sorrow was the anxiety that this would be the end of the string quartet. However, on 20 August 1918 he wrote to Frau Ronnefeldt:

"Now we are freed from our worries. The Graf has a worthy successor, a colonel who in civilian life was director of the court theatre in Gera and who knows a lot about music. Everything remains as it was. He has quartets played to him and, knowing the whole chamber music repertoire well, he chooses the programmes himself. He is a most attentive listener, so it's a real pleasure to play for him. I must tell you something funny: I have been made a corporal. Not on account of my bravery or any other military virtues, but simply because our colonel, the last time we played to him, took it into his head to promote me on account of it. If the war lasts much longer, I'll maybe finish up a captain!"

The armistice was now not far off. "You've no idea," he wrote to Emmy six weeks before, "how sick I am of this life. How much longer must this miserable existence go on? Will these stupid idiots of men never put an end to this fiendish war? Pity that I'm not religious, or I should long ago have declared war on God. These cursed people who keep prolonging it should be sent out here for a few weeks' holiday—that would soon teach them. But enough grumbling—it doesn't do any good."

He was released from the army at the beginning of 1919. As he entered his home in Frankfurt, his mother greeted him with the words; "Oh, so there you are." That same evening he returned to his place in the orchestra at the opera house.

Chapter 3

1919–22:

THE BREAKTHROUGH

THE GERMANY TO which Hindemith returned after de-
mobilisation differed little in its musical habits from the Germany he had left. The works in which he played at the Frankfurt
Opera were the works he had played before—the usual
repertory of Mozart, Verdi, Wagner, Puccini and Strauss—and
the few new operas were those of composers with a pre-war
reputation: in 1919 Delius (*Fennimore and Gerda*), Franz Schreker
(*Die Gezeichneten*) and Hindemith's former teacher Sekles
(*Schahrazade*). The only complete novelty was an early space-
fiction opera, *Die ersten Menschen*, by Rudi Stephan, a composer
of Hindemith's own generation who had been killed at the
front at the age of only twenty-six. This was given its first
production in Frankfurt in 1920, by which time a promising
new conductor, Eugen Szenkar, had come to join the established
team of Rottenberg and Gustav Brecher.

In that year too a younger generation of conductors emerged
at the Museum Concerts, with which Mengelberg had now
severed his connection. Fritz Busch and Bruno Walter appeared
as guests, and the new permanent conductor was Wilhelm
Furtwängler, then thirty-four years of age. In January 1921, a
few months after his appointment, he made an attempt to bring
the programmes more up to date with a performance of Schönberg's *Pelleas und Melisande*, but in general the Museum Concerts
did not venture much beyond Mahler and the tone-poems of
Richard Strauss, even when Furtwängler's job was taken over
in 1922 by a conductor whose interest in contemporary music
was even more active, Hermann Scherchen. However, the
important point for Hindemith, playing in the orchestra both
at the Opera and in the Museum Concerts, was that he came
into contact with three conductors (Busch, Furtwängler and
Scherchen) who were to prove important allies in the years to
come.

As far as his own compositions were concerned, he was still

dependent on his friends in and around the Hoch Conservatorium for performances, but the emergence of a number of small societies pledged to promote new music gave him a more promising opening than the established institutions, still so blithely unaware that art was standing on the threshold of a new age. What particularly appealed to Hindemith was that many of these new groups saw art as an instrument of social purpose. If he himself did not go so far as his slightly older contemporary in Vienna, Anton Webern, who collaborated actively with the Social Democrats and took part in concerts for the workers, nevertheless he was firmly convinced that music had a higher function than merely to provide relaxation for solid middle-class citizens. It was time, he felt, to rid it of its indulgent emotionalism and bring it back nearer to earth.

The organisation in Frankfurt which promoted the first concert of his works was entitled the *Verein für Theater- und Musikkultur* (Society of Theatrical and Musical Culture), and its declared principle was to promote "a culture based on the life of the community". Hindemith himself took part in the concert in the Saalbau on 2 June 1919 as violist in the Rebner Quartet (having now at his own request switched from the violin to the viola), playing his String Quartet No. 1 (the one written for the Ronnefeldts) and also his earlier Quintet, with Emma Lübbecke-Job at the piano. At the same concert she accompanied him in performances of two of his Opus 11 sonatas —that in E flat for violin, written while the war was still in progress, and that for viola, written early in 1919.

"Not everything that the young concertmaster of our opera orchestra has confided to paper during his silent hours sounds new and individual," wrote the critic Karl Holl a few days later in the *Frankfurter Zeitung* (10 June 1919). "Italian opera melody, Slav rhythms and impressionistic sounds have not been completely assimilated and made his own. But the composer's remarkable melodic invention, his surprisingly assured mastery of form and the powerful impetus of his works entitle us to speak of a creative talent far beyond the average."

On the recommendation of Sekles, Hindemith submitted all the works played at his first concert to a publisher. He chose the time and place well. The mainstay of the old established firm of Schott und Söhne in Mainz during the pre-war years had been the works of Richard Wagner, in which the copyright had

run out in 1913. They were thus urgently in search of new
composers and had not so far had marked success in finding
them. The firm's head, Geheimrat Ludwig Strecker, now in his
sixties, was not in sympathy with modern trends, and his two
sons, Ludwig and Willy, who joined him in the business after
the war, were as yet relatively inexperienced.

"We looked around for new composers," Ludwig recalled in
a letter to Hindemith dated 14 November 1955, "and various
new things were published. Our good old father observed these
activities with the greatest mistrust. Then one day a new man
arrived, and his name was Hindemith. We were convinced that
this time we were on the right path. We approached our
father, who put up a stern resistance (without looking at the
manuscript) before yielding with the words: 'But it's the last
experiment I shall be prepared to allow you as long as I still
have some say in the matter.' I can still remember how outside
in the corridor Willy and I dug each other in the ribs with
delight over our victory."

Willy Strecker's letter of 1 July 1919 accepting the string
quartet for publication showed, however, all the inborn caution
of his breed: "A publisher cannot unfortunately live for his
ideals alone," he said—and offered an outright fee of one
hundred marks. Hindemith replied sturdily: "I think I can
assume that you also well know how difficult it is for a composer
to believe in his ideals when for a work on which he has had to
lavish weeks and months of loving care he is offered the paltry
sum of one hundred marks. This does not pay even for the
paper and the copying of the parts, let alone for the time and
trouble of composing the work." Strecker hastily apologised for
hurting the composer's feelings and raised his offer to one
thousand marks, to cover the two violin sonatas and the viola
sonata of Opus 11 as well as the quartet (the quintet was not
accepted). Hindemith accepted this offer, at the same time
pointing out that he would expect royalty payments on any
future editions of the works.

It was the beginning of a lifelong association that was
eventually to prove as profitable to the composer as it was to
the publishers, though not without some moments of strain to
both. With the Strecker brothers, Ludwig and Willy, he remained throughout his life on friendly terms. Willy Strecker in
particular, who was eleven years his senior, proved a truly

congenial spirit, even if, with the emotional reticence common to them both, they kept a long time to outward formalities. Fourteen years after their first meeting they were still addressing each other as Herr Hindemith and Herr Strecker, in spite of having been frequent visitors in each other's homes and even taking their holidays together. Their backgrounds were as disparate as their physical appearance (Strecker was as tall as Hindemith was short), and their initial sympathy certainly rested to a great extent on their shared disdain of German provincialism, however differently based. Strecker was a worldly man: through his marriage he had acquired Argentinian nationality but, as a German-born person working at the Schott establishment in London, he had spent the whole of the war in internment in England. Now back in Germany, he had settled down in an elegant house in Wiesbaden, where he lived surrounded by a growing collection of original impressionist and contemporary paintings.

It was a life in complete contrast to Hindemith's own. He was still living with his mother and sister (Rudolf was now studying in Berlin) in a modest flat near the Opera, supporting them on his by no means lavish salary as an orchestral player there. He had, as before the war, his more prosperous social contacts—with the Ronnefeldts, with Dr Schmidt in Friedberg and, increasingly, with the Lübbeckes, who since 1917 had been living in a house in Frankfurt on the banks of the river Main known as the Schopenhauerhaus, because the philosopher had once lived there. Here he would often spend the night, having gone there after the performance at the opera house to make music with Emma. In her home he met not only musicians, but painters and sculptors as well. On 30 October 1919, Fried Lübbecke writes in his book *Der Muschelsaal*, "our friend the painter Reinhold Ewald from Hanau drew a double portrait of Paul Hindemith in our visitors' book". Their closest friend, Richard Petraschke, made a bronze bust of the young composer.

These were signs of the increasing attention he was beginning to attract in artistic circles, but his own opinion of himself as a practical musician willing to turn his hand to any job that would help pay the rent remained untouched. On 24 March 1920 he wrote to Willy Strecker to ask whether he would be interested in publishing "foxtrots, Bostons, ragtime and other junk of that kind? When I run out of any decent ideas I always write such things. I am very good at it, and I can imagine you would do better with that sort of stuff than with the very best of my chamber music. (Besides, good *Kitsch* is very rare.)" Though Strecker consented to look at the manuscripts ("We can use such things, unfortunately," he wrote), he was given no time to make up his mind, since within a few days Hindemith demanded them back. He needed them, he said, for a dance in the Frankfurt Palmengarten at which he was engaged to play.

All this time he was busy composing—works for the stage as well as instrumental music and songs—and Willy Strecker was becoming a little worried. "You have given us a hard nut to crack with your new piano sonata and the songs [Three Hymns on Texts by Walt Whitman for Baritone and Piano]," he wrote on 9 April 1920. "We are completely puzzled by your sudden change of direction. Your new radical style seems to us to obscure those individual characteristics we so much admire in you."

Hindemith rushed to his own defence in a revealing letter dated 11 April 1920:

"It is all true and natural music, not in the least bit 'forced'. ... I am still writing just as easily as before, and the difference between my earlier and my present things is not basic: it is only a question of degree. I could not write in this way before, because I was still too undeveloped technically (and as a person). All the 'disturbing' features you don't like in my new music can be seen in the other things, though in an incomplete, immature form. ... In the Whitman Hymns I have almost succeeded in pinning down the things that have been going around in my head from the start. But they still cling in many places to all sorts of old-fashionedness. (Atavism is a tiresome illness which can only be cured by patience, hard work and a lively and ever ready power of invention!)"

Willy Strecker was not convinced, and neither the piano sonata nor the Whitman songs were published. Hindemith was not worried by such apparent setbacks. Always modest about his own composing talents, he simply put completed works aside and got down to others.

The Rebner Quartet, of which he was still a member, gave several successful performances of his first string quartet. "During our extensive concert tours to Holland, France, Spain, etc.," Rebner writes in his reminiscences, "I could observe how prolific Hindemith was and what good use he made of his time. He could concentrate on his composing just as well in a railway carriage as in waiting-rooms or the restaurant car. The rest of us gradually got used to his 'preoccupations'. If there was no porter at the station, Hindemith would tie his suitcase, his music case and his viola together with a broad strap, which he then slung over his shoulder. We called him the 'modern troubadour'. He took our good-natured teasing in good part, though he often retaliated wittily in his own very earthy manner of speaking."

Hindemith's patience with Rebner, whatever impression this sunny picture may give, was quickly wearing thin. He was irritated both by the Quartet's unadventurous repertoire and by his former teacher's soulful attitude to the established musical masterpieces which were its mainstay. At a rehearsal of Beethoven's C sharp minor Quartet, Peter Cahn tells us in the *Hindemith-Jahrbuch II*, Rebner once quoted Wagner's opinion of the adagio as the most melancholy piece ever to have been given musical expression. Hindemith's reaction to this (though he waited until Rebner left the room before uttering it) was: "That's nonsense. All Beethoven wanted to do was to write a good fugue." The remark is neither perceptive nor particularly amusing, but it is typical of the young composer's feeling that musical problems demanded musical, and not verbal, elucidations. He severed his connection with the Rebner Quartet in 1921.

Hindemith's compositions were so far not of a sort to cause scandals. *Lieder* and sonatas, even if they bear such markings as "$\downarrow$=600–640, tearing tempo, wild, tonal beauty is incidental", as the 1922 sonata for solo viola does, usually reach only small audiences, and in the groups to which Hindemith's works were initially played he was addressing special audiences which would approve rather than condemn such iconoclasms.

The position was, however, very different when he ventured into the staunchest of the conservative strongholds, the opera house, as he did in 1921 with two Expressionist one-acters. The conductor Fritz Busch writes in his autobiography *Pages from a Musician's Life*: "I myself was only a young man, hardly past thirty. I felt completely at one with young people and was glad when I could co-operate with them. At a guest performance at

Frankfurt I noticed in the opera orchestra a young violinist who played with spirit. I found that he was called Hindemith and composed modern music. I took his first operas to give them performances at Stuttgart."

The theatre was the Landestheater, and the first performance took place on 4 June 1921, Busch himself conducting. The earliest of the operas, *Mörder, Hoffnung der Frauen* (Murderers, the Hope of Women), had been written in 1919, and was a setting of a little play by Oskar Kokoschka, who in his younger days was active as a writer as well as a painter. The second, *Das Nusch-Nuschi*, was also by an Expressionist writer, Franz Blei, who in the days before the war had been associated with the dramatist Carl Sternheim in editing the periodical *Hyperion*. This piece, described as "a play for Burmese marionettes", tells an Oriental story about a philandering character who is punished by being castrated for his sins—an episode which Hindemith clothed musically with a quotation from King Marke's music in Wagner's *Tristan und Isolde*.

"Now the Swabians were not prudes," Busch continues in his account, "and especially at that time, when after a war much was permissible, were not narrow-minded where dramatic events were concerned. On the other hand, they were completely lacking in tolerance—and I must now say quite rightly— to make them put up with an insult to their most sacred treasures, as they understood the quotation from *Tristan* to be. There was a scandal which increased the more when the newspapers attacked the affair."

It is legitimate to wonder, in view of that parenthesis, whether Busch was the right person to have launched these works. Hindemith's use of the *Tristan* quotation (*Mir—dies?*— This—to me?) was certainly no more than a piece of high-spirited mischief, and indeed, according to the reminiscences of Philipp Dreisbach, who played in the orchestra at that performance, Busch in rehearsal found it amusing, as did the players. If he had recognised in time the scandal it would cause, he would no doubt have refused to present the opera, as he refused to present the third of Hindemith's one-acters "owing to its obscenity". Ludwig Rottenberg, however, was made of sterner stuff. On 26 March 1922 he presented all three one-acters at the Frankfurt Opera.

Das Nusch-Nuschi, still with its *Tristan* quotation, this time caused less shock than the third piece, *Sancta Susanna*, which was being seen for the first time. It is admittedly strong stuff, with its story (by August Stramm) of a sex-obsessed nun who tears the loincloth from a crucified Christ. "A perverse and entirely immoral affair," wrote a critic in the *Zeitschrift für Musik* of July 1922, adding regretfully that, to judge by the number of performances the little operas were given, the public seemed to enjoy them.

It was the most widely publicised event of Hindemith's whole career to date, and inevitably it brought flocking to the theatre the young German intelligentsia, who detected in this new composer a kindred rebellious spirit. "We all went to Frankfurt to see his provocative one-act operas," the dramatist Carl Zuckmayer writes in his autobiography *Als wärs ein Stück von mir*. Very soon Paul Hindemith was a welcome visitor at the home of Dr Wilhelm Fraenger, the young director of the Institute of Art History in Heidelberg and an acknowledged leader of the *avant garde* intellectuals. After a concert in Heidelberg at which Hindemith's playing of his viola sonata was greeted with booes and hisses, Zuckmayer tells us, "we carried the little *Musikant* (for so he liked to call himself), who was always ready for laughter and jokes, on our shoulders through the town to our favourite haunt, the Goldener Hecht, near the old Neckar Bridge. . . . It was then an old and smoky den with wooden tables and benches, and in it the street porters and cabbies of Heidelberg drank their pints as well as unassuming artists and intellectuals. In the corner stood a wobbly piano, on which 'Paulche' Hindemith introduced us to his seal's piano. Using his hands flat, like flippers, he played delicious parodies of well-known pieces without sounding any individual notes, looking himself all the time like a trained seal. Liszt, Chopin and Wagner, played with seal's flippers, gained quite a lot in humour."

Of course Hindemith enjoyed such occasions, and of course he enjoyed being talked about, but one may legitimately question whether in spirit he was entirely at one with these revolutionary young intellectuals. The three one-act operas which started it all he himself regarded as apprentice work, and he very soon disowned them (though he made an attractive orchestral suite out of some of the music of *Das Nusch-Nuschi*). Later, when the Nazis came, these operas were to prove a

distinct burden to him, forcing him into the category of "decadent artists" to which by nature he never in fact belonged. His
choice of subjects for his first efforts at dramatic music had
probably been dictated mainly by the prevailing fashion of
Expressionism—particularly strong in Frankfurt, where plays
by Hasenclever and Kaiser and others had their first performances—and not by any deep personal identification with it.
Prolific as he was, he spent little time at this early stage of his
career in reflection, but was guided much more strongly by
impulse. The main task was to find new things to do and new
ways to do them, and his interest was always exclusively musical.
This is not to say that he did not enjoy shocking his elders: like
all young people, he obviously did. But his efforts were directed
solely towards breaking down *musical* complacency, and they
were the expression of juvenile mischievousness rather than
revolutionary zeal. Hindemith was not in fact particularly
interested in the wide public, whether inside concert halls or
outside. His main concern was always with the people who
played music or who were able to listen to it with true understanding, preferably at informal gatherings.

Such, by definition, was the new music festival at Donaueschingen, which opened in the summer of 1921. The manner
in which Hindemith came to be associated with it is told in
various ways. According to Preussner, a string quartet which he
had written for a competition organised by Mrs Coolidge in the
United States, but which was rejected, was sent by the Lübbeckes, unknown to him, to Donaueschingen in response to a
newspaper advertisement calling for new works. The first
Hindemith knew of it was the arrival on the doorstep of his
home in Frankfurt of the festival organiser, Heinrich Burkard,
bringing the news that the quartet had been accepted for
performance. Max Rieple (a pupil of Burkard) tells another
version in the *Hindemith-Jahrbuch II*. He says that Burkard
wrote to Hindemith, asking him to submit some compositions,
but received no reply. Burkard then approached Emma
Lübbecke-Job, who sent him the manuscript of the quartet. A
less romantic story perhaps, but one that takes account of
Hindemith's reputation as a rising composer whose name would
not be unknown to any new festival seriously interested in
contemporary music.

It was certainly, after the scandal in Stuttgart concerning

Paul Hindemith (*left*) with his parents and sister Toni

Paul Hindemith (*front, second from left*) with members of the summer orchestra in Heiden, Switzerland, 1914

Paul Hindemith as a soldier in the First World War, 1918

Das Nusch-Nuschi, quite widely known when he arrived in Donaueschingen two months later to present his new quartet. The Havemann String Quartet, with whose leader, the violinist Gustav Havemann, Hindemith was later, in the Nazi years, to have much to do, had refused to play the work—either because they could not understand it or found it required more rehearsal than they had time for. Hindemith at once proposed that he should perform his work himself with his brother Rudolf and a couple of violinists whom he would find. Out of this rescue operation the Amar Quartet was born. It took its name from the first violinist, Licco Amar. Of Turkish extraction, Amar had become concertmaster of the Berlin Philharmonic Orchestra in 1915 at the age of twenty-four, and in 1920 moved to Mannheim, where he now occupied the same position at the Nationaltheater. To complete the quartet, he brought with him a fellow violinist from Mannheim, Walter Casper. They not only successfully launched Hindemith's Second String Quartet (which is dedicated to his brother), but went on, in that same year and in the ensuing ones, to become throughout Europe one of the foremost protagonists of modern chamber music. Rudolf Hindemith, who from 1921 to 1924 was a solo cellist at the Vienna State Opera, was the only member who did not play regularly with the quartet throughout its existence. His place as cellist was then taken by Maurits Frank, Paul Hindemith's former colleague in the Rebner Quartet.

A letter written from Frankfurt to Emmy Ronnefeldt in September 1922, after an appearance at the second festival in Donaueschingen had established his reputation beyond doubt as a composer to be reckoned with, conveys vividly the excitement and confidence with which Hindemith, now in his twenty-seventh year, faced his present realities and future prospects:

"A pity you are not around to see the new zest we are bringing into musical life here. The spirit of enterprise has seized hold of me. Last year I finally left the Rebner Quartet, but in May I founded a proper quartet of my own: the Amar Quartet. We play only modern music and are kept very busy. In the summer we played at both the Donaueschingen and Salzburg festivals—with very great success. We are off soon to Denmark and Czechoslovakia and in the winter to Paris. At both the above festivals I succeeded once again in scoring over all the other composers, and since then my affairs have been blooming beyond all expectations. All over the place my things are being performed—my operas are to be done in Dresden, Prague and Kiel and have already come out here. Publishers are falling over one another to get me, and I am making use of the favourable constellation to pick out the one who will pay me the most, and then I shall get out of the orchestra and spend my full time composing and playing in the quartet.

"But my finest achievement has been to establish a 'music community' here in Frankfurt. We play modern music at Zinglers in the Kaiserstrasse (once every 2 or 3 weeks) before an invited audience of about 80: a purely musical gathering without any financial complications. The audience pays nothing, the players get nothing, and the very small expenses we settle among ourselves. So here at last we have got music for music's sake! Personal ambition has no say in the matter, and there are no newspaper reviews. And the best thing of all: none of the Frankfurters is allowed in!! I have had a lot of trouble about that, for they all seem to think they ought to be there. Nothing doing! And then, on top of this, we (the quartet) are shortly going to give seven musical evenings devoted exclusively to brand-new chamber works from all countries. We're even doing some Russian ones—never heard anywhere in Europe before. Great, isn't it? I must think up all sorts of new ideas like this before very long—it's urgently necessary.

"I've discovered a new sport: I'm playing the viola d'amore, a magnificent instrument that has been quite forgotten, and for which very little music exists. The loveliest tone you can imagine, indescribably sweet and soft. It's tricky to play, but I play it with great enthusiasm and to everyone's delight. . . .

"What else have I done this year? A lot of orchestra, a great many concerts, a lot of touring. And an awful amount of composing: a song cycle *Die junge Magd* with six instruments, a piano suite, a symphony for small orchestra, a wind quintet, a solo viola sonata, a sonata for viola d'amore and piano, the *Marienlieder*, another set of songs with two violas and two cellos, a sonata for viola and piano, a ballet (to be performed on 1 December in Darmstadt), a solo cello sonata and a Christmas fairy play which is to be done here and in five other theatres. Most of these things are being published too. I've got a chronic mania for work, and doubt if I'll ever get rid of it."

The list of new compositions contained in this letter is indeed impressive, not only for its length, but also for the variety of styles and combinations it embraces. Here, side by side with the vigorous and iconoclastic *Kammermusik No. 1*, which (like the piano suite) makes use of jazz, we find the two song cycles *Die junge Magd* (an Expressionist work) and the very important *Das Marienleben*, in which Hindemith first fully discovered his true roots in the polyphonic style of the early eighteenth century. Then there is his first venture into ballet (*Der Dämon*, a ballet pantomime by Max Krell, received its first performance in Darmstadt not in December 1922, as his letter suggests, but on 1 December in the following year), as well as a stage work for children, *Tuttifäntchen*, which was presented for the first time in Darmstadt on 13 December 1922 and three days later in Frankfurt under the direction of Ludwig Rottenberg.

All the works mentioned in this list, with the single exception of the sonata for viola and piano, were subsequently published and have since been extensively performed. Of the "music community" in Frankfurt, however, nothing more was heard, and one can assume that it gradually faded out under the pressure of other work and the growing inflation in Germany, which made financial considerations a necessity even for idealists. The "community" is nevertheless significant as an indication of how Hindemith's keenest enjoyment was derived from playing music in congenial company rather than from winning applause and money with it. His attitude towards fees tended towards the casual. "Our terms?" he once wrote to the promoters of a concert of this club kind. "You already know them: in general, as much as possible; for the sake of art and for institutions without much money, less—but not disregarding the possibility of a generous rounding off upwards."

However, this quixotic attitude did not extend to those circles in which idealism self-confessedly played a secondary role to sober business. His opening shot against his publishers, contained in a letter to Willy Strecker dated 1 March 1922, was humorously phrased. He complained of the rising costs of production and the small income so far received from his published compositions, then observed wrily: "From my slowly oozing fame I can't even keep myself in writing paper (one mark per sheet—God help us, I shall now write nothing but duets for two violins!)."

Schotts assuaged him with an immediate lump sum of two

thousand marks "to compensate you at least for a part of your costs", but in those days of galloping inflation such gestures afforded only very temporary relief. At the beginning of November 1922 Willy Strecker received a letter which must have shocked him with its revelation that the modest and friendly young man with whom he had been dealing had a hard side to his character and a rough tongue with which to express it. Baldly, in his letter dated 31 October 1922, Hindemith accused Schotts of taking advantage of his lack of business sense and paying him badly. In order to live at all, he said, he had to continue work at the Frankfurt Opera and thus had little time left for composing. He had now had a much better offer from another publisher and, unless Schotts improved their terms, he intended to accept it. "Do not be unduly surprised by the somewhat unaccustomed tone of this letter," he concluded. "I too have now discovered that in matters of money friendship has no place."

Anxious not to lose what promised to be their main hope for the future, Willy Strecker asked Hindemith to visit him in order to discuss new terms. But Hindemith, no doubt distrusting his ability to remain adamant in a face-to-face interview, resolutely refused to see him. He insisted on negotiation by letter with the help of a lawyer. The battle lasted three months and ended in a resounding victory for Hindemith. Schott's finally agreed to pay him a regular salary, sufficient to enable him to leave the orchestra and concentrate on his composition. In addition to this he would receive royalty payments on his works. The battle over, Hindemith wrote to Willy Strecker on 19 January 1923:

"I am very pleased that the contract is now in order. It is a pity that this could be achieved only at the cost of a lot of bother, and you will probably not be able to forget that it was I who caused the bother. But you must not think I do not appreciate the fact that you have now reached this agreement with me. I am fully aware of the worth of the concessions you have made. But I do ask you to recognise that I too have made concessions, for at the end of December I turned down an offer from another publisher which would have given me, besides the same subsidiary terms, a regular monthly salary almost double what I shall receive from you. I found it vexing to have to negotiate music like a sack of potatoes, and I have therefore signed your agreement . . . I hope we shall both profit by it. You can be assured that my work will not let you down."

The peace offering was accepted with as much grace and sincerity as it was tendered. The loyal relationship thus formed led to a lasting alliance which, in difficult years ahead, brought much honour to both sides. At the moment, however, there was no sign of looming trouble. Germany was as anxious to receive Hindemith's compositions as he was to write them. He immediately handed in his notice at the Frankfurt Opera and began to enjoy the freedom of his new independence.

Chapter 4

1922–27:

EARLY MASTERY

DONAUESCHINGEN, IN THE beautiful and romantic south-western corner of Germany which contains the Black Forest and Lake Constance, has one natural claim to fame: it is the place at which the river Danube's twin sources unite. The family seat of the Princes von Fürstenberg, it is one of a whole host of small principalities, margravates and dukedoms which still, long after they have been abolished as centres of power, give Germany a particular cultural advantage. In no other country in the world are there so many separate artistic institutions and theatres of equal renown, and this is the direct outcome of the political decentralisation which prevailed in Germany up to the latter part of the nineteenth century, and even persisted in modified form right up to the end of the First World War. After that the various princes, margraves and dukes had no more say in the running of the country, but the cultural traditions they had built up in their little courts remained—and more particularly the theatres and galleries erected to house them.

The Fürstenberg musical tradition went back nearly two centuries. The ten-year-old Mozart spent twelve days in Donaueschingen with his sister Nannerl and their father in 1766, playing to the prince and their guests. In 1843 Liszt played and conducted there. Less august though still imposing names are Konradin Kreutzer, who was court musical director from 1816 to 1822, and Johann Wenzeslaus Kalliwoda, who succeeded him and was still director at the time of Liszt's visit (and indeed for ten years afterwards).

The head of the family at the end of the First World War was Max Egon Fürst zu Fürstenberg. He was aware that times had changed, and readily gave his approval to the plans of his young music director, Heinrich Burkard, to establish an annual summer music festival designed to promote the works of contemporary composers. He also agreed that this required a less patriarchal approach than in the past, and he appointed an honorary council to preside over the festival. Among its members were Richard Strauss, Hans Pfitzner, Franz Schreker, Ferruccio Busoni and Artur Nikisch. The choice was admittedly conservative, but it was reassuring, and therefore tactically sound. The council had no duties: the practical work of running the festival was given at the start to a committee of four: Burkard; the Bavarian composer Joseph Haas (a pupil of Max Reger); Eduard Erdmann, the pianist; and Willy Rehberg, head of the music conservatory in Basle. After the first two festivals Erdmann and Rehberg faded out, and Paul Hindemith took their place.

The prince did not see his own place in the festival in the same light as Arnold Schönberg, whom he invited in 1924 (at Hindemith's instigation) to conduct his *Serenade* in Donaueschingen. In his reply to the prince accepting the invitation, Schönberg spoke approvingly of "this enterprise that is reminiscent of the fairest, alas bygone, days of art when a prince stood as a protector before an artist, showing the rabble that art, a matter for princes, is beyond the judgment of common people". This was quite contrary to the prince's aim, which was thoroughly democratic, and the evidence is that he much enjoyed the company of the young composers and their friends who turned up each summer to transform his classic palace and formal gardens into something nearer in style to a fairground. "The prince was very tolerant and spent a lot of time with us," the clarinettist Philipp Dreisbach observes in his reminiscences, preserved at the Hindemith Institute in Frankfurt. He recalls that once at two o'clock in the morning a group of players assembled under the prince's bedroom window and played him a serenade.

Busoni came nearer than Schönberg to defining the spirit of Donaueschingen. The festival, he wrote to Burkard in 1923, "stands forth as a temple of youth and high spirits, qualities which for me are inseparable from the art of music".

During the early festivals there were inevitably some generation clashes. Both Schreker and Pfitzner had to be discouraged from regarding Donaueschingen as an automatic stamping-ground for their own pupils, and from feeling insulted when Burkard and his committee rejected their protégés' works. And at the first festival there occurred that encounter between

Richard Strauss and Hindemith which is recorded by Max Rieple in his book *Musik in Donaueschingen*. After the enthusiastic reception of the new string quartet, Strauss addressed the composer in his broad Bavarian dialect: "Why do you compose atonal music? You have plenty of talent." Hindemith replied in his equally broad Frankfurt dialect: "Herr Professor, you make your music, and I'll make mine."

Other young composers besides Hindemith whose work was played at that first festival were Alois Hába, Ernst Krenek and Wilhelm Grosz (all pupils of Schreker), Alban Berg (the piano sonata Opus 1) and Philipp Jarnach. The concerts were held in the Festhalle, a building in the grounds which looked like a gymnasium, and the members of the Amar Quartet slept in the building that housed the prince's swimming-bath. The common meeting place between concerts was a restaurant in the Kurhaus and, in a letter preserved in the Hindemith Institute in Frankfurt, the painter Else Clara Prechter recalls how she and Hindemith set about decorating its walls with drawings and paintings of their own. There were two ornate gilt frames hanging there, from which the original pictures had been removed (she says stolen). Inside one of these Hindemith drew, with crude detail, a caricature of the festival audience sickened by the music it was hearing, while she filled the other with a portrait of a massive soprano.

The first festival ended with a performance in the palace grounds of Mozart's *Eine kleine Nachtmusik*, played by the Amar Quartet from a platform erected inside an ancient ash tree.

All these anecdotes and reminiscences, of which there are several more, testify to the spirit of informality and camaraderie which characterised the Donaueschingen festival. It belonged to no particular faction: the only qualification for acceptance was legitimate experiment, and none of the organising committee (Burkard, Haas and Hindemith) was at that time committed to any narrow line. The composers whose work was presented there in the few years of its existence ranged from Delius, Pfitzner and Ravel to Bartók, Milhaud and Stravinsky (and included inevitably a few names since forgotten). Schönberg came to Donaueschingen in 1924 not only to conduct his *Serenade*, but to introduce the works of Webern. The fact that Webern's *Sechs Bagatellen*, given their first performance by the

Amar Quartet, were greeted with laughter troubled Hindemith not at all (after all, his own *Kammermusik No. 1*, presented at the 1922 festival, had had a very mixed reception too).

After that meeting in Donaueschingen, Hindemith and Hermann Scherchen decided to honour Schönberg's fiftieth birthday with a festival of his works in Frankfurt. Schönberg wrote to Scherchen on 12 August 1924: "Tell Hindemith that *I am extremely pleased with him.* By doing this he is making a splendid sign of a proper attitude to his elders, a sign such as can be made only by a man with a genuine and justifiable sense of his own worth; only by one who has no need to fear for his own fame when another is being honoured."

This, though rather comic in its condescension, is no less than just. Hindemith had not yet reached the stage of condemning any experiment as unfruitful, whether it was Schönberg's twelve-tone system, Alois Hába's quarter-tone compositions or any of the other novelties for which successive Donaueschingen festivals provided a platform. Speaking about Donaueschingen in a lecture delivered in 1949, Hindemith gave his own opinion of its significance:

"Impulsively, without much reflection, we did there what we thought worth doing and, looking back on that period of communal learning and trying things out, one can see with what sureness of instinct the problems of the day were recognised and dealt with." In his experience, he added, music festivals in the period after the Second World War lacked the intimacy of Donaueschingen, which brought composers together to work out their problems in a spirit of mutual co-operation. On the other hand, in festivals of so intimate a kind, there was a potential danger: more time might be spent in talking about music than in actually making it. However gratifying to the composer, he was not helped, Hindemith observed, by "cackling over eggs just laid or crowing over others about to be laid".

Hindemith did not see Donaueschingen as the only showplace for his new works: in fact, the festivals of 1923 and 1924 included no new works by him. He was also actively concerned, both as a performer and as a member of the selection committee, with the International Society of Contemporary Music, whose festival at Salzburg began in the same year as Donaueschingen. Here in 1923 the Amar Quartet and Philipp Dreisbach gave the first performance of his Quintet for Clarinet and String Quartet, and in 1924 he launched his first String Trio together with Amar and Frank. The first is dedicated to Werner Reinhart, a well-to-do Swiss businessman and himself a clarinettist, whom Hindemith met in Donaueschingen and who was to remain a lifelong friend; the second to Alois Hába.

Even if they had wished to, these two festivals could not have coped with his enormous output of new works, including songs, piano pieces, sonatas and chamber works. All were performed in Hindemith's presence or with his participation as soon as they were written (in some cases at the very last minute) at concerts arranged by various societies devoted to modern music. To these societies he returned again and again, making firm friends of the organisers. There were for example the Thalheimer sisters, who were active in the Gesellschaft für Neue Musik (Society for New Music) in Cologne. Both of them, Else and Margret, will be encountered in later chapters. After his first appearance in a concert of their society in 1923 (so successful that it had to be repeated), he invited the two sisters to Donaueschingen, and they were greatly impressed when he abandoned the table at which he was sitting with Prince Max Egon and came to join them at theirs. He probably did not even notice that his gesture may have appeared unusual. Always happiest making music with and among people of his own choosing, he had no particular respect for stars, and certainly not for aristocrats.

The centre of his work at this time was the Amar Quartet, and all his many compositions were produced at a time when the quartet was carrying out a very heavy programme of concerts throughout Germany and its neighbouring countries. The list of concerts for 1924 alone numbers 129 appearances. The players were close friends as well as colleagues and, when they were playing in Cologne, they all stayed in the Thalheimer home, where family and players spent many cheerful hours together.

Another close friend and working colleague was of course Emma Lübbecke-Job, Hindemith's invariable choice as pianist when one was required for the performance of his works. His loyalty to her was such that he insisted that she should be the soloist when his piano concerto (*Kammermusik No. 2*) was given its first performance in Frankfurt in October 1924, though his publishers would have preferred a more famous name. Hindemith wrote to Willy Strecker: "She took interest in my things when nobody else cared a damn about them and played them when it wasn't as easy as it is now to get Hindemith on to the concert platform. I should like to show her my recognition for that." It was not only affection and gratitude that influenced him in such cases. He did not trust musicians who had not worked with him to know how his compositions should be played. "Since virtually all musicians have been brought up in the wretched romantic way of rubato-playing and 'expression',", he once wrote, when Willy Strecker again recommended a famous soloist, "they almost always play my things wrong." For that reason he thought it better that first performances should be given by him or his associates. "After that, everyone can do as he likes."

It was not surprising that, in the face of all this activity, Hindemith's critics should begin to wonder aloud if he were not merely a clever practician who could produce music by the yard under any sort of conditions. One of the sceptics was Richard Strauss, who managed to get his own back for that earlier encounter at the first Donaueschingen festival. At a later festival he asked Hindemith (according to Strauss's biographer Ludwig Kusche) how long he had taken to compose the work he had just heard. "Four days," Hindemith replied. Strauss remarked: "That's just what I thought."

Hindemith was impervious to such innuendoes. He was brimming over with self-confidence. "Please do not be alarmed by my rabbit-like productivity," he wrote to his publishers on 28 August 1924. "So far I have noticed no falling off in quality —rather the contrary. The moment I saw that happening, I should apply the brakes at once. It is not that I lack awareness or self-criticism—simply that I can now write a lot because I know exactly what to do."

A high four-storeyed tower of brick and stucco, topped with a steeply sloping slate roof, in the Grosser Rittergasse, Frankfurt, today bears the inscription: *In der Zeit von 1923 bis 1927 lebte und wirkte in diesem Turm PAUL HINDEMITH. Hier entstanden seine Kompositionen Cardillac, Marienleben.* (In the years 1923 to 1927 Paul Hindemith lived and worked in this tower. Here his compositions *Cardillac* and *Marienleben* were written.) Another inscription tells us that the tower was one of nine on the city walls of Sachsenhausen, then a town in its own right on the southern bank of the river Main opposite Frankfurt. Built in 1490 and known as the Kuhhirtenturm (Cowherd's Tower), it was severely damaged by bombs in 1943 and restored in 1957.

Except for the burnt-out shell of the old opera-house, the restored Kuhhirtenturm is the only visible reminder of Hindemith's close ties with Frankfurt, now the gleaming centre of German finance and big business, and it is perhaps a little incongruous that he, the outwardly unsentimental, forward-looking representative of a modern age, should be identified with the last relics of Frankfurt's past romantic glory. Yet one can see a hint of poetic justice in it, for his roots lay deeper in the past than he himself at that stage of his life cared to acknowledge, or others were able to recognise. Nevertheless, the roots are clearly visible in the *Marienleben* songs, to which (though he did not on the evidence of his letter of September 1922 to Emmy Ronnefeldt compose them there) he certainly put the finishing touches in the Kuhhirtenturm.

They were first performed in Donaueschingen on 17 June 1923, outside the festival season, by Beatrice Lauer-Kottlar, the dramatic soprano of the Frankfurt Opera, and Emma Lübbecke-Job, to whom the work is dedicated. The singer was the wife of Otto Ernst Sutter, who spent considerable sums of money promoting modern music in Frankfurt, and they were thus friends of long standing in the Lübbecke circle. Hindemith, whose dedications are always a sign of friendship and sympathy, dedicated his Fourth String Quartet (written in 1923) to her.

Das Marienleben is a setting of fifteen songs by Rainer Maria Rilke dealing with events in the life of the Virgin Mary. Hindemith, though confirmed in the Protestant faith, was not religious in the orthodox sense, and this, his longest single work to date, was conceived from the first in dramatic rather than devotional terms. It is drama not in the Romantic sense of direct emotional statement but, to match the poems, a stylised form of recollection and contemplation. For his model Hindemith returned to the music of an earlier age, using above all Johann Sebastian Bach as his model. The style of writing, for the voice and the piano combined, is polyphonic, and the structural shape of each song—derived from the shape of the poem itself—imposes on the work as a whole a formal unity.

The harmonic language, on the other hand, is not retrospective: intervals and combinations once considered offensive to the ear and thus to be avoided are used with impunity. But this is now neither "atonality" (a word Hindemith considered meaningless) nor Expressionism, but the inevitable result of structural necessities, the whole being considered more important than the part.

"I definitely think they are the best things I have yet written," he declared when, shortly after the first performance, he sent the *Marienleben* songs to his publishers. They agreed with him. "It is a really wonderful work," they wrote back enthusiastically. For the Strecker brothers it was also a heartening assurance (if that were needed) that the young composer in whom they had put their faith was turning out to be much more than a mere passing sensation, gaining notoriety rather than fame by cocking a snook at elderly conservatives.

So far his reputation as a composer had hardly penetrated beyond the borders of Germany. "I have just come back from Paris and London," wrote Willy Strecker to Hindemith on 19 October 1923. "In London the *Nusch-Nuschi* dances are to be performed quite soon, and in general people there are beginning to show some interest in your work, although it always takes time for the public to get used to anything new." With this letter he enclosed an article from an American periodical, in which Percy Grainger had written enthusiastically about Hindemith. In Britain his earliest protagonists were Edwin Evans and Donald Tovey, who was a close and long-standing friend of Willy Strecker.

It had proved impossible to get a grand piano up the narrow stairs of the Kuhhirtenturm, which Hindemith had rented from the city and restored from his own earnings and where he was now living with his mother and his sister Toni. According to Fried Lübbecke, the piano had to be hoisted by a crane through a window on the top floor, where Hindemith had established his music room.

With his many concert engagements he could have spent little time in it, but somehow, during a brief visit to Frankfurt, he managed in the spring of 1924 to get married. "Quite by chance," Willy Strecker wrote to him on 7 June, "we heard that you have just been married. Why did you keep from us this joyful occasion? But none the less our heartiest congratulations. As a token thereof we are sending you by the same post a copy of the big *Meistersinger* score for your library."

The wedding had indeed been a very quiet one. The ceremony at a registry office on 15 May 1924 was followed by a reception in the Kuhhirtenturm attended only by members of both families and a few intimate friends. Since the bride's family contained the musical director of the Frankfurt Opera, his wife, the daughter of a former mayor of the city, and the head of the newly-established radio station in Frankfurt, one might have expected the event to attract a fair amount of publicity, but probably Hindemith's own reticence regarding his private life, which was matched by his bride's, overcame all efforts in that direction. Such information as I have been able to glean concerning the event comes from the bride's sister, Mrs Gabriele Flesch, and Mrs Flesch's brother-in-law, Dr Max Flesch-Thebesius, who was a witness at the wedding ceremony.

Gertrud was Ludwig Rottenberg's younger daughter. His elder daughter, Gabriele, had married Dr Hans Flesch in 1920. Flesch, one of the leading pioneers of German radio, was interested in new music and, as director of the Südwestdeutscher Rundfunk, Frankfurt's radio station, able to do something to promote it. He and Hindemith became close friends, and it was in his home in Frankfurt that Hindemith and Gertrud came to know each other well. They were of course already aware of each other's existence through Hindemith's position in her father's orchestra, but there had been no previous social contact between them.

At the time of their marriage Hindemith was in his twenty-ninth year, Gertrud in her twenty-fourth. Born in Frankfurt on 2 August 1900, she went to school at the Lyceum there and after that (at her own request, according to her sister, because she wished to learn French) at a finishing school in Paris. Intensely interested in both music and the theatre, she took lessons in singing and did some acting in both Frankfurt and Heilbronn. However, any ambitions she may have had to make a career in the theatre or opera house were rendered vain by her inability to conquer her stage-fright. After her marriage her stage appearances were confined to participation in choirs and ensemble groups and an occasional solo performance among informal gatherings of friends.

After a delayed honeymoon in the Austrian Tyrol in August 1924 following the Donaueschingen festival, Gertrud returned to the Kuhhirtenturm, while her husband resumed his touring with the Amar Quartet. A letter from her to Schotts, dated 19 October 1924 and atrociously typed (in all the subsequent years of writing her husband's letters she hardly improved her typewriting abilities), shows her for the first time in the role she chose from the start to assume in her marriage—that of her husband's amanuensis. Her first task was to introduce some order into his carefree bachelor ways:

"Since I am sitting at the typewriter writing a letter to you from my husband, I should like to make a request I have long had in mind. Here in our home we have not a single copy of any of my husband's printed works. If he himself is happy to lay his finished opusses aside like an old suit and treat them in the same way, I on the contrary feel the wish now and again to look through some of his 'early works'. Would you be good enough at some time to send me the collected works? I shall then have the single copies bound—to stop my visitors wresting them from me one by one."

Her slangy style of writing reflects her own individual mixture of self-deprecating humour and determination, which was to gain in confidence as the years went on. Energetic, impulsive, excitable, all those characteristics which caused the many people she at some time offended and even those who remained her friends to describe her as masterful, fit in with Hindemith's own representation of her, in countless caricatures, as a lion (curiously, never as a lioness). The direct reason for this was that Gertrud was born under the zodiacal sign of Leo, and Hindemith was always very interested in the science of the stars.

Since their personal correspondence has not yet been made available, any estimate of the relationship between Hindemith and his wife is bound at this stage to be speculative. Inevitably their marriage would have developed differently if there had been children, but in the early months an abnormal pregnancy, which had to be terminated by an operation, ruled this out for ever, to the great sorrow of both.

Whatever the still-undisclosed facts, it cannot be doubted that marriage made a considerable difference to Hindemith's way of life. The carefree Bohemianism, the late night parties, the casualness over fees—all this, if it did not stop entirely, was nevertheless noticeably modified. Gertrud was herself not lacking in high spirits, and she was very willing, when occasion offered, to join her husband and his friends in walking tours along the river Moselle or in convivial social evenings. But they were always very conscious of her watchful eye: when the time came to make a stop, it was she who made it.

On 15 April 1925 Gertrud sufficiently overcame her stage-fright to be able—at the home of Hindemith's friend, Dr Werner Reinhart, in Winterthur—to give the first performance of *Die Serenaden*, "a little cantata on romantic texts for soprano, oboe, viola and cello". Hindemith dedicated this rather austere little work to his wife, and it provides an indication of the change of attitude towards his music which began to take place in him about the time of his marriage. That it was deliberate is confirmed by a letter which he wrote around this time (on 2 April 1925) to his publishers. In it he advised them against bringing out a fantasy for salon orchestra on his music for the children's play *Tuttifäntchen*, written three years earlier. He felt that such naïve music would only provide his critics with useful ammunition. He went on:

"I am firmly convinced that a big battle over new music will start in the next few years—the signs are already there. It will have to be shown whether or not the music of our day, including my own, is capable of survival. I of course believe firmly in it, but I also believe that the reproaches made against most modern music are only too well deserved. . . . I am of the opinion that in the next few years the utmost orderliness will be called for, and I myself shall do all I can to achieve it. . . . I hope you will have noticed that I have been striving in all my recent things for the highest degree of purity and orderliness."

Having achieved this in *Die Serenaden*, as well as in *Das Marienleben* and in the Fourth String Quartet, he now felt the need to apply it on a yet larger scale: in an opera. He had long been searching for a suitable text. In a letter to Schott's dated 31 August 1923 he had written: "If I could find the proper libretto I should produce the biggest of operas in a few weeks. I know exactly what the problem of modern opera is, and I am sure that I could now solve it completely—as far as it is humanly possible."

The Strecker brothers had been persistent in putting forward suggestions. These included a *Faust* story, for which they thought the rising young dramatist, Bert Brecht, would be a suitable writer. Brecht, however, ignored Hindemith's letter of enquiry. They then suggested putting an advertisement in a newspaper inviting writers to submit ideas, a proposal which Hindemith rejected on the grounds that he would be bombarded with rubbish. That was already happening, even without an advertisement. "My mother sorts them out, my sister reads them and finally our dog busies himself with them in his own way."

The whole trouble, he said, was that what went under the name of modern opera was "eternally the same old sauce, just stirred around a bit differently". As far as he was concerned, an opera could be set "in a factory, in the streets of a large city, in a railway train or anywhere you like (all I am trying to say is that I don't think a good opera has to contain a heavy shot of romance), it doesn't have to be naturalistic, veristic or symbolic. The main thing is that one should be able to write some real music for it."

He was not interested in Ludwig Strecker's idea for a modernised version of *The Beggar's Opera* (three years later Brecht and Kurt Weill brought out their *Dreigroschenoper*), and contacts with leading writers in Germany and France (among them Romain Rolland) all came to nothing. At last, towards the end of 1925, Hindemith came into contact with Ferdinand Lion, who sent him the libretto of an opera based on a story by E. T. A. Hoffmann, *Das Fräulein von Scuderi*, which had originally been intended for Eugen d'Albert. This became the basis for *Cardillac*.

Ferdinand Lion had already written several librettos. One, based on the adventures of Casanova, with music by Volkmar Andreae, had been produced in Dresden in 1924, and another, *Der Golem*, with music by d'Albert, was first produced in Frankfurt in 1926, only five days after *Cardillac* came out in Dresden. What he had originally prepared for d'Albert—based on Hoffmann's romantic tale of the goldsmith Cardillac who murdered his customers because he could not bear to part with his creations—we cannot know, for he rewrote much in close cooperation with Hindemith. On 31 March 1926 Gertrud wrote to the publishers from the Hotel Nettuno in Alassio, where Hindemith had retired to work on the music: "The *Cardillac* text is now finished, and is, I think, good. We spent some fruitful days together with Lion in Venice, and the story has now been given a good human slant.... Everything is precisely motivated, there are no gaps and Cardillac should now arouse abundant sympathy."

Lion's libretto is both economical and expert. It could have been no easy matter to adapt the complicated story to conform with Hindemith's desire for a structure based on a succession of musical numbers in a variety of strict polyphonic forms. He saw this as an attempt to objectivise the action by deliberately clothing the romantic subject in a contrasting framework. At the time Hindemith wrote *Cardillac* Germany was enjoying a revival of Handel's operas in the new edited versions of Oscar Hagen, and the principles of Handelian opera were certainly foremost in his mind in the shaping of his work.

The music was completed within a few weeks, and was followed at once by his *Konzertmusik für Blasorchester* (English title: *Concert Music for Band*). This was his contribution to the Donaueschingen festival, which that summer was featuring works for military bands. The festival at which this work was played by a student orchestra of the German army under the direction of Hermann Scherchen (to whom it is dedicated) was the last to be held in the grounds of Prince Fürstenberg's palace. What had begun as little more than an experimental workshop for composers had now developed into a major international event that strained the limited resources of the little town beyond its capacity. Since Burkard was leaving the prince's employment, there was no longer any logical identification of the festival with Donaueschingen, and so he and Hindemith began to search for a new site. Hindemith's musical friends in Frankfurt were keenly interested, but an outburst of local patriotism defeated them: the people of the province of Baden were reluctant to see the festival move outside their boundaries, and a correspondence developed in the press which induced the local authorities to take action. They decided that from 1927 the festival should be held in Baden-Baden.

The last work to be played in Donaueschingen was another new one by Hindemith, and it marked the beginning of an interest which he developed more fully in the subsequent festivals at Baden-Baden: mechanical music. The Welte mechanical piano was worked by punched paper rolls, and the music Hindemith wrote for his *Triadisches Ballett* (Triadic Ballet) was punched on the rolls with his own hand. The ballet was devised by Oskar Schlemmer, a versatile member of the Bauhaus group who was both dancer, choreographer and producer. He had produced Hindemith's *Mörder, Hoffnung der Frauen* and *Das Nusch-Nuschi* at Stuttgart in 1921 and had then invited the composer to write a ballet for him. The *Triadisches Ballett*, an idea of Schlemmer's own, was an abstract work proclaiming the triad as the beginning of the collective concept, as opposed to the individual (one) and the alternative (two). The work displayed a variety of triple relationships: dance, costume, music; red, blue, yellow (the primary colours, used in the costumes); sphere, cube, pyramid (used in the scenery); and so on. It remains something of a mystery, except for the favoured few who witnessed its first production: since the music was designed for and punched direct on player-piano rolls, it has not so far been published.

At the conclusion of the festival Hindemith and Gertrud went off to the south of France. "Our holiday tastes really good after the heavy winter work," Hindemith wrote to Willy Strecker. Since money was short, he asked Strecker to give him an advance on royalties for *Cardillac*, which was to be produced in the autumn. He warned his publisher: "If you send it, you'll be cutting off your own nose: I shall get accustomed to lazing about, shall settle down here and write nothing more." Strecker sent him a thousand marks. "I am not frightened of educating you in the art of lazing," he declared. "I know that it is simply not in your nature."

Highly conscious of the interest likely to be shown in Hindemith's first full-length opera, Strecker had offered *Cardillac* to Erich Kleiber, who was then the chief musical director of the Berlin State Opera. Hindemith himself had privately made vague promises both to Fritz Busch in Dresden and to Otto Klemperer in Wiesbaden. Kleiber accepted the work, with the result, as Strecker wrote to Hindemith, that Fritz Busch was mortally offended. "We must see," he added, "how best we can smooth him down." However, since Kleiber proposed to present the work in the Kroll opera house, which the publishers considered unsuitable, they withdrew it and entrusted it after all to Busch, Klemperer being allowed to bring out the second production in Wiesbaden.

The first performance took place in Dresden on 9 November 1926. Though Busch spared no efforts to make it an important occasion, entrusting the roles to his best singers (Robert Burg sang Cardillac and Claire Born his daughter), it is doubtful whether he and his producer, Issay Dobrowen, presented the work to its best advantage. Hindemith, who was present throughout rehearsals, is said to have urged Dobrowen to keep the singers constantly on the move, acting on the assumption that the contrast between the turbulent happenings on stage and the cool commentary of the formally constructed music would enhance the dramatic effect. Since Busch in his autobiography makes no reference at all to this important production, one might assume that for some reason it did not figure among his pleasanter memories.

The opera aroused mixed reactions from press and public, as Hindemith's new works invariably did. There were critics who hailed it as an important advance in operatic form, and in the next few years it was produced in many other German opera houses, after Klemperer in Wiesbaden, more successfully than Busch (according to Willy Strecker), had shown the way. It has still not managed to win a place in the regular operatic repertory, but the growing frequency of its revival (in its original form more often than in the revision of it which Hindemith made in later years) suggests that *Cardillac* may yet establish its claim to be regarded as a significant contribution to twentieth-century opera. Hindemith's boast that he knew how "to solve the problem of modern opera" will perhaps in time be seen to have been less complacent than it first sounded.

Chapter 5

1927–32:

MUSIC TO SING AND PLAY

IN 1927 HINDEMITH accepted a post as teacher of composition at the Staatliche Hochschule für Musik, one of the state music schools in Berlin. The decision seems to have surprised himself as well as all his associates. The withdrawn academic life could hardly have appeared attractive to a vigorous composer of thirty-two whose whole outlook was that of a practising musician. And horror was indeed his own initial reaction to the offer from Berlin. As he later told his American pupil, Howard Boatwright, he thought immediately of his own teacher, Arnold Mendelssohn, with his black coat, his big gold watch-chain and his Olympian air. How could he think of turning his life in that direction?

To the enquiries of his friends he reacted with defensive facetiousness. "How am I settling down to professorial life?" he wrote to Else Thalheimer on 26 May 1927, a few months after his appointment. "I have grown a long beard, have a thick gold watch-chain and in the mornings yolk from my breakfast hard-boiled egg hangs on my waistcoat."

One reason which may have caused Hindemith to tie himself down to a teaching job was his increasing awareness of his own basic lack of learning and the feeling that in academic surroundings he would find both time and opportunity to educate himself. During his period at the Berlin Hochschule he did in fact teach himself Latin so that he could read in the original Boethius, St Augustine and other early musical thinkers. He also immersed himself in the music of medieval composers, teaching both himself and his pupils to play on the instruments (of which a large collection was on hand in Berlin) for which they were written.

Another clue to his state of mind can be found in a letter to Willy Strecker, dated 12 February 1927, in which he outlined his plans for a new type of music for the young:

"My ideas originate in the feeling that the over-cultivation

of 'music for music festivals' is leading us up a blind alley. Even
the people who are interested in modern music can do nothing
with it by themselves, because they lack the technical capabilities, and nothing exists for young people and for the early
educational stages."

The friends with whose help he intended to fill this gap were
Hans Mersmann, editor of the musical periodical *Melos*, and
Fritz Jöde, who was active in the *Jugendbewegung*, a youth
movement devoted to the joys of nature and natural living.
Both were music professors in Berlin and thus, when Hindemith
joined them there, they would be conveniently placed to develop their plans, beginning with the issue of an album of new
pieces.

"The music," Hindemith explained in his letter to Strecker,
"will be designed, according to the degree of difficulty, to be
not only of use for teaching purposes, but also to provide
material for amateurs interested in modern music." Such
pieces, easy to play, would constitute a new branch of music
literature, and for that a new name must be coined. His own
suggestion was *Haus- und Gemeinschaftsmusik* (music for home
and general use), but the title eventually adopted was *Sing- und
Spielmusik* (English title: *Music to Sing and Play*).

There was yet another possible reason for Hindemith's
decision to move to Berlin, and this was the opportunity it
would give him to spread his new ideas among the rising
generation of composers. He had, as his letter of 12 February
1927 to Strecker makes clear, come to consider that through
over-specialisation modern music was losing touch with the
public. This estrangement was as bad, he felt, for the composers
as for their audiences. Having spent years in sifting out new
works for presentation at Donaueschingen and Salzburg, he
had come to the conclusion that too many young composers
were using the freedom which he and others had made available
to them as a cloak to hide sheer incompetence, which the public,
lacking an effective yardstick, was unable to recognise. The
young composer was equally led astray, since he was receiving
from an uneducated public an adulation far beyond his due.
Novelty, Hindemith had come to feel, was not enough in itself,
and beauty, being a subjective concept, was a fallible guide.
The traditional rules of harmony, counterpoint and other
compositional techniques were no longer adequate, but nothing

had yet been devised to replace them. This was basically how he saw his task as a teacher: to concentrate on developing in his pupils a knowledge of the tools of their trade and an ability to use them, and at the same time to delve deeper into his own ideas on composition by examining them from a theoretical point of view—for his own benefit as well as his pupils'. In this way he might succeed in bringing the ideas into some sort of significant order.

Berlin, at the time Hindemith went there, was a city with a progressive musical outlook. It had three opera houses, and the main symphony orchestra, the Berlin Philharmonic, was under the direction of Wilhelm Furtwängler, a conductor who had always been interested in his compositions. The music director of the Staatsoper, Erich Kleiber, was less so, but his devotion to new developments had been decisively demonstrated in 1925 with the first production of Berg's *Wozzeck*. The Kroll Opera, which belonged to the Staatsoper, was more specifically dedicated to new and experimental work, and here another of Hindemith's champions, Otto Klemperer, was now in charge. Berlin's third opera house in Charlottenburg was more traditional but its musical director was Bruno Walter, a further illustrious name to add to the constellation which gave Berlin in the late Twenties and early Thirties the right to be considered the world's leading music centre. On the academic side too Berlin was very much in the vanguard. Schönberg was teaching at the Prussian Academy of the Arts, and the head of the Hochschule was Franz Schreker.

Hindemith's classes at the Hochschule were small—never more than ten—and confined to postgraduate students, chosen (by a faculty committee including himself) on the strength of previous examination results, recommendations from former teachers, and an interview. There was of course no lack of applicants eager to study with him. Among his German pupils were Siegfried Borries, Harald Gentzmer, Ernst Pepping and Franz Reizenstein. His first pupil from England was Walter Leigh, followed two years later by Arnold Cooke, both of whom had studied at Cambridge under Edward Dent, and a great point in their favour was (as I learned in conversation with Dr Cooke) that they arrived thoroughly grounded in traditional harmony. This won Hindemith's approval not so much for its

own sake as for the evidence it provided of a basic technical
knowledge.

All of his pupils, whatever accomplishments they brought
with them, had to start by writing two-part and three-part
exercises, and only after they had shown their facility in this
field were they allowed to embark on free composition. The
themes for the exercises were of the students' own devising, and
in working them out they were not restricted to the rules of
traditional harmony, but were permitted to make use of the
whole range of musical possibilities. The only criterion was
whether the solution "worked". Whether it did or not was
decided by the class as a whole. Hindemith himself was always
very critical, Dr Cooke told me, and he could at times be very
scathing, though he made great use of humour to banish possible
resentment or loss of confidence. He did not take advantage of
his position to lay down the law to his pupils, and there was
nothing formal or remote about his approach, yet his students
took no liberties with him: though not much older than they
were, he had a certain formidable quality that commanded
respect. Since each of his pupils was at a different stage of
development, he dealt with them individually. In the dis-
cussions of their exercises and compositions, however, the whole
class worked together.

When a pupil had satisfied Hindemith in the two-part and
three-part exercises, he was allowed to start on small compositions, the form of the piece and the combination of instruments
being specified by Hindemith himself. He always insisted that
a composer when writing a piece must bear in mind who was
to play it and for what kind of audience. He had no patience
with ivory tower attitudes: music was written for known combinations and occasions, he said, and should be playable and
understandable within those limits. If it should eventually
prove to have a wider and more permanent appeal, so much
the better, but this would be an additional reward, beyond the
composer's control.

His teaching methods, as this account based on the personal
memories of Franz Reizenstein, Arnold Cooke and other pupils
shows, were grounded on practice rather than on theory. It
was a preference that extended to performance as well as to
composition. He insisted that all his pupils should be able
to play more than one instrument, and he formed them into

what he called his "Robber Band" to try out their own compositions.

As far as musical techniques were concerned, there was still in the early years a lack of clear definition. The criterion whether a musical progression "worked" or not was perhaps a slender one on which to build a composition class, but it was the necessary preliminary to evolving a new theoretical system to replace or extend traditional, outmoded ones. Once Hindemith and his jury of pupils were agreed on a solution that sounded effective, he could set about analysing it in an attempt to find its axiomatic basis. This was the difference, in his view, between his method and Schönberg's. The twelve-tone system, as he saw it, was a preconceived set of rules to which the composer was obliged to conform. It was consequently restrictive. What he was aiming at was a definition of tonal and inter-vallic relationships which could serve composers as a guide, enabling them to move, freely but logically, in the direction their ear indicated. It was a long process of trial and error, but the axioms Hindemith eventually put on paper and published in 1937 under the title *Unterweisung im Tonsatz* (English title: *The Craft of Musical Composition*) were to a large extent the outcome of his work as a teacher at the Berlin Hochschule. I shall deal with the book in detail in a later chapter.

A year after beginning work at the Hochschule Hindemith decided that teaching was sufficiently to his taste to justify a permanent move to Berlin, and he rented a spacious apartment at Sachsenplatz 1 in the district of Charlottenburg. The departure from the Kuhhirtenturm in Frankfurt was celebrated with a farewell party. He festooned the walls of its rooms with oak leaves, and sausages were served on paper plates, the knives and forks tied with string to the table so that none of the guests could run away with them. The entertainment included a tableau in which Hindemith and his painter friend, Rudolf Heinisch, appeared as angels in a Raphael fresco, while Gertrud took the leading part in a bloodthirsty melodrama.

The Kuhhirtenturm was kept on as a home for his mother and sister, and the music room on the top floor left intact for use during his frequent visits. He did, however, take with him to Berlin his electric model railway. Carefully drawn plans of its intricate layout, made by Hindemith himself, together with detailed timetables, are still preserved in the Hindemith Institute in Frankfurt, and they suggest that this model railway was for him not just a toy, but a type of rigorous mental exercise, in which his delight in organisation found expression. But even if—ignoring his known passion for real trains and the claim of friends that he knew the complete European railway timetable off by heart—one concludes that the railway, to which he gave up three complete rooms in his Berlin home, was nothing more than an expression of the eternal child in him, it was a characteristic shared by many of his distinguished friends. He once confided to an American pupil at Yale, the late George Lam:

"On Sunday mornings my friends would come, and we would have a number of trains running—everything precise, everything on schedule. We had a timetable, and trains had to run on schedule, otherwise we would have collisions and collisions, since one train might start in one room and another express in another." The friends included the violinist Bronislav Hubermann and the pianist Artur Schnabel, and on one unfortunate occasion Schnabel's mother begged to be allowed to operate a switch. She made a mistake and there was a collision. "Schnabel turned on her with a fury that was incredible. You have no idea how brutal Schnabel could be."

In Berlin there was as little chance of a quiet domestic life as there had been previously in Frankfurt. The year 1927 contained a number of premières—the short opera *Hin und Zurück* (English title: *There and Back*) at the Baden-Baden festival in July, the viola concerto (*Kammermusik No. 5*) in November—and in 1928 some more: the organ concerto (*Kammermusik No. 7*) in January, and then in March the concerto for viola d'amore (*Kammermusik No. 6*), both having been written in the previous year. Apart from these, in most of which he was actively concerned, Hindemith was still giving concerts with the Amar Quartet and making solo appearances, including in May an important engagement in Paris, where he played his viola concerto under Serge Koussevitzky: the first move in Willy Strecker's campaign to establish him as a major figure on the international scene. Before that he had managed to put in a few weeks' work on his comic opera *Neues vom Tage*, and then it was time to prepare for the second summer festival in Baden-Baden.

The first had featured miniature operas (his own *Hin und*

Zurück among them). The second was to be devoted to cantatas in chamber style, film music and mechanical music. Darius Milhaud, who had contributed a miniature opera (*L'Enlèvement de l'Europe*) to the 1927 festival and had agreed to write a piece for Hindemith's collection of music for amateurs as well as to contribute to the Baden-Baden festival in 1928, paid him a visit in Berlin shortly before the festival. He describes it in his book *Notes Without Music*:

"Hindemith's concerts and classes took up so much of his time . . . that he was caught unprepared, and right up to the last moment was feverishly composing his pieces. . . . I shall always see him scribbling furiously and passing each page as he finished it to two of his students who immediately transcribed it on a pianola roll. It was a score for an imaginative film by Richter called *Vormittagsspuk*. For an animated cartoon, *Felix the Cat*, he used a synchronising apparatus invented by a German engineer, Robert Blum. By means of this it was possible to run off the film at the same time as a reel of similar size bearing two staves on which the music was written, so that the music could follow the slightest movement of the picture. During the performance, the musical score was thrown on the conductor's desk at the same time as the images were projected on to the screen. In this way the conductor was enabled to synchronise his playing exactly with the film. Hindemith proposed that I should experiment with this apparatus and, having nothing better to do, I accepted: I got hold of the newsreel of the week and, using the Blum machine, I wrote a suite of short pieces for a small orchestra."

Milhaud was, as one sees in this account, a kindred spirit: a practical musician who, like Hindemith, was always ready to turn his hand to anything new. Their work together at Baden-Baden was the beginning of a friendship that lasted, however long the gaps between their meetings, right up to Hindemith's death.

It was probably Hindemith's work on the Felix film (*Felix at the Circus*) that Else Thalheimer is referring to in the following reminiscence, preserved in manuscript in the Osborne Collection in New Haven, Connecticut (Bienicke Library):

"On the evening before the performance of films with mechanical music a rehearsal was held in the ball-room of the Kurhaus in Baden-Baden. It soon became apparent that all was not as it should be with the synchronisation. . . . A small

group of devotees—mainly composers and journalists—waited
anxiously with Hindemith for the historical moment when a
complete harmony of vision and sound would occur. It grew
later and later, but still the longed-for moment failed to come.
By general consent the experiment was abandoned for the
night. But when we made our way to the exit, we discovered to
our dismay that all the doors were securely locked. It had not
occurred to the night watchman that rehearsals might still be
going on at this late hour, and he had simply done his duty and
gone home. Nobody was more delighted about this act of *force
majeure* than Hindemith himself, for if it had so recently seemed
senseless to continue with the experiment, it would now have
been equally senseless—with all those hours of captivity looming
ahead—*not* to continue with it. And at seven o'clock the next
morning, in the very minute when the doorkeeper came along
with rattling keys to deliver us, the miracle at last occurred:
vision and sound began to function in harmony. Our captivity,
we could happily feel, had not lasted a moment too long: one
minute earlier and the experiment would have failed."

Milhaud's response to the invitation to provide a "cantata in
chamber style" for the 1928 festival was his *Cantate de l'Enfant
Prodigue*. Hindemith contributed *Frau Musica*, a piece to words
of Martin Luther for mezzo-soprano, baritone, mixed choir and
string orchestra (with wind instruments ad libitum). Milhaud's
account of the performance in *Notes Without Music* ("In the
course of a concert given in the forest, ancient music as well as
his cantata *Frau Musica* was sung by peasants") gives a rather
misleadingly romantic impression. The work was certainly
performed in the open air, but the singers were not peasants (a
social class long extinct in Germany). Most of them were
probably members of Jöde's Musikantengilde, the musical side
of the German Youth Movement, while the orchestra was a
scratch one of people attending the festival, including Hindemith himself.

There was in fact nothing in the least romantic or old-world
about Hindemith's series of pieces (including *Frau Musica*)
grouped under the general heading of *Music to Sing and Play*. It
was designed, as he himself defined it in the preface to the
printed scores which Schott's were bringing out under the
general title *Das Neue Werk*, as "interesting and modern practice
material for those who sing and play for their own amusement

or who want to perform for a small circle of similarly minded persons". Though the instrumental and vocal parts are technically within the grasp of most amateurs, there is no false simplicity in the music, which is in Hindemith's characteristic manner. It was a thoroughly serious attempt to bring contemporary music within the grasp of all and, to achieve this end, he reverted to a practice which had been common enough in earlier centuries, and was still common in the field of jazz: that of adapting the music to the forces at hand. "If wind instruments are available," he wrote in his preface, "they can be used to reinforce the vocal or instrumental parts. In the score I have indicated how I envisage the distribution of these additional parts. The opening and closing choruses should be sung by everyone present; before the performance begins these passages should be rehearsed with the help of a blackboard on which the notes are written."

These words might seem to suggest a village schoolmaster rather than a great composer, but they illustrate yet again what should by now have already become apparent: that Hindemith considered no practical detail too small for his personal attention.

There is a physical limit to what a single person, even with Hindemith's unbounded energies, can undertake, and he reached this point at the beginning of 1929. A tour of Russia with the Amar Quartet had still further delayed work on the new opera, and in the meantime he had accepted an invitation from Diaghilev to write a ballet. Becoming worried when the great Russian impresario insisted that he must have the piano score by March, Hindemith made a decision that could not have been easy for him: he broke up the Amar Quartet. At the same time he tried to persuade Diaghilev to give the ballet commission, for which he himself had so far found no ideas, to Bohuslav Martinu, "whom I consider very capable and who could write you a good score in a very short time". Diaghilev, however, was not so easily put off, and kept badgering him with lengthy telephone calls from Paris. "He was very distrustful," Gertrud complained to Strecker on 14 February 1929, "and could not understand that pure tiredness might prevent someone 'delivering' on time." Diaghilev, whose lack of understanding was probably due to the fact that he had heard this excuse many times before—far more often than Hindemith had ever made it—eventually relented, and a new delivery date was agreed for the end of the year. Before it was reached, Diaghilev died, and the ballet was never written.

Neues vom Tage (English title: *News of the Day*) was finally completed in March and put immediately into rehearsal at the Kroll Opera. The first performance, with Otto Klemperer as conductor, took place on 8 June 1929. It received the usual divided criticisms from the press, one critic praising it for its high spirits and humour, another denouncing it as an "insipid and below-standard job full of cheap effects, more suitable for production on a suburban stage than in the State Opera". Hindemith himself, as a letter dated 25 February 1930 to his publishers shows, was very dissatisfied with Ernst Legal's production, "which, to put it very crudely but accurately, was a load of crap".

The work, which has gone into history as being the first opera in which a prima donna is required to sing in her bath, has something of the nature of a problem child, and it aroused in its progenitor all the feelings of protective jealousy usually associated with that relationship. Neither in its original form nor in the revised version he made in 1953 has it succeeded in holding its place in the repertory though apparently it pleased its initial audiences. Could it be that the opera is misunderstood? Hindemith himself claimed that its picture of cosmopolitan life in the Twenties was satirical and, if one takes into account his conviction that an artist has a moral responsibility to society, one can accept the satirical intention while questioning whether the satire effectively comes through. Hindemith was a man of great humour, but he lacked the quality of cynicism that is an essential part of satire. His librettist, Marcellus Schiffer, who had also been responsible for the text of *Hin und Zurück*, was a writer of lyrics and sketches for variety and revue, and this tale of a married couple who in their attempts to get a divorce are hounded by the publicity media has all the brittleness and superficial cynicism of that form of entertainment. As a writer Schiffer was in a much lower class than his composer.

The next writer with whom Hindemith collaborated was one of a very different calibre. He had come to know Bertolt Brecht in 1927 in Baden-Baden, Brecht being the author of *Mahagonny*, Kurt Weill's contribution to the series of miniature operas (later expanded into the full-length *Aufstieg und Fall der Stadt*

Mahagonny). For the Baden-Baden festival of 1929 Brecht and Hindemith now set about writing what the composer described to his publishers as "a kind of folk oratorio".

Lehrstück (English title: *Lesson on Consent*) deals with an air pilot who, injured when his plane crashes, calls on his fellow men for help. It is a harsh parable on the unimportance of the individual, and it seems likely that Hindemith did not fully grasp the message of the piece or the nature of Brecht's dramatic method when he decided to set it as part of his music for amateurs. He prefaced his score with the following words: "Since the *Lehrstück* is only intended to implicate all people present in the actual performance and not in the first place to make any definite impression as a musical or literary utterance, its form can be adapted to the needs of the moment. The order of pieces in the score is accordingly to be taken more as a recommendation than a command. Omissions, additions and transpositions can be made."

The motto of that year's festival was "Making music is better than listening to it". Hindemith was concerned only in providing a piece in which the audience would be brought in as participators. Brecht was also interested in implicating his audience—but not just for the purpose of developing their musical awareness: he wanted to rouse their critical sense and to ram his moral home.

The scandal which the *Lehrstück* caused at its first performance on 28 July 1929 was due entirely to a scene in which there is hardly any music. It is a rather roughly written sketch in which a couple of clowns cure a giant of his aches and pains by sawing off the affected limbs one after another. The violent protest it aroused from an audience which included such venerable literary figures as Gerhard Hauptmann and André Gide may very well have been due to the uncomfortable way in which its moral struck home, and for that reason Brecht, standing on the stage, as Max Rieple tells us, in "a crumpled khaki-coloured suit", must have been well content. Hindemith, though he accepted the protests and hisses with his usual calm, was less so. His main concern was that the scandal would frighten off the people for whom his work was intended— namely, amateurs—and he gave instructions in the score, published after the festival, that the clowns' scene could if desired be left out.

Brecht objected. After a few performances had taken place without the controversial scene, he wrote to Schott's on 23 April 1930: "I must urgently request you not to permit this, but to insist categorically on the clowns' scene, and what is more with the original Baden-Baden masks by Porep." A few months later, when the publishers notified Brecht of an intended production in Berlin, he came up with new objections. "I have in the meantime done some more work on the previous fragment," he wrote to Schott's on 20 September 1930. "I do not wish the work to be performed in its old form." Strecker appealed to Hindemith to sort the matter out personally with Brecht. "I hope you know the magic formula with which we can pacify him," he wrote on 24 September. It seems Hindemith did not. He had neither seen Brecht's new version, nor was he interested in writing any new music for it. Brecht stuck to his decision not to permit a performance in the original form, and the matter went to the lawyers. The final outcome of the dispute was that the *Lehrstück* was withdrawn from circulation and was not performed again for nearly thirty years.

It was a sad fate for a work which is now generally recognised as one of the finest examples of Hindemith's *Music to Sing and Play*, though happily it has with time proved remediable. Not so, however, the missed opportunity of a collaboration on a major work between two of the twentieth century's main artistic figures. At the beginning of 1930, before the *Lehrstück* dispute had got under way, Hindemith was writing enthusiastically to his publishers about a "high life" opera text which Brecht had promised him, but this fell victim to the ensuing estrangement. All that arose from the short crossing of their paths, apart from *Lehrstück*, was a few musical numbers (the others being by Kurt Weill) for a radio play, *Lindberghflug*, which was also performed at the 1929 festival in Baden-Baden.

Following his success in launching Hindemith as a soloist in Paris under the auspices of Koussevitzky, Willy Strecker turned his attention to London. He wrote on 3 July 1929 to the composer, reporting on Mrs Courtauld and her plans to start a series of concerts in the Queen's Hall. "She has engaged Klemperer, Schnabel and others and is allowing for each work as many rehearsals as necessary—something hitherto unknown

Paul Hindemith's musical handwriting:
Left: from his sketchbooks: passage from unpublished Piano Sonata, Opus 17 (1920)

Below: clean copy: passage from *Nobilissima Visione* (Troubadour's Song) in his own arrangement for piano (1938)

Above: Paul and Gertrud Hindemith in 1924, the year of their marriage

Right: Paul Hindemith at Boston on his first visit to the United States, 1937

in England." This was the platform he had long been seeking, Strecker went on, to introduce Hindemith there.

Elizabeth Courtauld was the wife of Samuel Courtauld, chairman of the giant textiles firm. What he did with his wealth for art and painting, his wife decided to do for music. After financing three international opera seasons at Covent Garden, she turned her attention to symphony concerts, and it was her friend Artur Schnabel who suggested that she might try in London something along the lines of the series of concerts organised by the Volksbühne in Berlin for the furtherance of "proletarian culture". Mrs Courtauld, deciding that even for the proletariat only the best was good enough, engaged the London Symphony Orchestra and announced a series of concerts at the Queen's Hall. The public response to the "Courtauld-Sargent Concerts", as they were called (she had appointed Malcolm Sargent, then still in his thirties, as musical director) was so great that each concert had to be given twice.

It was certainly an excellent opportunity for introducing himself to the London public, but Hindemith had little feeling for the politics of fame. Before the date Mrs Courtauld offered him, he accepted an invitation from Edward Clark, head of the music department of the British Broadcasting Corporation, to appear at one of Sir Henry Wood's Promenade Concerts. There he intended to give the first performance of a viola concerto by William Walton.

Strecker was appalled. "The London affair is very regrettable," he wrote to Gertrud on 8 July 1929. "I want your husband, appearing there for the first time before the larger public, to do it in a worthy setting, and as a composer, not just as a soloist. An appearance with Wood to play a concerto by a moderately gifted English composer—and that is what Walton is—is not as I see it a début. Wood's Promenade Concerts are, like their conductor himself, a worthy institution, at which the playing is so-so, 30 to 40 soloists appear, and never a sensation of the sort I am hoping for. . . . Your husband should make himself harder to get."

But Hindemith preferred to remain true to his own standards, and in doing so showed himself a far better judge of the English than Strecker with his careful manipulations. He performed Walton's concerto on 3 October 1929, and that act of graciousness towards a young English composer certainly did

D

more to endear him to the British public than any contrived "sensation".

Hindemith played Walton's concerto for the best possible reason—because he liked it. He also liked and respected Sir Henry Wood, recognising in him a man of his own kind: one who set himself to make music competently and without fuss in the most practical way, unconcerned by thoughts of personal fame, either present or posthumous. Hindemith's playing of Walton's concerto was very brusque, as the composer himself told me. "His technique was marvellous, but he was rough— no nonsense about it. He just stood up and played." This encounter (not their first, for they had met in Salzburg in 1923 at the ISCM festival in which Walton's first string quartet was played) was the beginning of a lasting friendship between the two. Walton admits that in writing his work he had been much influenced by Hindemith's own viola concerto (*Kammermusik No. 5*). "I was surprised he played it," he told me. "One or two bars are almost identical."

Hindemith did eventually appear at a Courtauld-Sargent Concert. In November 1930 he played his own viola concerto, which the critics compared variously to "a toy Tower Bridge made from a Meccano set", "a flat pancake" and "patterns cut by a busy stencilling machine". On the whole, the English critics were never very kind to him, but nor was he very kind in his opinion of them. "In England the newspaper critics seem to consist of dunces," he once wrote to Willy Strecker. "I'd like to be there when they take their exams before starting on their career. That must be a curious sight."

In February 1930 Hindemith announced to his publishers that as regards composition he was going through a fallow period. "But don't cry," he added. "Even Beethoven had several years when he wrote nothing."

With Hindemith such periods could be measured in months, not years. After abandoning the Amar Quartet, it had not been long before his desire to play chamber music led him to form, with two colleagues at the Hochschule—Josef Wolfsthal, the violinist, and Emanuel Feuermann, the cellist—a new string trio. And for the summer festival in Berlin, transferred there from Baden-Baden following the *Lehrstück* scandal, he was soon busy composing a new work.

Wir bauen eine Stadt (English title: *Let's Build a Town*) was a further development of the series *Music to Sing and Play*. It was an attempt to write something for children with the co-operation of children themselves. Daily over a period of weeks he went to a school in Berlin and, having worked out a general idea with the children, made a note of what they themselves suggested. On the following day he would bring in his work based on their suggestions and rehearse it with them. Any objections the children then raised would be discussed, and alterations made. Never before, Hindemith told Strecker, had he had so hard a task and such uncompromising critics.

This little stage work, though held by some critics following its first performance in Berlin on 21 June 1930 to be beyond the capacity of children (Hindemith did not disclose publicly the manner in which it had been written), is a remarkable example of joint creation, whose value has been confirmed by the huge number of performances it has since received by children throughout the world and in many languages. Hindemith's own attitude towards it was fully in keeping with the spirit in which it was written. He told his publishers that he had no objection to people altering it as they liked to suit themselves. "The work is meant to be a creative game, and the more people tinker with it and alter it around themselves the better."

Of the other works composed in 1930 two were destined for America. The Concert Music for Piano, Brass and Two Harps was commissioned by that indefatigable collector of contemporary composers, Mrs Elizabeth Sprague Coolidge, who came regularly with her musical staff to the festivals of the ISCM to seek out likely candidates and reward them with a commission, generously paid. Hindemith was pleased to supply a work, though not to go to America to hear it. Emma Lübbecke-Job made the journey and played the piano part when it was first performed in Chicago on 12 October 1930. The Concert Music for String Instruments and Brass Orchestra was written at the invitation of Serge Koussevitzky to celebrate the fiftieth anniversary of the Boston Symphony Orchestra, and first performed there on 4 April 1931.

The outstanding success of these two pieces suggested to the Strecker brothers that the time was approaching when Hindemith himself should be launched in America. But he was in no great hurry to go there. Having now written in practically

every other known musical form, he was anxious in 1931 to try
his hand at the one remaining unstormed citadel: the oratorio.

His choice of the German lyric poet Gottfried Benn (1886–
1956) as his librettist may have owed something to the fact that
Benn also lived in Berlin where, besides writing poetry, he
practised medicine as a skin specialist. Ian Kemp, in his monograph on the composer, mentions a more compelling artistic
reason. Hindemith happened to hear a radio discussion between Benn and Brecht on the theme of the artist's influence on
society. Their attitudes were radically opposed, and Hindemith,
with the dispute over *Lehrstück* a very recent and still painful
memory, found himself on Benn's side.

The theme of *Das Unaufhörliche* (English title: *The Perpetual*),
shortly defined, is the evanescence of human endeavour in
contrast to the permanent values of the universal order. First
performed in Berlin under Otto Klemperer on 21 November
1931, it aroused respectful attention as well as the usual
sprinkling of abuse, but apart from a few performances—an
early one was in London under Sir Henry Wood—the work has
never managed to establish itself in the regular repertory.
Nevertheless, it is significant as a reminder of the contemplative
side of Hindemith's nature which, particularly in the years
devoted to *Music to Sing and Play*, was only intermittently in
evidence. Benn's mood of pessimistic resignation was perhaps
not in line with Hindemith's own more positive outlook, but
the theme of Man's place in a wider scheme more permanent
than himself was beginning more and more to dominate his
thoughts. Seen thus, there is a line which connects *Das
Unaufhörliche* with the final expression of Hindemith's views on
the human function in the opera *Die Harmonie der Welt*.

The year 1932 produced two new works of a widely differing
kind. The *Philharmonisches Konzert* was written at Furtwängler's
invitation to celebrate the fiftieth anniversary of the Berlin
Philharmonic Orchestra and was dedicated to both conductor
and orchestra, who first performed it on 14 April. Two months
later Hindemith brought out his *Plöner Musiktag* (English title:
A Day of Music in Plön), a whole series of instrumental and
choral pieces which he wrote for and rehearsed with the pupils
of a school in Schleswig-Holstein. The first performance began
in the morning with a fanfare from a tower. It was followed by

a short instrumental suite, played during lunch; and then came the most substantial item, a cantata entitled *Mahnung an die Jugend, sich der Musik zu befleissigen* (English title: *Admonition to Youth to Apply itself to Music*), the whole event being rounded off in the evening with an instrumental concert of six pieces.

If this work has not as a whole attained the popularity of *Wir bauen eine Stadt*, the reason lies in its even more purpose-bound nature. As Hindemith observed to his publishers: "The pieces allow, both in their layout and construction, for a lack of expertness in the players, and the teacher should not try to overcome it. To play pieces like this with the smooth brilliance of a highly-trained professional orchestra would be senseless, as it also would be to play them in the concert hall of a large town. The conditions for a 'day of music' are not everywhere as favourable as in Plön. Nobody should entertain for a moment the false idea of performing all the music at once just as it is: it is far more desirable to select from them and arrange them to suit the conditions and circumstances."

The *Plöner Musiktag* was virtually the last of that important body of work which Hindemith once rashly referred to as *Gebrauchsmusik*, then grouped together under the apter title of *Sing- und Spielmusik*. Its importance lies less in its actual musical content (though that is by no means negligible) than in its recognition of music as a social activity. Of course this aspect of music has never been entirely neglected, as the unbroken flow of dance music, salon pieces, fanfares and marches over the centuries shows, but it was Hindemith's purpose to demonstrate what composers before the nineteenth century, among them Bach and Mozart, already knew—that this type of composition is not beneath the dignity of even the greatest.

The fact that after the *Plöner Musiktag* Hindemith himself ceased to pursue this line actively, apart from a few pieces written in America, was due not to a change of attitude towards music, but rather to a change of circumstances. Within a few months of its first performance the German chancellor Heinrich Brüning would be gone and his place taken (following a couple of short-lived successors) by Adolf Hitler. Hindemith was, of course, well aware of the existence of the National Socialists—who could not be at that time?—but he had never wasted time in speculating what effect a National Socialist dictatorship might have on his own life and career. As far as he had any political convictions at all, he seems to have leaned towards social democracy: the fact that, beside his teaching work at the Hochschule, he also conducted an evening class in Neukölln, a workers' district in Berlin, is an indication. But his basic inability to take politics seriously can be inferred from a light-hearted exchange of correspondence between himself and Ludwig Strecker when in August 1932 he was on holiday in Switzerland.

It began with a mistake in Schott's despatch department. A letter addressed to a certain Herr Zehnter, rejecting an opera he had submitted for consideration, got into an envelope addressed to Hindemith. For fun Hindemith pretended to be Zehnter and wrote Schott's a furious letter. "You have rejected my *Söldner*, but the dreadful rubbish I have foisted on to you during the past ten years or so under the name of Hindemith you have printed without a murmur." In his reply Ludwig Strecker noted with surprise that the name Hindemith was a pseudonym, and invited "Herr Zehnter" to compose three or four operas on well-known car names such as Adler, DKW and BMW, "since we got along so famously with your Cadillac". He might also care to write a Hitler oratorio as well as a Brüning one—"for one can never know". Hindemith responded to this by writing back under the name of "Adolf Neuner, secretary to Herr Zehnter": "Nothing will probably come of the Brüning oratorio. The name of Hitler is completely unknown to us. We can only assume that it is a misprint, and that you really mean Hiller."

PART TWO

SEMI-EXILE

Chapter 1

1933–34:

A TRIAL OF STRENGTH

WHEN, IN JANUARY 1933, the Nazis came to power, Hindemith was busy working with the novelist and dramatist Ernst Penzoldt on the text of a new opera. Two months later, on 10 March, he wrote to the Strecker brothers in Mainz:

"To judge by what I now see happening in musical and theatrical affairs, all the key jobs will shortly be occupied by rigidly national types. Next spring, by which time the first difficulties should have been got over, the prospects for an opera by Penzoldt and myself should be very good, though maybe not for this particular text. Still, one never knows. But all the same, caution is called for, and I am in favour of shelving this particular subject for a while and seeking another. I have already been looking around and have come on something which is innocuous and interesting and will this year and next be highly topical. It deals with the building of the first railways. There are some very nice anecdotes, both in England and in Germany, from which one could easily make a comic opera."

The opera on which Hindemith had been working with Ernst Penzoldt (1892–1955) was called *Etienne und Luise* and concerned a love affair between a French prisoner-of-war and a German girl during the First World War. However unlikely a subject it might seem for a man of Hindemith's deliberately unromantic character, it had taken a strong hold on his imagination—to the exclusion of other suggestions which had even included one for a work based on the life of the painter Matthias Grünewald. Putting forward this idea, Willy Strecker wrote on 26 September 1932: "There would be a chance with the peasants' wars and the Renaissance of drawing parallels with present times." Hindemith's decision to put off *Etienne und Luise* after working the text out in complete detail with Penzoldt can be taken not as a cooling off of interest, but as what he said it was: a concession to expediency. In fact, he never took it up again. Nor did anything come of the suggested comic opera about the advent of the railways.

Expediency might also explain the nature of the piece of music he intended to write in place of the opera. Temporarily laid up with an inflamed foot, he wrote to Willy Strecker on 15 April 1933:

"Through this wretched foot and all the general muddle I have not done any serious work in the past weeks. I did a few songs, but what I really had in mind was a big thing for men's chorus, a sort of cantata with soloists and perhaps a very primitive brass band such as can be found in any village. . . . I am looking for texts in Novalis (the Night Hymns) and Hölderlin. Don't you agree that a kind of light and harmless, but still very serious piece would be just the thing for now? With the bigger things we shall have to wait a bit."

Strecker had already been perturbed by the dictatorial attitude of some petty Nazi officials belonging to the Kampfbund in Mainz towards some of the composers whose works he published: "Stravinsky has been put on the list of bolshevist Russian Jews and his works can no longer be played," he wrote to Hindemith on 5 April 1933. "You yourself are to fifty per cent condemned as a cultural bolshevist on account of your earlier works." Both Sekles and Hans Gal, he added, had been dismissed from the Hoch Conservatorium in Frankfurt. He asked Hindemith, as one "sitting at the source" in Berlin, to advise him on what might be done to get things put in order at the top, before too much milk was spilt.

Hindemith's reply, contained in the letter of 15 April already quoted, was reassuring:

"To judge by what is happening here I don't think we need worry too much about the musical future. One must just be patient for the next few weeks. So far in all the changes nothing has happened to me. Recently, just after my return from England, I had a long talk with some of the higher-ups in the Kampfbund. It concerned only educational matters, but I got the impression (after I had satisfied them that I was neither a half nor any other fractional Jew) that they have a good opinion of me there. Since then they have commissioned me (though not quite officially) to work out plans for a new system of teaching composition and musical theory. Since I know how mistrustful people are, and have also seen how several who tried to curry favour have sunk without trace, I am none too anxious to carry out this tidying-up operation just now: *I* have no desire to curry favour. . . .

"One of these days I shall have of course to get the Kampf-bund to intercede on my behalf, but it is too early yet for that. In the present state of general uncertainty it won't be possible anywhere to do much. . . . But the right course for us is not to show any fear or uncertainty. God knows, we've got nothing to hide. . . .

"Here in the school there's a grand old muddle. All the Jewish teachers have had to go of course, except for one or two like [Curt] Sachs and [Karl] Flesch who are indispensable. [Georg] Schünemann too, probably, having ruined everything by his vacillating."

It is easy, with the benefit of hindsight, to condemn this letter as not only blind, but remarkably heartless. Among the Jewish teachers who were instantly dismissed from the Hochschule was, after all, the cellist of his own string trio, Emanuel Feuermann. And Schünemann, who had taken over from Schreker as head of the Hochschule in 1932 and was not even a Jew, seems to have lost his job not on account of his "vacillating", but because the Nazis wanted a man of their own in the job. Hindemith thought that his successor, Fritz Stein, a professor of music at Kiel University, might be "not bad for our cause, although he is not exactly a model of courage and steadfastness". He possibly did not know that Stein had been a secret supporter of the Nazi party since 1925 and a member of the Kampfbund since 1932. Before assuming office at the Hochschule, Stein astutely demanded that all the professors considered undesirable by the Nazis (and they included Jöde, Hindemith's colleague in *Das neue Werk*, as well as Feuermann) should be dismissed so that he himself could start with clean hands.

Hindemith did not give the names of the Kampfbund officials with whom he discussed plans for a reorganisation of teaching methods, but they certainly included the violinist Gustav Havemann, whom he had known for many years. However disreputable Berta Geissmar makes him appear in her book *The Baton and the Jackboot*, Havemann, at the time the Nazis came to power, was a respected figure in musical circles, having been a teacher at the Hochschule since 1920. The Kampfbund, in which he held a leading position, was founded in 1928 by

Alfred Rosenberg to combat the "culturally destructive efforts of liberalism" and to promote "powers rooted in the German outlook". In the early months of Nazi rule it had sole control over cultural and artistic activities in Germany, and possessed a choir and orchestra of its own.

It is therefore not to be wondered at that all practising artists should have felt it expedient at the start to keep on the right side of the Kampfbund. Hindemith must certainly have thought that, by keeping a cool head and not protesting against summary dismissals of Jews and others, he was adopting a commonsense attitude: no doubt he believed that these demonstrations of excessive zeal would soon die down of their own accord. Strecker was convinced by his comforting assurances, "since they largely accord with my own feelings". Neither of them, obviously, saw the true nature of the men with whom they were now dealing.

Hindemith's initial attitude towards the Nazis was quite simply that of a citizen in a democratic country when the party he does not support comes to power. Since he was not a Nazi supporter, he did not find it necessary to give the Nazi salute when he entered the Hochschule. In his class, which included two Jews as well as an American, a Japanese and several Germans, politics were sometimes discussed. The late Franz Reizenstein (one of the Jewish students) told me: "Hindemith did not make any secret of his anti-Nazi convictions. He was not afraid of being given away to the authorities, though he could have been a hundred times over."

Nor did Hindemith see any reason why he should not continue to play chamber music in public with his Jewish colleagues. With Feuermann and Symon Goldberg, who had taken over the violin part in his trio in 1931 following the death of Wolfsthal, he gave the first performance of his new string trio in Antwerp on 17 March 1933. In May he went to Vienna to take part in the Brahms centenary celebrations, and his colleagues in a performance of the piano quartet were Bronislav Hubermann, Pablo Casals and Artur Schnabel. His letters to his publishers showed no interest in politics. Unless he was directly asked for a political opinion, he preferred to talk about his musical activities. He was very interested, for instance, in a new electrical instrument which one of his fellow professors at the Hochschule, Dr Trautwein, had invented. The trautonium, as it was called, was a single-string instrument which produced a clear note, and Hindemith found it useful in the experiments on intervals and overtones which he was busy working out with his students. He urged his publishers to issue an instruction manual on it. "It really has become a very useful thing," he wrote, "and I believe will soon be in great demand."

Nothing came of the trautonium, just as nothing came of a plan, initiated by Sir Robert Mayer, to transport the children of the school in Plön to England in order to perform the *Plöner Musiktag*; nor of the idea, following Sonya Korty's new production of *Das Nusch-Nuschi* in Antwerp in March 1933, to revive this work in Berlin under Furtwängler. But there is never a hint in his correspondence with his publishers that Hindemith was conscious of a connection between these non-events and Hitler's rise to power.

Yet by the end of the summer, 1933, he must surely have become aware that the persecution of the Jews was no mere passing excess of zeal. Besides those already mentioned, others of his friends and colleagues had by then been swept away. Curt Sachs, the specialist in old instruments, earlier described by Hindemith as "indispensable", had after all been dismissed; Mersmann, his colleague with Jöde in *Das neue Werk*, had lost his jobs both as teacher at the Technische Hochschule and as head of music in the Berlin radio station; Schreker, who had taken up a position at the Prussian Academy of the Arts after leaving the Hochschule, was dismissed from that and suffered a stroke from which he died a few months later; Schönberg and Leo Kestenberg had also disappeared from the Prussian Academy; and gone from their posts as conductors and performing artists were Otto Klemperer, Fritz Busch, Licco Amar, Beatrice Lauer-Kottlar and many other associates too numerous to mention.

Most of these emigrated, but some remained for a while to continue their careers within the confines of the Jüdischer Kulturbund, the Jewish cultural organisation which the Nazis fostered in the not unsuccessful hope that it would be accepted by the outside world as proof that they were not too inhuman towards their Jews. In Berlin alone the Jüdischer Kulturbund had 19,000 members and provided employment for 125 musicians and actors. The elder of the two Thalheimer sisters, now since her marriage named Else Lewertoff, remarks in her reminiscences: "It is one of the many ironies of those times that it was precisely within those organisations, with their ghetto implications, that the best of the forbidden names appeared once again on the programmes." She records that one of the first works the Cologne branch of the Jüdischer Kulturbund put on for performance was Hindemith's *Wir bauen eine Stadt*. Hindemith allowed her husband, Schlomo Lewertoff, to adapt the libretto, turning the town the children were engaged in building into Palestine, and he wrote for it a new orchestral intermezzo which enabled the work to be presented in two acts.

Hindemith did not see such gestures on his part as courageous: they were what anyone would do for his friends. Another act of the same sort, though it took place in 1934, is worth quoting here as a further striking example of Hindemith's refusal to allow political events to affect his personal loyalties. It was related by the late Franz Reizenstein in an article "Hindemith— Some Aspersions Answered", printed in *The Composer* of 1965, and it concerns a student at the Hochschule who was about to leave after studying there for six years. Reizenstein tactfully refers to him simply as X:

"Hindemith admired the quality of his workmanship and, when two concerts of students' works were planned, he decided that one of these should be entirely devoted to X's works. The other concert was to consist of compositions by an American, a Pole, a Japanese and two German Jews of whom I was one, but this programme was also to include one of X's works which did not fit into the other programme. X, pretending false modesty at first, suggested that his work should be taken out of this mixed concert, as he already had the lion's share. We all felt a little uncomfortable, as this did not ring true. When hard pressed by Hindemith to state the real reason for his request, he stammered that it would be a bad thing for his career now if his work was sandwiched in between two Jewish compositions! X was on quite friendly terms with all the other members of the class. He was not really a Nazi, but his cowardly attitude was very typical of millions of his fellow countrymen.

"Hindemith, who was of a calm and level-headed disposition, had on this occasion the only outburst of furious temper that I have ever witnessed in all the years I have known him. X was told by his beloved master that with his mentality he was unfit to be a creative artist, as he lacked some essential qualities of character. Then Hindemith released a whole flood of bitter words against the Nazis, saying that he would sooner die than fight for these criminals if it came to a war. He spoke passionately for toleration, freedom of the individual in society and preservation of human rights. Amongst the class who listened to this tirade there were several young Germans whose political views were unknown to Hindemith and who could have denounced him. It goes almost without saying that X's request was ignored and his piece performed in the mixed programme as planned."

Willy Strecker's suggestion of an opera about the painter Matthias Grünewald, disdained by Hindemith in 1932, now began to take possession of his thoughts. He decided, after his difficult experiences with past librettists, to write the text for it himself. On 26 July 1933 he wrote to Strecker: "I am making very good progress. True, at the moment I am still ploughing through books, but quite a lot of the action is already fixed, and musically also I have plenty in mind." At the beginning of August he and Gertrud visited Strecker at his home in Wiesbaden, and on the following day (4 August 1933) Strecker wrote for his brother Ludwig an account of the meeting:

"He told me that in Berlin views and leading personalities are being changed much more often than shirts. Nobody dares to touch him, and both Havemann and Furtwängler swear by him. How long Havemann will last nobody of course can say. Furtwängler is behaving admirably, has also seen to it that all his Jewish orchestral players are kept on, and Fräulein Geissmar of course too [Berta Geissmar, Furtwängler's Jewish secretary]. . . .

"Hindemith is expecting a complete change of direction in a few months' time, and till then one should just keep quiet and do nothing rash. . . . He said: 'Let them go ahead and put on a few poor operas. It may work the first time or two, but then no more, for bad works can't be pushed indefinitely, and the people they are now digging out are all complete mediocrities.' . . .

"Hindemith is clearly conscious that he must write in a more popular way, and he believes that he can do it. For the Grünewald opera he is writing four preludes and interludes based on pictures from the Isenheim altar, and designed more or less to set the scene for each of the four acts. Since Furtwängler badly wants something new by Hindemith for a concert at the beginning of December and his ensuing tour, Hindemith wants to give him these pieces in the form of a suite, thereby demonstrating that a composer can write in a decent modern way and still remain popular. Furtwängler intends to make great propaganda with this work, which at the same time will provide a good advertisement for the opera.

"The basic material for that is already more or less fixed. In the past fourteen days he has read no fewer than 130 books in order to collect material and study the historical background. The first concrete result of that, he told me, was to arouse in him a huge contempt for scientists, who all did nothing but stolidly read books and copy each other's conclusions. If one of these gentlemen had a good idea, he would be dismissed by the others as 'unserious'. His study of all scientific books of the Reformation period, he says, has strikingly confirmed this judgment.

"He is full of enthusiasm for the subject, which suits him extremely well. This can become *the* German opera. The figure of Grünewald, who went his own way in spite of being misunderstood, and resisted the foreign influence of the Italian Renaissance, is of course a reflection of himself, and that is why it interests him so tremendously. There are even two sketches for love scenes in the story, both of which turn out negatively in Hindemith's version, but are of great human interest. Two acts are set in Frankfurt (Römer, cathedral, election of the emperor, etc.), one in Mainz and one in Oppenheim, where he (Mathis) meets Luther—a magnificent scene with a grand finale of *Eine feste Burg* and confession of faith as choral piece. He is so gripped by the subject, the atmosphere in which he is steeped, the overall parallels between those former times and our own, and above all the theme of an artist's lonely fate, that he will work with an inspiration and self-involvement as never before.

"He is a truly remarkable person, extraordinarily sensible and practical—a man who has digested his experiences, knows exactly what is needed and what he himself wants, and is in no need of advice. The theme is big and German, yet of international interest. And since he feels he has the power to work it out himself, and above all is so blissful at the prospect of writing the words to the music and not the other way round and being able to plan it all accordingly, I am confident we can expect something very exciting.

"Our evening together was most impressive, and it was so characteristic of Hindemith the way he constantly—and almost shyly—tried to conceal the human connections with his own personality, dragging in irrelevant historical happenings to hide the essential point."

Strecker was right in his assumption that Hindemith would probably alter the details, but not the overall theme, of his opera. In its final form none of the projected scenes in Frankfurt appear, and nor does the meeting with Luther occur. With great skill Hindemith managed in the ensuing months to reduce the story of an artist's struggle with his conscience to its clearest and most human form, contrasting Matthias Grünewald (?1480–?1528), an artist with a social conscience, with his employer Albrecht von Brandenburg, the art-loving archbishop of Mainz, a politician with a social conscience. He sets them against the conflicting background of the Peasants' War (1524–25), in which Catholics and Protestants, otherwise in bitter rivalry, are united in their opposition to the rebellious peasants. Also humanly involved in this drama of irreconcilable interests are Ursula, the daughter of a prosperous Protestant citizen of Mainz, who, though in love with Mathis, is required to make a political marriage with the archbishop; and Regina, the young daughter of the peasant leader Schwalb.

The months during which Hindemith wrestled with this complicated material were months during which his own life was being forced towards a showdown, against a muddled background of public denunciation and private tolerance. Five days after his meeting with his publisher in Wiesbaden, his brother-in-law, Hans Flesch, was arrested in Berlin and taken to the concentration camp at Oranienburg.

Flesch, who had moved from the radio station in Frankfurt to the Berlin radio in 1928, had already been deprived of his position in Berlin on account of his Jewish blood. Now he was to become one of the principal victims of Goebbels's plan to seize complete control of the German radio network. After a protracted trial, in which Hans Bredow (1879–1959), the founding father of German radio, Flesch and others were accused of corruptly diverting sums of money from licence fees into their own pockets, they were sentenced on 13 June 1935 to fines and terms of imprisonment. The longest sentence—one year's imprisonment—was imposed on Flesch.

The Nazi pressure was now beginning to come uncomfortably near home. Flesch was married to Gertrud's sister Gabriele, and though their father, the completely Jewish Ludwig Rottenberg, had mercifully escaped persecution by dying in 1932, Hindemith himself faced the difficulty of possessing a "non-Aryan" wife. That this had not been officially brought up against him he owed probably to the fact that quite a number of prominent German musicians, including Richard Strauss, the president of the Reichsmusikkammer, had family connections with Jews. The Nazis, alarmed by the fall in quality of the artists willing to remain in the country, were prepared—for the moment—to make concessions.

They were anyway at this time engaged in a struggle for power among themselves. Goebbels was trying to wrest control of the cultural front from his rival Alfred Rosenberg. His Reichskulturkammer, which covered music, theatre and other cultural activities, was designed as an active instrument of the Propaganda Ministry. That division of it which covered music, the Reichsmusikkammer, had a representative in every German town with a population of more than five thousand, and all programmes had to be submitted in advance to this representative for approval.

Rosenberg, his monopoly as cultural dictator now broken, secured from Hitler the right to make himself responsible for the overall education of the Nazi party in philosophical and intellectual matters. In 1934 his Kampfbund was given the new title of Kulturgemeinde. Rosenberg's general influence was nevertheless still immense for, in addition to his other activities, he was the editor of the Nazi party's official daily newspaper, the *Völkischer Beobachter*.

Many of the people who were active in Rosenberg's Kulturgemeinde (or its predecessor, the Kampfbund) were also implicated in Goebbels's Reichskulturkammer and its divisions. Among them were both Stein and Havemann at the Berlin Hochschule, and it was certainly due to their efforts, together with the support of Furtwängler, the Reichsmusikkammer's vice-president, that Hindemith was not at this time openly under attack.

Busy as he was with his Grünewald opera, he was in any case little before the public eye. The few concert appearances he made in the winter of 1933–34 were mainly abroad. In October 1933 he was in Copenhagen, in January 1934 in Brussels and in London, where, together with Goldberg and Feuermann, he made (for Columbia) his first commercial gramophone records. To fill a blank side he rose at five on the final morning, and by eight had completed a Scherzo for viola and cello, which he and Feuermann at once recorded. After the session there was a party. Walter Legge, who was present, told me: "Hindemith, in high spirits, took Feuermann's cello and walked round the room, holding it vertically and playing (among other extremely funny improvisations) variations on the *Barbiere di Siviglia* overture." It is evident that, whatever his worries, he had not lost his customary humour.

In February 1934 the prospect of being entrusted with the initiation of a new educational venture arose once more. This time the sponsor was the Deutsche Arbeitsfront, which three months earlier had launched its new cultural organisation, Kraft durch Freude (Strength through Joy). Modelled on the Italian Dopolavoro, it was intended to bring culture within the reach of the working population.

Hindemith, though determined to sell his body as dearly as possible, was tempted by the offer. As he wrote to Willy Strecker on 9 February, it would "provide the basis for the most ambitious programme of popular musical education (together with appropriate composer training) the world has ever seen. One could literally have the musical enlightenment of millions in one's hand." But he added, more cautiously: "I myself intend, as before, to steer clear of any official position, trusting to achieve all the more in the background. In particular I want to take over the composer training myself, though not as an addition to my work: I would, I hope, be able to drop my teaching at the school."

Another sign of growing official favour was an invitation to conduct his Concert Music for String Orchestra and Brass Instruments at a concert in Berlin devoted to works by composers of whom the Nazis officially approved: Paul Graener, Siegmund von Hausegger, Hans Pfitzner and Richard Strauss. Willy Strecker listened to this concert on the radio, and wrote on 27 February commenting on the sounds of protest he heard among the audience. "A little opposition never does any harm. It simply shows that you do not yet belong in the category of senile old men."

Hindemith's work on the text of his Grünewald opera, which he had now decided to call *Mathis der Maler*, and on the orchestral interludes was being delayed both by his concert activities and his constant alterations and revisions. Originally he had intended to write four orchestral pieces, one for each act, but with the changing shape of the libretto that plan had run into difficulties. The first piece (*Engelskonzert*) was completed in November 1933 and the second (*Grablegung*) in January 1934. In the suite he intended this to be the last of the four pieces, but on 5 February, after his return from London, he wrote to Willy Strecker from Lübeck: "I could find no ideas for the third piece, though I sweated a lot and tried all sorts of things. In the end I gave it up and decided to leave it at the two pieces. Since yesterday, however, things have begun to move again, and I am working on the *Versuchung*."

The idea of using the Temptation (*Versuchung*) of St Anthony as the dramatic climax of his opera was a late inspiration which solved many structural difficulties. Mathis, rejecting the archbishop's plea that he should compromise, joins the peasants in their rebellion. Disgusted, however, by their brutality, he defends a countess from rape. When the troops overwhelm the peasants, she intercedes for him, and he is allowed to go free. He takes refuge in the forest, where, tired and hungry, he has a vision. Each of the characters in the opera appears to him in a symbolic form, resembling figures in his paintings of the Temptation of St Anthony: the countess as Voluptuousness, the dean of Mainz as a trader, representing the mercenary view, Ursula in three forms as beggar, seductress and martyr, the archbishop's political adviser as a philosopher, the peasant leader Schwalb as a warrior. All seek to persuade him to their single-minded view of life, taunting him with his indecision. Finally it is the archbishop, in the form of St Paul, who rescues him from his agony and persuades him that he can best help his fellow men by using the gifts God gave him. The opera ends with Mathis returning to his painting.

With this fine temptation scene Hindemith was able to simplify his structural plan, reduce the number of scenes from eleven to seven, and eliminate the meeting with Luther, which Willy Strecker had criticised in draft form as "stuck on and meteoric". Once it had occurred to him, his musical inspiration began to flow. He wrote an orchestral piece, which he called *Die Versuchung des heiligen Antonius*, and placed it after the two pieces he had already written. He completed this just in time for the first performance of the suite, which was given by the Berlin Philharmonic Orchestra under Furtwängler on 12 March 1934.

The *Mathis der Maler* Symphony, as it was finally named, was an immediate success, not only with the public but with the critics as well, some of whom (as good Nazis) were by no means Hindemith's friends. The Telefunken company at once made a gramophone record of it, on which the Berlin Philharmonic Orchestra was conducted by Hindemith himself. He also conducted the symphony in Duisburg, while in other German towns conductors vied with each other for the privilege of including it in their programmes. It seemed to everyone concerned that Hindemith's acceptance by the Nazis was now complete, and nothing stood in the way of the opera on which the symphony was based. In May he settled down temporarily in the quiet little Baltic seaside resort of Scharbeutz to start work on the first scene, and his publishers opened negotiations with the leading opera houses. Hamburg and Frankfurt, as well as Berlin, were eager for the honour of launching the opera.

The first cloud on the horizon appeared in the following month. Hans Rosbaud was refused permission to perform the *Mathis der Maler* Symphony on Frankfurt Radio. The reason, Rosbaud told Strecker, was that a report had come in from Switzerland that while on a visit there Hindemith had made some critical remarks about Hitler. Until the alleged offence had been investigated, none of Hindemith's works could be broadcast. Even if he were to be cleared and the total ban lifted, Rosbaud told Strecker, radio stations would still need to obtain permission from radio headquarters in Berlin if they wished to broadcast anything at all by Hindemith.

Strecker could not find out who was behind this order. Whoever it was—and he suspected Hindemith's enemies in the Reichsmusikkammer, perhaps even Richard Strauss himself— he was well aware of its implications for the production of Hindemith's opera. "It shows that our feelings against Berlin were not completely groundless," he wrote to Hindemith on 28 June 1934, "and we should not venture to give the première there without definite official permission. Furtwängler seems to be holding his end up splendidly, and we must give him all the support we can."

Hindemith, who had now moved on to Freudenstadt in the heart of the Black Forest, reacted not at all to Strecker's cries of alarm. His letters were concerned almost exclusively with his opera, and they show him in an uncharacteristic state of self-absorption. On 25 July he sent Strecker the text of the fifth scene, groaning over his continuing difficulties with the libretto. The music, he said, would cost him only a tenth of the trouble the words were causing him. On 29 July he sent the text of the sixth scene, remarking: "When I now look back, I am amazed at the rash way in which I began this really horribly difficult task." Two days later he sent the text of the seventh and last scene, adding that he hoped to finish the music of the third scene by the end of the week. On 6 September he told Ludwig Strecker that he was composing the scenes out of order. "Interruptions or visits during this huge job would be very unwelcome," he added. On 11 September Gertrud wrote to both Strecker brothers: "The vision scene is done. Paul is working without a break." On 17 September Hindemith wrote that he was going to visit Grünewald's Isenheim altar and would then compose the second scene.

It was October before the Streckers received a reaction from the Hindemiths on the radio ban, and it came not from him, but from Gertrud. It was surprisingly laconic. The ban was not official, she said. Presumably she owed this information to Furtwängler, who had been to visit them. Furtwängler, she added, intended to approach Hitler personally, requesting permission to bring out *Mathis der Maler* in Berlin. "There are only two courses. Either Fu does the opera, which is as good as certain. Then there is no hurry, and the others can follow on. Or Fu doesn't or can't. Then there will be so much fuss and bother that you won't need to do any advertising."

This extraordinarily simple view might of course have been Gertrud's own. At any rate Hindemith's first action on returning to the Hochschule in Berlin for the new term suggests that he was more alive than his wife to the pressures that had been building up against him while he was shut away writing his

opera. The Nazi press had been losing no opportunity to denigrate him. Immediately after the successful first performance of
the *Mathis der Maler* Symphony the *Deutsche Zeitung*, for instance,
criticised him for allowing a piece of his to be played at a festival
of modern music in Florence, "which is dominated by Jews".
His two most virulent journalistic opponents, who set the
general tone, were Fritz Stege, music critic of the *Völkischer
Beobachter* and editor of the *Zeitschrift für Musik* (official organ
of the Reichsmusikkammer), and Friedrich Herzog, editor of
Die Musik, which was the official organ of Rosenberg's Kulturgemeinde.

Armed with his press cuttings, Hindemith went straight to
Havemann and threatened to leave the country if these vicious
attacks on him did not stop. The outcome of his ultimatum he
described in a letter to Willy Strecker dated 15 November
1934:

"Faced with this impending catastrophe of a passionate
patriot forced into emigration, he sank down in despair and
promised to do everything to divert it. Today it happened.
There was a meeting of the Musikkammer. Havemann spoke
first, and suddenly I heard myself being placed beside Strauss
and Pfitzner as the only true composers and articles of export.
Afterwards I was taken to see State Secretary [Walther] Funk,
who is the big boss in the Propaganda Ministry as far as we are
concerned, and there I could hardly get a word in, for Havemann and Stein overwhelmed him with such panegyrics about
me that my ears burned. . . . He promised to talk tomorrow to
the Führer. The latter, he told us, had once a long time ago
walked in horror out of a concert in Munich where something
of mine was played, but he (Funk) had no doubt at all that
things would be all right."

To this letter Hindemith added a postscript: "Don't you
think it would be better if *Nusch-Nuschi* and *Sancta Susanna* were
to be taken off the market for a while? It's making things too
simple for these fellows if they can easily get hold of these bits
of folk poison."

Willy Strecker, who received this letter on his birthday,
described it as the "best birthday present I could have wished
for". He had another in the shape of a report in the *Frankfurter
Zeitung*, which revealed that at a meeting of the Reichsmusikkammer in Berlin the head of the Reichsmusikerschaft, Professor

Dr h.c. Gustav Havemann, had "paid tribute to the significant contributions of such outstanding creative personalities as Richard Strauss, Hans Pfitzner and Paul Hindemith in furthering the reputation of German music abroad". He had never, Willy Strecker wrote to Hindemith (with whom he was at last, after fourteen years of friendship, on Christian name terms), ceased to believe in the triumph of the good. "Now you will probably have to be protected from your friends, for there is a certain danger in a too sudden change of atmosphere." He added that *Das Nusch-Nuschi* and *Sancta Susanna* had already been "placed in the poison cupboard, and will only be given out with my personal permission".

If they now thought they had finally beaten down the opposition, their illusions were short-lived. When Furtwängler applied to his chief, Goering, for permission to produce *Mathis der Maler* at the Berlin State Opera, he was told that this could only be done with Hitler's personal permission. Now Hitler was known to have disapproved of Hindemith ever since he had once seen *Neues vom Tage* and been shocked by the sight of an unclothed soprano singing in her bath. How could they persuade him to change his mind?

The strategy Furtwängler and Hindemith evolved to win Hitler's consent is described in a letter which Hindemith wrote to Willy Strecker on 18 November 1934. Furtwängler, he said, would write an article exposing the efforts of certain people in the Nazi party to denigrate him. Before visiting Hitler, armed with a copy of the *Mathis der Maler* libretto, Furtwängler would make sure that he had seen this article. In addition, Hindemith would write to Hitler, inviting him to visit his class at the Hochschule, and he would arrange for the cantata from the *Plöner Musiktag* (Admonition to Youth to Apply itself to Music) to be performed during the visit. "No one has ever been able to resist that piece," Hindemith told Strecker confidently.

The plan was a total failure. Furtwängler's article *Der Fall Hindemith* (The Hindemith Case) appeared on Sunday, 25 November 1934, on the front page of the *Deutsche Allgemeine Zeitung*, a Berlin newspaper whose editor, Dr Fritz Klein, still had liberal ideas about the freedom of speech (needless to say, he did not survive much longer in his job). Hindemith himself had no hand in the writing of it and did not know what it contained until he read it in the *DAZ*. Willy Strecker, who also read it there, immediately wrote to Gertrud: "I think the article excellent—as sensible as it is diplomatic."

Sensible it certainly was, with its sympathetic assessment—not free of legitimate criticism—of Hindemith's achievements, its defence of his right to make his own artistic mistakes and its admiration for his talents as a teacher. In a normal democratic society it could even pass as diplomatic in that it dismissed the reproaches of Hindemith's Jewish associations as merely irrelevant and made its main point—the relation of art to politics—reasonably and with moderation. Referring to the great success of the *Mathis der Maler* Symphony eight months previously, Furtwängler pointed out that since then its composer had been left in relative peace. "Though he has published nothing else since, attempts are now being made to make up for lost time, to defame him publicly and—for that is what it finally amounts to—to drive him out of Germany. No means, it seems, are too petty: there are those who are even prepared to hold up against him old burlesques of misunderstood Wagner and Puccini which he once wrote—as if Hindemith did not know who Wagner was! Naturally, with a composer who has written so much and whose works are constantly available in print, it is easy enough to seek out 'youthful sins' to hold up against him. Hindemith has never been politically active: what is to become of us if political denunciation is to be applied in the fullest measure to matters of art?"

It was this incautious reference on Furtwängler's part to political denunciation which succeeded in uniting in one single stroke the whole Nazi hierarchy against him. Goebbels's Reichskulturkammer rushed to the defence of Rosenberg's Kulturgemeinde. Its spokesman, Bernhard Rust, issued a statement, rejecting the suggestion that the attack on Hindemith was an act of political denunciation. "In the rejection of Hindemith by the Kulturgemeinde the value or lack of value of his creative work is beside the point. National Socialism puts the personality of a creative artist before his work. The fact that before the new regime Hindemith showed signs of an un-German attitude disqualifies him from taking part in the movement's cultural reclamation work." Goebbels's own newspaper *Der Angriff* came out on 28 November with a huge headline right across the front page: *Warum Vorschusslorbeeren für Konjunktur-Musiker Hindemith?* (Why Advance Laurels for Musical Opportunist Hindemith?),

accusing him among other things of having used his position in
the Reichsmusikkammer (of which, it should be noted, he was—
and as a practising musician was obliged to be—simply an
ordinary member) to push his own works to the exclusion of
other composers.

A few days later both Goebbels and Rosenberg joined in
personally, the first in a speech in the Berlin Sportpalast on 6
December and the second in a leading article in the *Völkischer
Beobachter* on 7 December 1934. In both the message was the
same: in the new Germany it was the rulers who decided what
was art, and the artists who did not like it could go. Goering
took private action: he telephoned Hitler, who at once cancelled the meeting arranged between himself and Furtwängler.
"Goering was said to have been particularly angry about the
article," Furtwängler later told his biographer Curt Riess,
"because he saw in it an attempt on my part to influence his
decision. Nothing had been farther from my mind. But from
that moment the ban on *Mathis der Maler* was absolute."

This was not the only miscalculation Furtwängler made.
"When I wrote my article on Hindemith," he told Riess, "I was
of the honest opinion that it would help the cause, that is to
say, Hindemith." It achieved, in terms of what Hindemith
himself was striving for, exactly the opposite. Instead of winning,
if not approval, at any rate tolerance for Hindemith's musical
activity, it ensured that all doors to reconciliation were closed.
The battle, hitherto confined to sniping in the back streets, had
been brought out into the open. There were public demonstrations in favour of Furtwängler in the Staatsoper, in support
of Hindemith at the Hochschule. The Nazis had been forced
into a position in which any signs of relenting would have been
seen as a political defeat. Furtwängler reaped the first consequences of the rout: he had no alternative but to resign from all
his positions—Reichsmusikkammer, Staatsoper and Berlin
Philharmonic Orchestra. But it was Hindemith against whom
the whole vindictiveness of the Nazi hierarchy was ultimately
directed. That Goebbels made completely clear in his speech at
the Sportpalast on 6 December, though he did not mention
Hindemith by name. He did not need to: after all the publicity
everyone knew whom he meant when he said: "Purely German
his blood may be, but this only provides drastic confirmation of
how deeply the Jewish intellectual infection has eaten into the

body of our own people. To reach that conclusion has nothing in the least to do with political denunciation. Nobody can accuse us of trying to inhibit true and genuine art through petty or spiteful regulations. What we wish to see upheld is a National Socialistic outlook and behaviour, and no one, however important he may be in his own sphere, has the right to demand that this be confined to politics and banished from art. Certainly we cannot afford, in view of the deplorable lack of truly productive artists throughout the world, to turn our backs on a truly German artist. But he must be a real artist, not just a producer of atonal noises."

This speech, greeted with prolonged applause, was followed by the reading out of a telegram congratulating Goebbels on his success in "weeding out undesirable elements". It bore the signature of the president of the Reichsmusikkammer, Richard Strauss. Strauss subsequently denied that he had ever sent this telegram. Whether or not he did, Hindemith was deeply hurt by it. He could bear Goebbels's abuse, however inopportune for his hopes and plans, but such a judgment from a fellow musician whom he respected, even when he disagreed with him, wounded as much as it angered him. He may, as Berta Geissmar observes, have developed "a sort of Siegfried hide" in relation to the Nazis, but it was an outward shield that hid a lot of inner suffering. On 20 November 1934, at the height of the battle, the conductor Johannes Schüler was intrepid enough to play the *Mathis der Maler* Symphony in Essen. After the performance Hindemith wrote him a touching letter:

"The unearthly amount of filth that has been poured over me in the past few days has made me more than usually sensitive to the pleasant aspects of this world. You are one of them, and I thank you for it. Your refusal to be got down by this tangle of falsehood and abuse has been very heartening to me."

To his publishers, however, Hindemith continued to show his customary mood of confident optimism. On 18 December 1934, after the open battle had subsided, he wrote to Willy Strecker:

"Nobody is now probing the wounds, and it seems both to me and most of the others here that everybody is now hoping for a gradual recovery. I think we should just quietly wait. Next season will be early enough for the opera to come out. In any case, through all these events I am so behindhand with my work that I couldn't possibly have had it ready in time."

He added that he was going to London the following day for a concert and would be careful not to get involved in any public arguments. But he would pay a visit to the German Embassy, so as to ensure that reports on the concert would appear in Germany. As we see, he was still attempting to keep all possible doors open. Yet the policy of wait and see, so assiduously culti- vated both by himself and his publishers, was beginning to look less like prudence than an inability to know what to do next.

At the end of 1934 the Hochschule granted him a period of extended leave. He left Berlin with Gertrud and settled down in Lenzkirch in the Black Forest to orchestrate *Mathis der Maler*, which he had completed in piano score just a fortnight before the storm broke.

Chapter 2

1935–37:

THE UNINTENTIONAL AMBASSADOR

"SKI-ING AND NOTATION are my only occupations besides eating and sleeping," Hindemith wrote to Willy Strecker from Lenzkirch on 28 January 1935. His attitude towards the Nazis was now rather like that of Achilles in his tent before the battle of Troy: he was still ready for a reconciliation, but unwilling to make the first move himself. He expressed his feelings in a dignified letter to Havemann, written on 3 February 1935:

"I have been urged to write you a letter defending myself against all the aspersions and false accusations. You know me long enough to understand that it is not my habit to grovel. I have often enough spoken personally to you about all these things. If I am now so important that it is thought necessary to bring up the heaviest guns against me, at least the people concerned might have listened to what I had to say, instead of relying solely on the one-sided and blatantly prejudiced opinions of 'friends'. Or, if that was considered inexpedient, they might at least have sought the opinion of truly objective and qualified party members.

"I remain as before willing to talk to any official department, but I must refuse to answer charges based on compositions written fifteen years ago. As long as the point of view revealed by so many published statements is adhered to, I feel powerless to answer the slanders and false accusations made against me. One talks of acknowledging the musician while rejecting the man, and that seems to me to emphasise the lack of real substance in the attacks. I know of none among my accusers who know me well enough to express so summary a judgment—one which has led to consequences apparently embarrassing to all concerned. Everybody knows that it is impossible to separate the man from the artist, and anyone who seriously wants to form an impression of my aims and capabilities would do better to seek it in the long list of my published compositions and from people with whom I have had to do as composer, teacher and private individual. Meanwhile I shall carry on with my 'opportunist' policy of writing music as well as I can, hoping in that way to do German art a better service than is being achieved by this rejection of me. Time judges fairly and without envy, and I put my trust in it and in my good intentions. But I thank you personally for the good opinion you have so long held towards me."

Hindemith had reason to be grateful to Havemann. Whatever damage he may have done to other musicians (and there is evidence that he was both fanatic and ruthless), he had protected Hindemith as far as was within his power from Nazi persecution. But Havemann's power was very limited. Hindemith's unrepentant letter, addressed to this junior level, would not effect his rehabilitation, as he well knew. To achieve this, he would have to go to the lengths that Furtwängler went later in the same month. Furtwängler sought an interview with Goebbels, and on the following day a statement appeared in all German newspapers: "Dr Furtwängler declared that he had written his well-known article about Hindemith with the sole intention of treating a musical question from a musical point of view. He regretted the conclusions of a political nature which had been drawn from his article all the more, since it had never been his intention to interfere in the control of artistic affairs in the Reich. This was in his opinion a matter to be properly decided by the Führer and Chancellor and his appointed ministers."

This wholesale capitulation had the effect of restoring Furtwängler to favour, if not of securing his reappointment to the posts he had given up. It was a compromise which suited both sides, for it gave the Nazis the public victory while enabling Furtwängler to retain (with their knowledge) his private opinions.

Since Hindemith was not personally prepared to go that far, Willy Strecker decided to make the attempt on his behalf. His letter, dated 9 March 1935, was addressed to Havemann. Hindemith's work, Strecker claimed, had never been opportunist, but could be seen throughout his composing life as a logical development of his talents; his aim in his music was to overcome post-Wagnerian influences and to return to the strict polyphony of the old German masters; his harmonic language was not atonal, but followed understandable laws of logic.

Interspersed with these valid arguments, however, were others which show the futility as well as the distastefulness of trying to argue with the Nazis on their own level. Hindemith, said Strecker, had never written "cheap successes" such as *Die Dreigroschenoper* or *Jonny spielt auf*; he did not owe his success to Jewish cliques and critics—on the contrary, he had often had trouble with Jewish critics; he avoided the use of "fashionable instruments typical of a destructive age", such as vibraphones and wind-machines; and his positive, constructive music could not be compared with "the decadent intellectual musical efforts of a Schönberg", to whose ideas he had always been sharply opposed.

Strecker sent a draft of this letter to Hindemith, who surprisingly approved it. He even made a handwritten addition to Strecker's list of his musical aims: "A search for concise expression, for clarity of melody and harmony." The most surprising thing of all was that he not only allowed the wounding reference to Schönberg to stand, but asked Strecker to add a reference to his rejection of twelve-tone music generally: "I think I have been accused of that too." It was an uncharacteristic moment of weakness which can perhaps most charitably be explained as a symptom of his current anxiety.

As far as his financial position was concerned, he had no immediate worries. He was still on the payroll of the Hochschule in Berlin—a job he was in any case thinking of giving up soon so that he could devote himself to writing a book on the theories he had evolved there with the help of his pupils. After conducting a concert in Basle, he was offered a tour with the Swiss Radio orchestra, and he had also been invited to teach at a musical course at Basle. Though he did not say so in his letter to Strecker, he no doubt owed these opportunities to the good offices of Paul Sacher, with whose chamber orchestra in Basle he had played frequently since its inception in 1926.

More attractive than these prospects, however, was an invitation he had received from an official in the Turkish Ministry of Education, Cevat Bey, to establish a school of music in Turkey. "I shall probably go there soon to take a look around," he told Strecker. "I wouldn't want to settle there permanently, but for a few months, why not?" He added: "But it wouldn't be bad if despite this I could go on living in Germany."

He was still clinging to this hope when, at the beginning of April 1935, he and Gertrud left for Ankara. There was no thought of a final break. Just before his departure he was assured by Stein that the Reichsmusikkammer and even Richard Strauss himself, its president, were on his side. Not for the first time, but also not for the last, Hindemith could write to Willy Strecker on the eve of his departure: "I believe the worst is now behind us."

Turkey, under the benevolent dictatorship of Mustafa Kemal Atatürk, was at that time making strenuous efforts to adapt its traditions to the Western way of life. Its music, Arab in origin and style, was tending in the same direction, which meant that its composers went to Europe for their education. They were thus in danger of losing contact with their native traditions. Hindemith's task was to provide ideas for the organisation of a training ground on Turkish soil on which composers could learn advanced musical techniques without losing touch with the needs of their own people. The school was to be in Ankara, the new capital which Gertrud described on arrival as "a juxta-position of archeology and America, Hittite ruins beside the latest in material comfort, all of it in an impressive desert landscape".

Hindemith's official duties, on this first visit, were confined to studying existing conditions and making suggestions on how to improve or replace them, but it was not in his nature to miss the opportunity of a little practical music-making. Within a fortnight of his arrival he was writing to Willy Strecker in Mainz, asking him to send copies of the Bach Brandenburg Concertos and the complete *Plöner Musiktag*, which he planned to present at a concert at the end of April. "It is extremely interesting here," he wrote on 16 April. "I go around inspecting whatever music there is, make proposal after proposal, and if everything is done as I suggest (and the will is there) I shall be able to flatter myself with having put Turkish music on its feet. . . . Meanwhile we spend our time eating mutton and yoghurt, watching the innumerable storks, and can almost hear the city growing."

So impressed were the Turkish authorities with their energetic inspector that they asked the German Embassy in Ankara to apply through the Foreign Ministry in Berlin for a week's extension of his leave from the Hochschule. The extension was granted. He conducted the concert. "Paul has worked like mad with the Turkish musicians," Gertrud reported. "To begin with they could only play loudly and out of tune, but he was determined to show what one can do with what there is here, when one goes about it properly."

On 16 May 1935 they left Ankara to return home, charged with commissions to engage teachers and musicians in Germany to staff the new school and to buy instruments and musical scores for the library.

Back in Berlin, Hindemith wrote a report for the Turkish authorities on his work in Ankara and gave a copy of it to Havemann, who promised to ensure that it was seen in the proper quarters in Germany. Whether or not this report persuaded the Nazi bosses to regard Hindemith with a more favourable eye cannot be definitely established, but it is significant that within a few weeks of receiving it Goebbels let it be known that he had no objection to a production of *Mathis der Maler* in Frankfurt. And when the Turkish authorities invited him to return to Ankara, Hindemith felt strong enough to make conditions. He would only go there again, he said, if he were to be fully rehabilitated at the Hochschule in Berlin and allowed to draw the material he required for Turkey from there. Both Foreign Ministry and Hochschule agreed to his terms without a murmur.

The orchestration of *Mathis der Maler*, interrupted by the trip to Turkey, was finally completed in Berlin in July 1935, and Hindemith turned his attention back to composition. The outcome was *Der Schwanendreher*, a concerto for viola and small orchestra which, like the opera *Mathis der Maler* written immediately before, directly reflects his interest in folksong as a musical basis. This, though intermittently discernible in his earlier works, had grown in importance through his association with Jöde's Youth Movement and the *Music to Sing and Play* which arose from that. It was an integral part of his effort to bridge the gap between the composer and the listener. His aim was obviously not mere popularisation, but the establishment of a common basis through which the listener could become involved in the composer's thought. One of his Berlin pupils, Silvia Kind, recalls in the *Music Journal* of March 1966 that Hindemith liked

E

to give his students German folk melodies to use as the basis of their counterpoint exercises. Among these were the melodies he subsequently used himself in *Mathis der Maler* and in the *Schwanendreher* concerto.

Though, as far as anyone was prepared to admit, there was no official ban on Hindemith's music in Germany, no conductor was inclined to take the risk of launching a new work by him. For the first performance of *Der Schwanendreher*, therefore, he went to Amsterdam, where on 14 November 1935 he played it together with his old *bête noire*, Willem Mengelberg, and the Concertgebouw Orchestra. In January 1936 he went to London to introduce the new concerto there. On the eve of the concert King George V died, and the programme had hastily to be rearranged. Hindemith explained what happened next in a letter to Willy Strecker dated 23 January 1936:

"There was great despair at the BBC. Boult and Clark wanted me to take part in the concert at all costs—it was held in the studio, not in the Queen's Hall. We debated for hours, but no suitable piece could be found, so we decided that I should write some funeral music myself. As I read yesterday in the newspaper, a studio was cleared for me, copyists were gradually stoked up, and from 11 to 5 I did some fairly hefty mourning. I turned out a nice piece, in the style of *Mathis* and *Schwanendreher* with a Bach chorale at the end (*Vor deinen Thron tret' ich hiermit*—very suitable for kings). It is a tune every child in England knows, though I did not find that out till later. Maybe you know it—they call it 'The Old Hundred' or something like that. We rehearsed it well all yesterday, and in the evening the orchestra played with great devoutness and feeling. It was very moving. Boult was, by English and his own personal standards, quite beside himself, and kept thanking me. My various pupils are now busy writing articles about the affair, they are very proud that the old man can still do things so well and so quickly. . . .

"Shouldn't we perhaps make use of this story? Would you like to circulate it to the German press? It is after all no everyday occurrence when the BBC gets a foreigner to write a piece on the death of their king and sends it out over the complete network. I'm now going to specialise in deceased persons—maybe there'll be some more opportunities."

Hindemith's account of the origin of his *Trauermusik* (English

title: *Music of Mourning*) is accurate, however much he may
contrive in his self-deprecating way to make it sound like a
newspaper story. The piece, written for viola and string
orchestra and performed by himself on 22 January 1936 with
Sir Adrian Boult conducting, is a shining example of an
occasional composition which long outlives the occasion for
which it was written. In its original form or in its piano reduc-
tion (in both cases the solo part being playable on the violin or
cello as well as the viola) it has remained one of his most
frequently performed pieces.

An account of the affair found its way into a few German
newspapers, and a friendly article appeared in the periodical
Deutsche Zukunft. The Nazi régime, however, though willing
enough to accept the benefits of Hindemith's unofficial (and
unintended) aid to its foreign relations, did not on that account
feel obliged to welcome him publicly back to the fold. The fact
that Goebbels did not now object to the production of *Mathis
der Maler* was not sufficient in itself to ensure its performance:
there were other permissions to be sought, in particular that of
Rosenberg, who was still proving intractable.

There were plenty of opera houses abroad seeking the
privilege of launching Hindemith's opera, but both publishers
and composer were anxious that this work, which they regarded
as his finest, should be seen first in Germany. Though this final
goal still eluded them, they now felt sufficiently confident of the
improved atmosphere to risk the performance of a new work—
the little Sonata in E for violin and piano which had had its
first performance earlier in the year in Geneva. The concert
took place in Baden-Baden in April 1936, when the work was
received (in Willy Strecker's words) "warmly, though not
demonstratively", and the second of the two movements was
repeated. The critics wrote favourable reviews, thus encouraging the publishers in their view that the future now looked
brighter.

At the time of the concert in Baden-Baden Hindemith and
Gertrud were back in Ankara, preparing for the opening of the
new music school. "Things are very different this year," Gertrud
wrote on 1 April 1936 to the Strecker brothers. "There is after
all a distinction between travelling around on tours of inspection
and in a practical way diving into a sea of chaos. The first days

were difficult enough, with resistance and revolt in the orchestra. I typed one bloodthirsty edict after another. Luckily the ministry, headed by the minister himself, backed Paul's orders and even summarily dismissed one of the main trouble-makers. Now he has been re-engaged, and all is peace. The trickiest job was to get our brave Germans firmly into the saddle. . . . But the orchestra is running along nicely now, statutes have been worked out, pianos ordered. . . . Now it's the turn of the school. I am busy working on a puzzle: how to fit 150 pupils, 17 teachers and 30 rooms into a working week of 24 hours."

The head of the school was a German, Dr Ernst Praetorius, and a Berlin friend, Eduard Zuckmayer, brother of the dramatist Carl Zuckmayer, came to Ankara on Hindemith's persuasion to occupy a teaching post. Another of the teaching staff was his old colleague Licco Amar, himself Turkish by birth, and for that reason almost certainly instrumental to some extent in securing Hindemith's appointment in the first place. Hindemith's function in the new enterprise was that of general organiser, but it was never his way simply to supervise. "I am really worried," Gertrud wrote to Willy Strecker on 3 May 1936. "If you could see how Paul is working here, you would certainly feel the same. . . . A normally functioning person would spread such a mammoth undertaking over ten years. He has now set up in nine weeks a huge apparatus which is always generating new questions and problems of its own. Paul deals with them all himself, and is doing practically everything on his own, from polishing violins to thinking out rules and regulations—there is no one from the humblest scholar to the minister himself who doesn't receive the benefit of his highly personal instructions. The Turkish bosses dimly realise that they could scarcely hope to find another such man anywhere in the world, and they are already pushing for him to come back in September to carry on. A return next spring is fixed in any case."

She feared that the double burden of the Hochschule in Berlin and the new school in Ankara would ruin his health. Would it not be better, she asked, if he were to give up Berlin entirely, spending six months of the year in Turkey and the other half writing in some quiet spot in the Black Forest? Willy Strecker's reply, dated 11 May 1936, strongly urged them not to give up Berlin. A firm foothold in Germany was essential to his chances of rehabilitation. He should be careful, Strecker went on, not to bind himself too tightly to the school in Ankara. There were plenty of offers of work on hand: the Russian Ballet in Monte Carlo, for instance, was crying out for a ballet from him. Strecker, who had now discovered that the German ambassador in Ankara, Dr von Keller, was a close friend of his wife's family in Buenos Aires, suggested that the embassy might be persuaded to make representations to Germany on Hindemith's behalf. "He himself is too modest," Strecker added, "to present the significance of his work there in the proper light."

It is possible that the ambassador, with whom the Hindemiths immediately established cordial relations, may indeed have sent a favourable report to Berlin, for very soon after his return there in June 1936 Hindemith, much to his surprise, was approached by representatives of the German Luftwaffe. Would he, they asked, be prepared to write a piece for a "highly official" concert in the coming autumn? He accepted the commission. "I want to give them something really good," he told Willy Strecker on 8 July 1936. "I am quite certain that this piece, if reasonably successful, could mean *Mathis* in the Staatsoper. . . . I have discovered that the English *Trauermusik* had a far greater effect than we knew of at the time. It seems that this was the first blow that started the change of mind about me."

Another surprise was the sudden *volte-face* of his old enemy Friedrich Herzog, who sought an interview with Ludwig Strecker to offer his services in the rehabilitation process. He had never been against Hindemith as a composer, he explained: the only real objection to Hindemith lay in his Jewish connections, and in that matter his employer Rosenberg was thoroughly obstinate. However, Herzog declared, if he could be given a copy of *Mathis der Maler* he would be willing to discuss the case with—and perhaps even play the work to—Rosenberg.

Hindemith was highly sceptical. He had heard, he told Ludwig Strecker in a letter dated 1 July 1936, that Rosenberg's Kulturgemeinde was in financial difficulties. He advised caution: "I would consider it entirely wrong to sell myself now, when the worst has been proudly endured."

He showed his own caution in the ensuing months by supporting the BBC's plan to present a concert performance of *Cardillac* in London, whereas Willy Strecker would have preferred to see this earlier work replaced by *Mathis der Maler*. That would only lead to new trouble, he told Strecker. For the same reason he vetoed a projected performance of *Hin und Zurück* in Switzerland. His hopes of rehabilitation were centred on two performances scheduled for Berlin in the autumn. Georg Kulenkampff was to play his violin sonata of the previous year and Walter Gieseking to launch his first piano sonata, which he had begun in Turkey and completed on his return to Berlin. He had sent that to Schott's at the beginning of July, together with the second sonata. "So that you won't think senility is setting in," he wrote, "I'm enclosing another smaller brother. . . . It is the lighter counterpart of the rather weighty first." He was, he added, now making a piano score of the *Schwanendreher* concerto and composing a few songs. These, to conclude from Gertrud's letter of a few days later (14 July 1936), were some of the new *Marienleben* songs. He was thinking, she said, of rewriting them all and reissuing them with an introduction as a harbinger for his theory book, on which he was also now hard at work.

A walking tour in the Eiffel with Willy Strecker and Hans Flesch, who since his release from prison had been working in the country as a physician, was followed by a visit to Bavaria. But even on holiday he could not relax his mental activity. Besides putting in some work on his book, he wrote a number of limericks praising Henkell Sekt. Willy Strecker also wrote some, and sent their efforts to the firm of Henkell, who rewarded them with twenty bottles of their popular sparkling wine.

Hindemith was still in Bavaria when the first concert took place in Berlin. On the following day Kulenkampff, who had played the violin sonata, was called to the Propaganda Ministry by Goebbels's second-in-command, Walther Funk, and admonished. At the same time Gieseking was ordered to remove the piano sonata from the programme of his forthcoming concert.

The reason Hindemith heard from Gieseking when he reluctantly returned in October to the "Berlin mill". The authorities had been disturbed by what they considered the "demonstrative" applause the violin sonata had received, and considered it expedient for the time being to ban further performances of all Hindemith's works. They had nothing against Hindemith personally, Funk assured Gieseking, and it was possible that in time the situation would change again. "If there are a lot of good new works," he declared, "it will not be possible to conceal their existence for ever."

Hindemith attempted to assess the situation in a letter to the Strecker brothers dated 1 November 1936:

"Either things will move in the opposite direction in the near future, which I do not expect, nor (to be honest) really want, or the existing tension will mount even further." Funk's assurance that the objection was not personal was, he thought, confirmed by the fact that his plan to found a new string trio with Kulen-kampff and the cellist Enrico Mainardi had not so far been opposed. Nor had the Luftwaffe commission been withdrawn. But he was in no hurry to carry it out. "I do not on any account wish to give the impression of getting to my goal the sooner by creeping into another hole—not even an air hole. A bit of pride might now stand us in better stead than haste."

The small ray of hope offered by the projected string trio did not last long. Kulenkampff and Stein thought it opportune to approach Funk during a party to seek his assurance that there would be no official objection to the trio. Funk, surrounded by film stars and flushed with wine, was, according to Gertrud's letter of 4 December to the Strecker brothers, not best pleased to be interrupted. The trio, he said, would not be welcomed. It is more than probable that the answer would have been the same even if a more suitable moment had been chosen to put the question, but one can sympathise with Gertrud's comment: "Paul is really unlucky in the clumsy way he is fought over."

The plan for the trio was abandoned.

In January 1937 the Hindemiths left once more for Ankara. Some chapters of the theory book, *Unterweisung im Tonsatz*, which he had almost completely rewritten during the latter part of 1936, had by now been set up in type, and Hindemith gave his pupils at the Hochschule proof copies to work on during his absence. The visit to Turkey, his third, was only a short one of three weeks, of which he spent one week in bed with influenza, but, since the main bulk of his work there was now done, the loss of time was not serious. "He is very happy with Ankara," Gertrud wrote to the Strecker brothers on 16 February. "Zuckmayer has been working magnificently, so this time Paul is spared all the petty detail and can spend more time at the ministry. In spite of a few little blemishes the higher-ups are very satisfied and faithfully do all that is asked of them. The orchestra is already presentable—Praetorius has done an unbelievable training job in these eight months."

Though Hindemith was to pay a fourth visit to Turkey later in 1937, his work there was by now virtually complete, and a short review of his aims and achievements might for the sake of convenience be made at this point. It is based on two reports which Hindemith made to the Turkish authorities in 1936 and 1937, copies of which are preserved at the Hindemith Institute in Frankfurt.

In view of his own preoccupations at this time with folksong as a musical starting point, it is not surprising that Hindemith emphasised the need of Turkish composers to acquaint themselves with the musical desires of their compatriots. "At the moment," he wrote in his 1936 report, "the composers are much too involved in the petty demands of their daily professional routine to be able to assess the role that music plays in Turkish life. They should be sent to the provinces to listen to the music of their own people, living among them for a period of months. They now know nothing of the musical capabilities or needs of large sections of the populace. Only when they are familiar with these will they be able to apply their talents in the right direction. They must find out once and for all, through freely exchanging ideas and making music with non-musicians, what part music and the composer play, and in the future can come to play, in the life of the people. That does not mean that the music of the future will emerge from the lathe or the weaver's loom, on plantations or from behind machine-guns. That romantic illusion of a mechanically-obsessed age has long been abandoned in Europe, and it is to be hoped that the talents of Turkey's composers and intelligent efforts by the state will discover the right approach. Certain as we may be that Bach, Mozart and Beethoven did not spend their lives in factories, we can be equally certain that they did not moulder in sour seclusion behind their writing desks."

No effective training would be possible, he went on to say, without a library of Turkish folk music to work on, and it would be a useful exercise for Turkish composers to set about making such a collection. Strictly functional work of this kind "would force them to do the best they can with restricted means within a small framework—an indispensable preliminary to their later free compositional work".

Hindemith certainly knew, when he offered that advice, that another European composer, Bela Bartók, had already been approached by the University of Ankara to supervise a collection of folk music. Bartók, for his part, was anxious not to get at cross purposes with Hindemith. "I am on very friendly terms with him," he wrote to Laszló Rázonyi, professor of Hungarian studies at Ankara, on 18 December 1935, "and hold him in high esteem; therefore we must at all costs avoid even the slightest suggestion that I might want to interfere with his work. But there is no need for this to happen: he gives advice on the organisation of music, and I should only give advice in relation to the collecting of folksongs—something not in his line." Hindemith, while not a close personal friend of Bartók, knew him and respected his work very highly, and he would certainly not have disagreed with that analysis. However, in his 1937 report he did criticise Bartók's suggestion of forming a library of recordings of Turkish folk music, on the ground that this did not take the country's climatic conditions sufficiently into account.

But the nature of their interest in folk music was, as Bartók rightly observed, different. Hindemith was less interested in it for itself than as a starting point. He saw it as providing the basic language in which the composer could freely express himself, and in his analysis of this language he drew a sharp distinction between the two types of music he found existing side by side in Turkey:

"The urban type, Arabic in origin, has reached the apex of its development—perhaps even passed it. Through its concentration on a single voice its technical potentialities have with the passage of time been exhausted. All that can now be done with it is to repeat past discoveries. Nor can the expressive content be much changed: the basic scales are, because of their differentiated structure, melodic patterns rather than neutral bricks for the composer to build with, and adherence to them produces a musical uniformity which may be very fascinating for the connoisseur, but excludes a whole host of expressive uses. Finally, the subtle shape of the Arabic scales is unsuited to polyphonic treatment—and in all attempts to develop music an ordered combination of various voices is essential."

In the old Turkish folk music which still persisted in country districts Hindemith saw a more promising source. "It is so simple in its tonal, rhythmic and formal structures that it can be used in all sorts of ways. Its emotional scope offers rich inspiration. It is fresh and unsullied, the melodic line has not yet become over-polished, and it is readily amenable to polyphonic treatment."

In spite of his belief in contrapuntal methods, which the German band of teachers imported by him could doubtless be guaranteed to teach, Hindemith stressed in his 1937 report with even more vigour his belief that the composer had a duty to make himself understandable to the listener. If Turkish composers wished to bypass the European experience of writing music stifled by too much technique, they must radically alter their approach:

"Instead of the question: 'What compositional technique should I use?' they must ask themselves in future: 'How can I make myself comprehensible to my compatriots?' Comprehensible does not mean making concessions to ignorance or bad taste. It means learning from the natural feelings of music-loving people and leading them to an understanding of genuine art based on their own music; it means subjecting modes of expression always to the aim of making oneself as easily understandable as possible; and ceasing to hanker for European recognition or to cling to foreign techniques.

"An artistic endeavour of this kind—and it is the only genuine kind—will create its own technical means of expression. Whether one works with seven beats to the bar, whether the melodic line strays outside the bounds of major and minor tonality, whether the harmonic pattern is in broad strokes or subtly variegated, whether compositions are cast in large representational forms or in the most intimate chamber music style—all these questions will take second place to the one true desire of making oneself understood. Even if it is unusual in method, music of this sort will be convincing and will be met with deep understanding in distant lands, since the overall search for truthful expression, if present in all aspects of the work, will everywhere be recognised."

It is of course very sound advice, but there is no evidence that Turkish composers, either at the time or since, paid much attention to it. Perhaps if Hindemith had been more closely involved with the teaching at the school, or if his supervisory association with it had been more prolonged, he would have achieved even more in Turkey than he actually did. As both the extracts already quoted and other passages in his reports dealing with more specific cases suggest, he was anxious to avoid pressing Turkish music into a European mould. Yet the very way in which he organised and staffed the school inevitably led in this direction, and it was a direction which the students themselves were very willing to take. The signs of discontent with which, on each of his short visits to Turkey, he had to deal, could usually be traced back to the feelings of the natives that they were being treated, not as different, but in some way as inferior. It is a frame of mind with which colonialists everywhere are certainly familiar. Hindemith was no more successful than most colonialists in knowing how to deal with it. There was a young student named Sabahattin who had, in the opinion of the Turkish authorities, a rather too big idea of himself. He had already, before entering the school, written 89 large-scale works, and he was not prepared tamely to confine himself to the demands of a petty school routine. Hindemith, after interviewing him at the request of the despairing authorities, found himself in lively sympathy with the young man, whom he proclaimed to be the most talented pupil in the school. But the only solution he could suggest to cure Sabahattin of his frustrations was that he should be treated as a special case—and sent to Europe to complete his studies.

It was ironic that Hindemith should feel obliged to write those lines about a composer's duty to make himself understandable to his own people at the very time when he himself was being ostracised by his fellow countrymen. He returned to Berlin via Vienna at the beginning of March 1937 to find the situation even worse than before. The only people who now showed interest in him as a musician were almost exclusively foreign. Apart from the Turks, there were the Americans, who had invited him to make his first visit to the United States in June. And in March Nadia Boulanger came from Paris to see him in Berlin. She had read the proofs of his new theory book and was full of enthusiasm—so much so in fact that she wished to translate it into French herself. She had her doubts, it seems, about the application of Hindemith's theories to classical music, but felt, if she were allowed to express her reservations in her translation, that she could safely put her name to it. Hindemith had no objection to this arrangement: he thought she would probably change her mind in time. Unfortunately for posterity, this projected "collaboration" between two of the most influential musical teachers of the twentieth century never materialised.

Hindemith's reception on his return to Berlin, at best indifferent, had at last convinced him that he could no longer hope for a change of attitude from the Nazis. He decided, before leaving on his trip to America, to hand in his notice at the Hochschule. Gertrud wrote to Willy Strecker on 14 March: "You know that Paul never does things over-hastily or on blind impulse, but that all his decisions mature slowly but surely inside him. And why should he let himself be kept in this straitjacket when nobody here wants anything to do with him? . . . I leave him in peace to decide for himself, don't try to persuade him one way or the other: I know exactly what it means to him not to be able to continue working in and for Germany. Poor man!" To this letter Hindemith added a postscript: "All the above confirmed herewith in haste. From autumn on I intend at last to live like a real composer. I shall of course take my leave in sweet accord."

Willy Strecker's hopes were now centred on the theory book, which was shortly to be published, and he urged Hindemith at least to keep his home in Berlin intact: his firm would almost certainly be forbidden to send royalty payments abroad. Hindemith saw the sense of this argument and gave up his plan to relinquish his apartment. But on the day of his departure for New York on the liner *Deutschland* he wrote to Stein, dating his resignation from the Hochschule at 30 September 1937.

Stein's formal reply accepting the resignation, dated 1 April 1937, contains a handwritten postscript: "I cannot send off this 'official' communication without expressing the hope that everything to do with 'the Hindemith affair' will change. I recently wrote to Furtwängler, so that he would have everything on hand for his forthcoming interview with the Führer. His reply to me was very optimistic. So let's continue to hope."

Whatever the purpose of Furtwängler's projected talk with Hitler, Hindemith was content now to leave such illusions to those who believed in them. From the ship he wrote to Willy

Strecker: "I am travelling in a blessed state of complete incognito. I sit by myself at my little table and have a pact with the stewards to say nothing about me. On people who still persist I just turn my back, and so keep my peace. I am already looking forward to June, when I shall at last be able to compose again unmolested."

Chapter 3

THE CRAFT OF MUSICAL COMPOSITION

IN JULY 1937 Donald Tovey wrote to Miss Weisse, his former teacher: "The great event in musical history at this moment is the appearance of Hindemith's harmony book."

If it was this, the event passed virtually unnoticed by any but a few. Willy Strecker, who had predicted that *Unterweisung im Tonsatz* would produce a sensation, wrote to Hindemith a month after publication that the book was selling slowly but surely—five or six copies a day. As far as Germany was concerned, this was not surprising, for German newspapers were forbidden to review it. Plans to publish an English translation simultaneously, with a foreword by Tovey, had been frustrated by the dilatoriness of the chosen translator, a young friend of the Hindemiths named Gassmann. The English version, eventually translated by Arthur Mendel under the title *The Craft of Musical Composition*, did not appear (in New York) until 1942.

The Strecker brothers, in view of the Nazi attitude towards Hindemith, displayed considerable courage in publishing the book at all. They would, Willy Strecker had told Hindemith in October 1936, bring it out without applying for any official permission and "wait to see what happens". He advised Hindemith to give a copy of the proofs to Stein in order to cover himself if any trouble should arise. Hindemith did so, and he also, as we have seen, left proof copies with his students at the Hochschule (undoubtedly with Stein's approval) to work on during his absence in Turkey.

As it turned out, there was no trouble. This was probably due as much to the discretion with which the publishers launched the book as to the obviously non-political nature of its contents. Hindemith himself was anxious that it should not be made to appear that he was using the book "as a prayer for good weather just before the doors close shut" (to use Gertrud's words). He gave directions that presentation copies should be sent only to real friends, among them Stein, Furtwängler, Mengelberg, Kulenkampff, Gieseking, Schnabel, Werner Reinhart, Emma Lübbecke-Job and his brother Rudolf. The addition of Rudolf to his list was no doubt due to a stirring of his sense of family duty: his relations with his brother had long been cool. There was a warmer and more genuine impulse behind his dedication of the book to his mother. She would not understand it, he declared, but the dedication would please her.

In the two years devoted to the writing of his book following the completion of *Mathis der Maler*, Hindemith had produced (to judge him by his own standards) very little music, and none of it had been on a large scale. But it would be too facile to suggest that his musical silence was due to his difficulties with the Nazis and his turning to literary work an attempt to fill in time. Had circumstances been different, he would still, almost certainly, have written his book at the time he did. With *Mathis der Maler* he had reached a stage of complete technical mastery. The years of trial and error which had preceded it had produced many fine works, but he alone knew how much of their quality they owed simply to accident or to the unaccountable factor of inspiration. If basically he was an instinctive composer, there was also inside him a deep desire to be the master and not the slave of his invention. His book—a deliberate effort to construct a new and firm foundation for the technique of composition to replace the outmoded system on which he had himself been brought up—was an essential part of the process of getting to know and understand himself. That he cast it in the form of a textbook was, besides being the natural expression of his practical nature, the result of his own teaching experiences in Berlin, where he was too often able to offer only his own taste as a criterion. The only available textbooks were those he had himself used in his student days. Added to that was his conviction that the mature artist had a social duty towards the younger generation and was morally bound to pass on to them the benefits of his own experience. All these things, as well as other autobiographical undertones, are clearly discernible in the introductory chapter:

"I am not animated by any desire to freeze into permanent shape what I have been teaching for years, either to get it out of my system or to be rid of the burden of continually improvising new forms of the material which I have often handed out. Anyone who has for years taught students who wish to know why the masters are free to do what is denied to them, why one theme is good and another poor, why harmonic progressions may be satisfactory or irritating, why sense and order must prevail even in the wildest turmoil of sounds, and why such order cannot be arrived at with the traditional tools; anyone who has not sidestepped this unending struggle with the Why of things, and, at the risk of laying himself bare before his pupils, has taken each new question as a stimulus to deeper and more searching study—anyone who has faced these issues, I say, will understand why I feel called upon to devote to the writing of a theoretical work the time and trouble which I would rather spend in composing living music.

"I have experienced the needs of the teacher as well as the strivings of the composer. I have lived through the transition from conservative training to a new freedom perhaps more intensely than anyone else. The new land had to be explored if it was to be conquered, and everyone who took part in this process knows that it was not without danger. The path to knowledge was neither straight nor smooth. Yet today I feel that the new domain lies clearly spread out before our eyes, that we have penetrated the secrets of its organisation. This was not accomplished by the stubbornness of those who simply put up a pretence of strength by persisting in their accustomed disorder, or by those who were so self-righteous that they never experienced temptation. Anyone who is familiar with the development of music after the First World War will find step by step in these pages, which are intended to afford entrance to the newly won territory, traces of struggle with external circumstances as well as of that inner strife whose aim is the perfection of one's own work. But even a wider circle of readers will understand, at this first stopping-place on the road to complete clarification of both contemplation and action, that an attempt to explain the music of the present day had to be undertaken, if only to satisfy a personal need to pass on to new learners what had been acquired by learning, and to shorten for them the paths which until now have been inevitably roundabout."

The reference to "that inner strife whose aim is the perfection of one's own work" is a revealing sign that Hindemith had not allowed the apparent ease with which he had won his position at the head of Germany's young post-war composers to deceive him into believing that he had achieved all there was to achieve: the divine spark of artistic discontent was still gnawing inside him. This being so, what led him to think that he had finally penetrated the secrets of the "new domain" so thoroughly that he could venture to set them out in a book?

The answer is provided by the book itself, which turns out to be no blueprint of the right way to compose, but an identification and analysis, more thorough than anything published before, of the actual materials of musical composition. A sound knowledge of one's tools, Hindemith observes, is no guarantee of an ability to use them to good effect, but it is an essential prerequisite.

"The road from the head to the hand is a long one while one is still conscious of it. The man who does not so control his hand as to maintain it in unbroken contact with his thought does not know what composition is. (Nor does he whose well-routined hand runs along without any impulse or feeling behind it.) The goal must always be such mastery that technique does not obtrude itself, and a free path is prepared for thought and feeling. The man to whom the tones are a necessary evil with which he must wrestle; or who sees in them a perfectly tractable medium in which he can express himself without any restraint; or who climbs up on them as on a ladder, or wallows in them as in a bog—such a man is simply adding to the infinity of pieces that are written every year without moving a human ear or spirit. The initiated know that most of the music that is produced every day represents everything except the composer: memory, cheap compilation, mental indolence, habit, imitation, and above all the obstinacy of the tones themselves. Our principal task is to overcome the latter. To do this we need precise knowledge of the tones and of the forces that reside in them, free from aesthetic dogma and stylistic exercises such as have characterised previous methods of instruction, but leading the composer rather according to natural laws and technical experience."

The introductory chapter of *The Craft of Musical Composition* does not end with this admirably direct statement of purpose, but takes a sudden plunge into the dangerous world of metaphysics:

"What did tonal materials mean to the ancients? Intervals spoke to them of the first days of the creation of the world: mysterious as Number, of the same stuff as the basic concepts of time and space, the very dimensions of the audible as of the visible world, building stones of the universe, which, in their minds, was constructed in the same proportions as the overtone series, so that measure, music and the cosmos inseparably merged. . . ."

It may have been unwise of Hindemith to introduce such ideas into his outline of a new musical theory. Unfashionable at the time the book was written, such a statement hints even today, when minds are somewhat more amenable to imaginative speculations about the invisible universe, at a certain spirit of crankiness, and tends to confirm the impression of Hindemith as basically a backward-looking theorist whose ideas Time has now left behind. But such ideas were, however unexpectedly, an integral part of his nature—the escape route perhaps of that innate romanticism which he was so anxious to keep in check, if not entirely to repress. One may regard them, as far as others are concerned, as limiting, but for Hindemith himself they were one of the liberating factors of his imagination.

The starting point of Hindemith's attempt to overcome "the obstinacy of the tones themselves" (to use his own graphic phrase) lies in the overtone series, a natural and—at least in its earlier stages—measurable phenomenon which means that if (for instance) the fundamental tone C is sounded, we hear vibrating with it the octave, the fifth, a fourth, a third and so on in diminishing intervals to infinity. This is a natural quality of sound, as immutable (Hindemith assures us) as the series of colours, familiar to us in the rainbow, that constitute light. From this fixed series Hindemith proceeds to derive his tonal scale and arrives, after calculations based on vibrations and adjusted for practical purposes by tempered tuning (as in the diatonic scale) at—the existing chromatic scale.

It is not really an anti-climax. As Hindemith explains, he has, through his system of tonal relationship based on vibrations, liberated those notes which have no place in the diatonic scale from their subservient position as passing notes and given them a legitimate place of their own in what, with his usual flair for the revealing analogy, he describes as his "tonal planetary system", each note in his chromatic scale revolving round the sun of the central tonic at a distance established by its degree of relationship. The result of this arrangement, he claims, is that it frees the composer from "the tyranny of the major and minor".

"The actual dethronement took place in the last century. In Wagner's *Tristan* the rule of major and minor was overthrown. Unquestionably, the diatonic scale was here replaced by the chromatic as the basis for all lines and harmonic combinations. But the revolution came too soon. The decision and the consistency of this bold step were unique, and at first no one followed the new trail. For decades *Tristan* remained the only work based on chromaticism, and even its creator never again made so mighty a forward step into the new domain. Not until the turn of the century did the outlines of the new world discovered in *Tristan* begin to take shape. Music reacted to it as a human body to an injected serum, which it at first strives to exclude as a poison, and only afterwards learns to accept as necessary and even wholesome. What we have experienced, instead of a true understanding of the chromatic world of music, has been first the penetration of an ever minuter chromaticism into the linear and harmonic aspects of our music, then the disintegration of every element, a lapse into complete absence of plan and rule, and finally pure anarchy.

"If today, from our point of vantage over the whole field, we definitely adopt the chromatic scale as the basic material for composition, we are only continuing what was begun eighty years ago."

At the beginning of Hindemith's system stands the triad, formed of the notes with the closest relationship to the tonic in the overtone series. "Music," he writes, "as long as it exists, will always take its departure from the major triad and return to it. The musician cannot escape it any more than the painter his primary colours, or the architect his three dimensions. In composition, the triad or its direct extensions can never be avoided for more than a short time without completely confusing the listener. If the whim of an architect should produce a building in which all those parts which are normally vertical and horizontal (the floors, the walls and the ceilings) were at an oblique angle, a visitor would not tarry long in this perhaps 'interesting' but useless structure. It is the force of gravity, and no will of ours, that makes us adjust ourselves horizontally and vertically. In the world of tones, the triad corresponds to the force of gravity. It serves as our constant guiding point, our unit of measure, and our goal, even in those sections of compositions which avoid it."

Is this a confession of a conservative outlook? Hindemith regarded it as simply realistic: "All tonal phenomena are based upon inescapable facts, and these facts cannot be overlooked if order and purpose are to reign in music."

Having established his basic principle, he now begins to develop his ideas on its practical application. Single tones, as he points out, are not music. "Music arises from the combined effect of at least two tones. The motion from one tone to another, the bridging of a gap in space, produces melodic tension, while the simultaneous juxtaposition of two tones produces harmony. Thus the *Interval*, formed by the connection of two tones, is the basic unit of musical construction." Just as the notes of the scale have a natural order, based on the overtone series, so too have intervals, which are governed by combination tones, involuntarily produced when groups of tones are sounded simultaneously. "They are usually so weak that the superficial ear does not perceive them, but this makes them all the more important for the subconscious ear."

From these combination tones Hindemith deduces mathematically (his calculations being based on sound vibration ratios) that intervals have root tones. "Numerous experiments have convinced me that the feeling that one tone of an interval has more importance than the other is just as innate as the ability to judge intervals exactly—everyone hears the lower tone of a fifth as the principal tone; the ear cannot be persuaded to attribute primary importance to the upper tone." The interval values thus deduced are arranged, like those of the tone values, in an order of relative strength, and from these Hindemith extracts two fields of force—the harmonic and the melodic, which he shows to be at variance with each other: the strongest harmonic interval, for instance, is the fifth, whereas the strongest melodic interval is the second. On the basis of these tonal contrasts Hindemith proceeds to categorise chords into groups in relation to their individual strength and the degrees of tension existing between them.

It is not the purpose of this chapter to provide a complete summary of Hindemith's book, which anyone who wishes to can read far more profitably for himself (and savour in doing so the vigour and clarity of his literary style). But a certain amount of definition has been necessary in order both to show the nature of Hindemith's technical ideas, based always on considerations of practicality and commonsense, and to dispel the notion that he was trying to establish any exclusive system of composition. His aim was rather to show that combinations traditionally considered impermissible could in fact be seen as legitimate within the natural laws of sound and—more important—could be purposefully used when fully understood:

"The familiar theory of harmony prevents chords from the free unfolding of their vital urge. For it proclaims as the highest harmonic law the relationship of tones and chords in a key. The diatonic scale with its limited possibilities determines the position and rank of the chords, which are the mere satellites of this power. The chord must blindly subordinate itself, and attention be paid to its individual character only as the key allows." The new system produces a different result. "The key and its body of chords is not the natural basis of tonal activity. What Nature provides is the intervals. The juxtaposition of intervals, as of chords, which are the extensions of intervals, *gives rise to the key*. We are no longer the prisoners of the key. Rather, we now have a free hand to give the tonal relations whatever aspect we deem fitting. The different harmonic tensions which we need for this purpose are indicated by the ranking of the interval-values."

In a later chapter on harmonic fluctuation, Hindemith enlarges on the subject of tension: "Conventional harmonic theory does not provide, of course, any key to the construction of complicated designs of fluctuating tension; for this we must employ our detailed knowledge of chord-values. Whoever possesses such knowledge can create harmonic structures of the most daring thrust and tension without having to rely on the uncertain method of trying out each individual combination by ear—a process that soon becomes more a guessing game in pursuit of concealed possibilities than a form of creative work. We thus add to the time-honoured practices of harmony—voice-leading, and the production of tonal relations—the observation of the rise and fall of harmonic tension as an exact and completely reliable procedure. . . . The secret of good arrangement of this rise and fall is completely open to the composer in our table of the chord-values."

In attaching to his book a table of specific chords Hindemith might appear, in spite of his good intentions, to be coming perilously near to a doctrinaire approach, and it is easy to see how so many minor composers, sticking all too religiously to these, have since tended to produce music of so characteristically Hindemithian a stamp that the reproach often levelled against him of making all his pupils write like himself begins to appear justified. However, Hindemith's division of chords, amounting to six general categories with only a few subdivisions, leaves room enough for individual invention. And in fact, in his own analyses of various compositions, he is able to accommodate his new theoretical system convincingly to works as different in sound as Wagner's *Tristan* Prelude, Stravinsky's Piano Sonata and Schönberg's *Klavierstück* Opus 33a, as well as others of an earlier period.

The Craft of Musical Composition, for all its didactic form, is rich in biographical implications, and never more so than in the passage towards the end in which Hindemith himself answers the question which many readers will certainly have been asking: "What good is a new theory of composition if it leads straight back to the old, 'worn-out' concept of tonality?" His reply has all the force of a personal artistic credo:

"We have seen that tonal relations are founded in Nature, in the characteristics of sounding materials and of the ear, as well as in the pure relations of abstract numerical groups. We cannot escape the relationship of tones. Whenever two tones sound, either simultaneously or successively, they create a certain interval-value; whenever chords or intervals are connected, they enter into a more or less close relationship. And whenever the relationships of tones are played off one against another, tonal coherence appears. It is thus quite impossible to devise groups of tones without tonal coherence. Tonality is a natural force, like gravity. Indeed, when we consider that the root of a chord, because of its most favourable vibration-ratio to the other tones, and the lowest tone of a chord, because of the actually greater dimension and weight of its wave, have greater importance than the other tones, we recognise at once that it is gravitation itself that draws the tones towards their roots and towards the bass line, and that relates a multiplicity of chords to the strongest among them. If we omit from consideration the widely held notion that everything in which the ear and the understanding are not at once completely at home is atonal (a poor excuse for a lack of musical training and for following the path of least resistance), we may assert that there are but two kinds of music: good music, in which the tonal relations are handled intelligently and skilfully, and bad music, which disregards them and consequently mixes them in aimless fashion. There are many varieties between these two extremes, and of course it does not follow that all music in which the tonal relations are beautifully worked out is good music. But in all good music account is taken of them, and no music which disregards them can be satisfying, any more than could a building in which the most elementary laws of the vertical and horizontal disposition of masses were disregarded. For the creation of tonality it is all the same, being a matter of style and period, or of the manner in which a composer works, what kind of chord material is employed. A piece that consists primarily of very harsh and grating chords need not be atonal; and, on the other hand, limitation to the purest triads is no guarantee of clean tonal relationships.

"The only music which can really be called atonal, therefore, is the work of a composer who is motivated perhaps by a consciousness of the inadequacy of old styles to the musical needs of our day, perhaps by a search for an idiom that will express his own feelings, perhaps by sheer perversity, to invent tonal combinations which do not obey the laws of the medium and cannot be tested by the simplest means of reckoning. Such a man is not impelled by the instinct of the musician, who even in what seems his blindest groping never loses the true path entirely from view. . . .

"There are today a considerable number of composers who issue works that they call atonal. Doubtless these composers see in their freedom from tonality a liberty that will lift their art to the infinity of time and space. Apart from the fact that I consider it impossible to abolish the inherent characteristics of the medium, I do not believe that liberty is achieved by substituting mere variety for the principle of natural order. Nowhere does Nature give us any indication that it would be desirable to play off a certain number of tones against one another in a given duration and pitch-range. Arbitrarily conceived rules of that sort can be devised in qualities, and if styles of composition were to be based upon them, I can conceive of far more comprehensive and more interesting ones. To limit oneself to home-made tonal systems of this sort seems to me a more doctrinaire proceeding than to follow the strictest diatonic rules of the most

dried-up old academic. Is it not strange that the same composers who worship harmonic freedom—or what they mistake
for freedom, which is only a dead end which they have not yet
recognised as such—have been taken in as regards musical
structure by a formalism that makes the artificialities of the
early Netherland contrapuntists seem like child's play? . . .

"A true musician believes only in what he hears. No matter
how ingenious a theory is, it means nothing to him until the
evidence is placed before him in actual sound. . . . Just as in the
literature that is written in letters, so in that written in notes
everything must be clear and completely analysable to the
person who knows how to read it. The true work of art does not
need to wrap any veil of mystery about its external features.
Indeed the very hallmark of great art is that only above and
beyond the complete clarity of its technical procedure do we
feel the essential mystery of its creative power."

One does not need to accept all Hindemith's arguments,
theoretical or philosophical, to come to the conclusion that *The
Craft of Musical Composition* is an important book. There have
been attempts since its publication to discredit both Hindemith's mathematics and his axioms derived through them (for
instance by Norman Cazden in his article "Hindemith and
Nature" in the *Music Review*, XV, 1954), but such attempts,
successful or not, do not deprive the book of its significance as
a unique insight into the thought processes of an important
composer. Victor Landau, having analysed Hindemith's works
in the light of his theories, was able to demonstrate (in "Paul
Hindemith: A Case Study in Theory and Practice", *Music
Review*, XXI, 1960) that they conform most closely to his
definitions during his earliest compositional period (1917–21)
and again during the period 1937–41. In the years 1937–41
Hindemith was of course most consciously influenced by the
definitions he had just committed to paper. The earlier period
is more interesting: it leads one to conclude that basically his
theories were a rationalisation of his own inborn mode of
expression. That he strayed from his path in the years between
was surely due to the fact that he was deliberately experimenting, and it was indeed what he felt to be the unprofitability
of aimless experimentation that gradually awoke in him the
need to seek some sort of order in his ideas. His later divergences
were the result of second thoughts and new discoveries. Clearly

his musical development could not be expected to cease at the age of forty. The first volume of *The Craft of Musical Composition*, written at about this age, was not his last word on the matter. In subsequent years he added a second volume, *Übungsbuch für den zweistimmigen Satz* (English title: *Exercises in Two-Part Writing*). A third volume was begun in America, but its completion was constantly delayed. This may have been due, as his American pupil Howard Boatwright has suggested, to doubts in his own mind about some of his earlier conclusions: he often talked, Boatwright told me, of eventually revising the whole work. He never did so. The third volume, *Der dreistimmige Satz* (Three-Part Writing), was not published until after his death.

Chapter 4

1937–40:

GOOD MUSIC AND A CLEAN CONSCIENCE

HINDEMITH'S FIRST ENGAGEMENTS in the United States were in Washington. Since the great Mrs Coolidge was sponsoring his concerts there, Ernest R. Voigt, president of Associated Music Publishers, Schott's representatives in New York, cautiously refrained from stealing her thunder, and so Hindemith on his arrival in New York was spared the lavish public reception at the docks then considered obligatory for visiting celebrities.

Voigt did, however, manage to provide the human touch so dear to American hearts when he himself went to meet Hindemith, armed with an orange handkerchief to ensure recognition. On the quay, he reported in his subsequent letter to Willy Strecker, "we were joined by his old uncle, the eldest brother of his father, I think, who has been in this country since the early 80's and has never been back nor seen any of his family since then. The meeting was quite touching, and Hindemith showed that fine, unassuming, democratic side of his character which has endeared him to everybody over here who has met him."

Not surprisingly, considering Hindemith's lack of family feeling, this old uncle disappeared from the scene as swiftly as he arrived on it. Hindemith's ability, as Voigt approvingly put it, "to accommodate himself so readily and efficiently to new conditions" did not, as far as relatives were concerned, go beyond the bounds of ordinary politeness. More in his line, probably, was a visit to the Cotton Club in New York where, as Voigt reports, he enjoyed Duke Ellington's floor-show "like a kid", and was impressed by the fun which the players themselves got from their performance.

Hindemith's own first performance in Washington was on 10 April in the Library of Congress, and it began with the solo viola sonata of 1922. In this series of concerts, given under government auspices before an invited audience, his music was not unknown—works of his had been played there in 1928, 1929 and 1933—but it was the first time the audience had seen him personally and, as Voigt reported, they "rose as one man and applauded him to the echo. His charming, disarming stage presence immediately won the crowd."

Mrs Coolidge herself was among the audience, and also Marshall Bartholomew, who later became a friend at Yale University. Bartholomew noticed that as Hindemith began to play Mrs Coolidge, who was listening through her old-fashioned ear trumpet, looked increasingly dismayed. She removed the trumpet from her ear, shook it, then tried again. Apparently achieving no improvement, she gave up and laid the ear trumpet in her lap.

This first concert, in which Hindemith was joined by the pianist Jesus Sanroma and the flautist Georges Barrère, was according to Voigt "a really genuine, unequivocal success", whereas the first performance of the *Schwanendreher* concerto only went "pretty well". The orchestra, "a heterogeneous body of musicians who had never played together", was directed by Carlos Chavez, a Mexican conductor who was Mrs Coolidge's latest protégé, and Hindemith was unable to establish a sympathetic relationship with him.

The *Schwanendreher* concerto was played in each of the five cities included in Hindemith's first tour—Washington, Boston, New York, Chicago and Buffalo—each time under a different conductor. Voigt reported with particular approval of Arthur Fiedler in Boston. "Thoroughly in sympathy with Hindemith and his music, he achieved a fine performance, considering the short rehearsal time. The Boston concert took place at the Boston Chamber Music Club, Koussevitzky having declined to consider engaging Hindemith on the threadbare ground that his rostra of soloists for the season was complete. . . . However, he saw Hindemith—in fact he and his orchestra acclaimed him informally and vociferously on the occasion of a rehearsal which Hindemith attended. He did not come to the concert, although he had promised to, but sent a long apologetic telegram pleading indisposition, à la prima donna. If you knew Koussevitzky, you could hardly expect him to lend his august presence to any such unofficial occasion." But he did promise Hindemith an engagement in the following season.

Hindemith's own summing-up of his first encounter with the United States was contained in two letters, both written on

3 May on board the *Europa* during the return journey. "The success was sufficient," he told Willy Strecker. To Oliver Strunk at the Music Division of the Library of Congress in Washington he wrote in less detached terms: "I left with a heavy heart, much to the amazement of so hardened a traveller as myself. . . . It seems like a whole year since those days in Washington, the weeks were both busy and eventful, and I am returning home not dissatisfied. Now another life faces me with the work in Italy, a lot of teaching and my work for the Turks. And with it much vexation and unpleasantness. . . ."

Léonide Massine's account of the origins of the ballet *Nobilissima Visione* gives the impression that it was a lucky accident. "The idea for this work (known later in America as *St Francis*)," he writes in his autobiography *My Life in Ballet*, "came to me from Paul Hindemith, whom I happened to meet in Florence. He had just come from the great church of Santa Croce, which contains the frescoes by Giotto depicting the life of St Francis of Assisi. He had been deeply impressed by them, and taking me by the arm he hurried me back to the church to see them. I too was struck by their spiritual beauty and could well understand why they had so profoundly moved Hindemith. But when he suggested that we should do a ballet together on the life of St Francis, I hesitated."

The meeting with Massine was not quite the chance it is there made out to be. Even before his departure for America Hindemith had started work on a ballet for Colonel de Basil's company, of which Massine was then a member, and the intention of discussing it during the Maggio Fiorentino, where Hindemith had been invited to give a lecture on his musical theories, had always been envisaged. It is, of course, possible that, when they met in Florence in May 1937, Massine was not impressed by Hindemith's original ideas for a ballet. In this case the idea of writing a ballet about St Francis would simply have been a sudden (and inspired) second choice.

Massine, taken by surprise, asked Hindemith to give him time to think it over. While he was doing so, Hindemith continued work on his original score, remoulding it in the form of a concert suite to fill a commission from the BBC. Under the title *Symphonic Dances* it was given its first performance in London on 5 December 1937.

This, together with two organ sonatas, was his main compositional work during that year. A third sonata for solo viola, written on a train journey to Chicago during his American tour and publicly performed the same evening (19 April), was probably no more than a nostalgic exercise, inspired by opportunity, in the habits of his youth: the work has remained unpublished. And his editing of the Schumann Violin Concerto, the odd story of whose "rediscovery" by the Hungarian violinist Jelly d'Aranyi with the help of an ouija board is told by Joseph Macleod in his book *The Sisters d'Aranyi*, was a routine job in which he claimed no proprietorial rights.

The old game of tactical warfare with the Nazis was still being played, and it was certainly this, combined with the necessity of working out his time at the Hochschule in Berlin, which Hindemith was thinking of when he wrote to Strunk of "vexation and unpleasantness". Rosenberg had in the meantime read the text of *Mathis der Maler* and appeared (in spite of its book-burning scene) to have been completely converted. At any rate, he was now anxious that Hitler should at last be told the truth about the work, and there was even the suggestion of a meeting between Rosenberg and the composer.

This development arose as the Strecker brothers, with Hindemith's approval, were discussing plans to produce the opera in Vienna, with Carl Ebert as producer and Furtwängler or Victor de Sabata as conductor. In view of Rosenberg's change of front it was thought expedient to shelve this project in order not to queer the pitch for a production in Germany.

After reading many books and making a journey to Paris to consult the writer François Mauriac, Massine, who had now parted from Colonel de Basil and was forming a company of his own, had come to the conclusion that he would be willing to co-operate on a ballet depicting the life of St Francis. He invited the Hindemiths to visit him at his home on Sirens Island in the Bay of Naples. "They came for several weeks in the summer," he writes in his autobiography, "and we began work on the ballet. After selecting the episodes which seemed most suitable for our purpose we discussed each one carefully. I described the scene as I saw it, improvising the choreography so that Hindemith could visualise it more easily. In his precise way he would then make careful notes, and afterwards play

over a number of liturgical chants on the piano, for he had
decided to base his score mainly on early French religious
music, particularly that of the great fourteenth-century composer Guillaume de Machaut."

A series of picture postcards of Positano, where the Hindemiths were staying in a hotel, crossing the water every day to
Massine's island, informed his publishers that work was going
well—on the *Symphonic Dances* as well as the ballet synopsis.
Between working hours time was found for an excursion with
Massine to nearby Amalfi, where Hindemith was delighted to
find a military band playing in the piazza; and to the ancient
temples at Paestum with Stravinsky, who was also temporarily
settled in Positano, writing his Concerto in E flat.

Hindemith was still in Italy when, on 30 September 1937,
his connection with the Hochschule in Berlin officially came to
an end, but the severance of this final link with the land of his
birth passed without mention. From Italy he and Gertrud went
at the beginning of October to Ankara, where he found the music
school running smoothly. With no new problems to face, he
found time to write the last of his four *Symphonic Dances*. He also
wrote a detailed sketch, including passages of dialogue, of an
opera on a Turkish subject, but this was never completed.

"Best greetings from this land of limited impossibilities,"
Hindemith wrote from New York to Willy Strecker on 21
February 1938. His second tour of the United States, undertaken like the first alone, was on a more modest scale, being
confined mainly to appearances at smaller centres with chamber
works. Among these was an engagement at Yale University,
where on 27 February, for a fee of only two hundred dollars,
Hindemith and Sanroma gave a recital of his works in the hall
of Jonathan Edwards College. It was his first contact with the
university that was very soon to become his home. Owing to
the disapproval of the dean, Stanley Smith, the recital was not
officially sponsored by the School of Music, but among the
younger staff it attracted a great deal of attention.

Hindemith returned to Europe to find himself involved
simultaneously in preparations for the launching of two major
works, and two which, in spite of the lapse of time between their
composition, had striking similarities in theme and treatment:
Mathis der Maler at the opera house in Zurich and *Nobilissima*

Visione (which he had completed before leaving for America) in Monte Carlo.

Even the incorrigibly optimistic Willy Strecker had by now to acknowledge that their hopes of staging the first production of *Mathis der Maler* in Germany were no longer feasible. A few months earlier Goebbels had hinted that he would not object to three private performances at Frankfurt as a way out of the impasse but, when this proved impossible, Strecker at last acknowledged defeat and yielded to the persuasions of Zurich.

The tide in Germany now seemed to be set solidly against Hindemith. In the very week of the *Mathis* première, an exhibition opened in Düsseldorf under the title *Entartete Musik* (Degenerate Music). Hindemith's books and music were prominently displayed, his *Unterweisung im Tonsatz* sharing a cabinet with Schönberg's *Harmonielehre*. "Who eats with Jews, dies of it", was the motto of the exhibition, and Hindemith, as the *Hamburger Nachrichten* observed in its review, was one composer who had proved its truth.

Zurich may not have enjoyed a very high reputation among the opera houses of the world, but the production of *Mathis der Maler* by Karl Schmid-Blos and Hans Zimmermann, the musical direction of Robert F. Denzler and the singing of Asger Stig in the title-role were widely praised as worthy of a work which was an instant success from its first performance on 28 May 1938. Critics from all countries wrote enthusiastically about it, and only in Germany was there complete silence: by official order no mention of the occasion was permitted in the German newspapers.

Massine, having rehearsed *Nobilissima Visione* with great dedication in Monte Carlo, gave its first performance in London on 21 July. Hundreds of priests from all over England were among the first audiences at the Drury Lane Theatre, Massine tells us in his autobiography, thus expressing his wonder at his own temerity in attempting to portray so revered a saint on the stage. His apprehensions were shared by Mauriac, who contributed an explanatory note to the programme in an effort to forestall criticism. They need not have worried: the reception in London was friendly and untroubled.

"*Nobilissima Visione* was not really a ballet at all," Massine comments. "It was a dramatic and choreographic interpretation of the life of St Francis in which Hindemith, [Pavel]

Tchelichev [the designer] and I tried to create and sustain throughout a mood of mystic exaltation. . . . I was gratified . . . by Mauriac's comments after he had seen the production. He said he had at first thought the idea impossible, almost sacrilegious, because he had not realised that 'the dance, as this great artist (Massine) has conceived it, can express what is most beautiful and sacred in this world: the love of God taking possession of the soul of a young man'."

Hindemith himself, who conducted the first performances in London, did not see his work in such narrow dogmatic terms. He was not a Catholic, and his inherited Protestantism did not arouse in him any sense of partisanship. The common ground of *Mathis der Maler*, with its Protestant hero, and *Nobilissima Visione*, with its Catholic one, cannot be found in any denominational belief, but in the composer's sense of moral responsibility. The painter Matthias Grünewald and the saint from Assisi were human beings seeking the balance between their duty towards their fellow creatures and their own souls. The two works, written during the period of his own conflict between his love for the land of his origin and his abhorrence of its present political direction, are surely first and foremost the sublimation of Hindemith's own inner suffering.

On his return from London Hindemith went with Gertrud to Berlin to close the apartment in the Sachsenplatz which had been their home for the past ten years. They had decided, after the nomadic existence of the past few months, to make themselves a new permanent home in Switzerland, and had rented a small Alpine villa at Blusch near Sierre in the canton of Valais.

Germany did not let him go without a final kick. Arriving at the Swiss border near Freiburg in the middle of September, he was stopped: a police certificate in his passport had expired. He was obliged to spend the whole weekend in Freiburg before the authorities, after checking with Berlin on Monday morning, allowed him across the border. Gertrud, travelling separately, joined him in Basle on the following day. Stopping at Blusch only to drop their belongings, they went on to Venice, where Hindemith conducted the orchestral suite he had made from the music of *Nobilissima Visione*.

In a long letter to Willy Strecker, written from Lugano on

Left: Paul and Gertrud Hindemith in Minneapolis, 1945

Below: Paul Hindemith with pupils Sam Bonaventura (*left*) and Yehudi Wyner (*right*) at the Yale School of Music, 1953

Mural painted by Hindemith in May 1953 for farewell party in his New Haven home

Christmas and New Year greetings card, 1950

20 September 1938 while waiting to take over their new home, Hindemith at last gave vent to the bitterness he felt over his virtual banishment from the country of his birth. The trenchancy of his language is this time not softened by his customary humour:

"I read in the *Frankfurter Zeitung* a detailed review of the Venice festival, in which my *Visione* is not mentioned at all. That is by current standards hardly surprising—it just proves to me that the decision I have now made was entirely right. A change in the obstinate insistence on a completely idiotic system can hardly be expected any more. There are only two things worth aiming for: good music and a clean conscience, and both of these are now being taken care of. Looked at from this point of view, all our previous efforts were a waste of time—and when I see yet another shit-pants being taken seriously, as happened last year, when it is of no interest to anybody what he says, good or bad, about a work—or even if he ignores it entirely—then I could kick myself retrospectively."

This was followed two weeks later by another letter from Blusch:

"First news from the happy house-owners—the very happy ones in fact, for the little house is tailor-made for us and the countryside is the loveliest one could wish—woods and meadows surrounded by the most magnificent things. Behind us the southernmost chain of the Bernese Alps, facing us the snow-capped giants of the Valais (Weisshorn, etc.) and deep below the Rhone valley, which we can see along to a distance of about 40 kilometres. Added to that a solitary position in a tiny village full of cows with tinkling bells, a house with veranda and a garden full of fruit trees—what more could one want? Besides the composing there's plenty of housework: sawing and chopping wood (with oak logs, very healthy exercise!), looking for mushrooms and in springtime the garden to dig. And an ideal place for winter ski-ing."

The fifteen months the Hindemiths spent in Blusch were probably the happiest of their lives. He had warned Willy Strecker, who was one of their first visitors, not to disclose their address, "otherwise we shall be besieged". They were clearly anxious, after the unsettled, nerve-ridden existence of the past few years, to enjoy their quiet life undisturbed. Their love of the countryside, confined up till now for enjoyment to a yearly

F

rambling holiday, could be indulged without stint. With none but their pet dog Alfi as companion in their childless home, they lavished their attentions on the village children or those of their friends old and new.

One of these was Georges Haenni, head of the Conservatoire in the neighbouring town of Sion and director of a choir, the Chanson Valaisanne. "We saw each other several times a week," he writes in the *Revue Musicale de Suisse Romande* of June 1973 (a special number devoted to Hindemith). "I remember a *raclette* undertaken with our mutual friends, M. and Mme. Darius Milhaud, in the forest of Plan Mayen. . . . Paul was devoted to my four children and played with them in a thousand ways—I can see him now, crawling on all fours with one or the other of them on his back. . . . My happiest memory is of an evening at Blusch: we were deciphering a cantata by J. S. Bach —Gertrud, my wife and our four children, Paul improvising the whole score on his viola, myself at the piano. It was moving and unforgettable."

Another friend of both, besides the Milhauds, was Werner Reinhart. Among the many artists this rich Swiss businessman had generously helped was the poet Rainer Maria Rilke, whose gratitude had found expression in a number of French poems. Haenni, on that "unforgettable" evening, had the idea of showing Rilke's *Quatrains valaisans* to Hindemith in the hope that he would set them to music for his choir. "After a moment's hesitation he selected six quatrains, which he set to music in a record time. On the next day, before the meal at which both of them were our guests, I found on my plate these six songs with the dedication: 'To my good friend G. Haenni and his Chanson Valaisanne, with best wishes from the new Valaisans to the old.'"

Another memory is recorded in the *Revue Musicale* by Hélène Riéder, who was connected with a musical group in Lausanne specialising in contemporary works. Hindemith agreed to take part in one of their concerts, and one day Gertrud invited Mme. Riéder and the pianist Maurice Perrin to visit them at Blusch.

"'But I warn you,' she added, 'nobody comes to our house without bringing an instrument he has never played before.'

"My son, a medical student, took his child's recorder. I brought an alto flute and Maurice Perrin a silver trumpet playing the chord of D flat. We arrived at Blusch in the snow, our instruments slung over our shoulders with pink ribbons. Hindemith was just embarking on the clarinet, his wife the cello.

"Hindemith considered the situation, fetched a huge sheet of paper lined with staves and, taking no notice of the general conversation, wrote in half an hour a quintet based on the incapacities of each of us. Gertrud wanted no flats, Perrin had two of them, my flute refused to emit more than four or five tones. We worked at it for over an hour, with the aid of much bullying. It is a pity that this quintet, with everybody playing wrong, has never had the honour of a public performance."

Mme. Riéder also recalls Hindemith pretending to be a seal, using his hands as flippers to reproduce on the piano parodies of Wagner and Verdi. Many years had passed since this particular feat had figured in his friends' reminiscences: we have already met it in Carl Zuckmayer's account of the early 1920's. But there is no need to suppose that, in the troubled years between, Hindemith had lost his capacity for playing the fool in private. That blessed quality never deserted him, whatever the worries on his mind.

However, these worries were now, in the relaxed atmosphere of Blusch, considerably lessened. In a letter to Willy Strecker written on 23 December 1938 when—as always with Hindemith —the spirit of Christmas tempted him into revealing his true feelings, we get a glimpse of his new-found tranquillity:

"We are sitting here in deep snow and today for the first time I put on my skis again (I can still manage them). In all the happiness which we enjoy here in full measure I feel a real need to express my heartfelt thanks: in general to my publishers as such and in particular to you and your brother Ludwig. A year ago the future looked murky indeed: I could not see how I could ever extricate myself from the tangle I was in. It has now all turned out much better than I could have dreamt, and for that you are to a large extent responsible. Your understanding of my position and my need for peace and a quiet place to work made my path here so much easier. I believe that you too will profit indirectly from the beauty and the utter rightness of this corner of the earth, for I hope to work here a lot, well and successfully."

In his study with its panoramic view of the Alps he worked on the second part of his book *Unterweisung im Tonsatz*. The first part had been devoted to the theory: the second dealt with its practical application. His compositions during 1939, apart from a violin concerto commissioned by Mengelberg in Amsterdam, were mainly sonatas. These covered such a wide range of instruments, among them clarinet, horn, trumpet and harp, that Willy Strecker was provoked into comment: "I am willing, as a spur to your imagination," he wrote, "to send you a list of instruments which have perhaps escaped your eagle eye." But Hindemith's reply shows that there was nothing artificial in his project of writing solo pieces for all the instruments of the orchestra in turn. Not only did they fill a gap in existing literature, "they also serve as a technical exercise for the great coup which I hope to bring off next spring: *Die Harmonie der Welt* (that or something like it will be the Kepler title)."

He did not, in fact, progress very far with this opera, which did not finally emerge until eighteen more years had passed, and one of the reasons for that was probably that his life in Blusch, tranquil though it might have been, was by no means uninterrupted. During 1939 he made several concert journeys—to Italy, France, Holland and Belgium as well as his third to the United States. He found it necessary to do so for financial reasons. There was difficulty, now that he was living abroad and had no permanent address in Germany, in receiving his royalty payments. Though *Mathis der Maler* was doing well (thirteen performances in nine months—a record for Zurich, Hindemith noted proudly), the money was still going to Germany. His earnings in Switzerland from concert-giving were not sufficient to keep him and Gertrud going until the transfer arrangements (for they were now registered as emigrants) were completed.

For the sake of economy he made most of his trips alone, leaving Gertrud in the villa at Blusch with only the dog Alfi for company. His third journey to the United States at the end of January 1939, was made on a small Dutch ship. This may also have been an economy measure, though Gertrud declared it was by choice. "Paul doesn't care for the ocean giants, from which you see nothing of the sea: he prefers to be rocked across more slowly and cosily (??) with less tonnage."

His tour of America was this time on a much larger scale, geographically as well as musically, and seems to have been arranged with a curious disregard for convenience. After Cleveland, he went to San Francisco for two concerts with Pierre Monteux, returned for four concerts at colleges in the state of New York, then back to California for a symphony concert in Los Angeles, taking in Denver on the way. The return was via Philadelphia to New York City at the end of April. The long railway journeys were of course very much to his taste, and on one of them he drafted out a ballet on the subject of the Children's Crusade, to be danced to the music of his *Symphonic Dances*. This was intended for George Balanchine, who had asked for a work for his new American Ballet. However, when Hindemith returned to New York it was to find that Balanchine's plans had fallen through for lack of engagements, and so the ballet was never performed.

Massine, who had successfully brought out *Nobilissima Visione* (under the title *St Francis*) at the Metropolitan Opera three months earlier, was also in New York at the time, and he was none too pleased to find Hindemith discussing plans with Balanchine. He wanted a new ballet himself, and Hindemith worked out for him a comic piece about pirates and a girls' school. Massine, however, had set his heart on a subject they had previously discussed, based on paintings by Pieter Breughel. Detailed synopses of both the Children's Crusade and the Breughel projects, written in pencil in Hindemith's own hand, are contained in a notebook preserved in the Hindemith Collection at Yale. There is no trace of the comic piece.

One of the last concerts of this third American tour took place at Wells College, where the composer Nicholas Nabokoff was head of the music department. Nabokoff was making plans for a summer school in composition in the following year, and he invited Hindemith to take part in it. No definite promises were made, and Hindemith returned to Europe at the end of April with no thoughts but to write his violin concerto for Mengelberg and his Breughel ballet for Massine, with whom he had now signed a contract.

Although he had severed virtually all connections with Germany, he found the cat and mouse game with the Nazis still continuing across the borders. He had orchestrated four songs from the *Marienleben* cycle, which were to have been sung by the German singer Elisabeth Ohms in Amsterdam: the Reichsmusikkammer refused her permission to sing in Holland.

Hindemith wished to entrust the first performance of his violin concerto to Kulenkampff, but Kulenkampff (probably on orders from above) did not even reply to his invitation. In consequence Hindemith was somewhat sceptical when a new and elaborate plot was initiated to get *Mathis der Maler* produced in Berlin. The story is worth telling in some detail for the rather ludicrous light it throws on the devious methods which were necessary if one wished to get the better of the Nazis and their system.

The Zurich company gave some performances of the opera in Amsterdam in April 1939, and there the scenic designer of the Berlin State Opera, Emil Preetorius, saw it. Before going, he took the precaution of asking Goebbels for permission. Goebbels not only gave it, he also asked Preetorius to tell him on his return what he thought of the work. Preetorius then asked Schott's if he might give Goebbels his opinion. Strecker, knowing that Preetorius had been impressed by the work, consented. At this point Heinz Tietjen, the director of the Berlin State Opera, intervened: he asked Preetorius not to speak to Goebbels, since he himself wished to raise the question of a production with his own chief, Goering. Willy Strecker, after consulting with his brother Ludwig in a homemade code (Ludwig being away from the office at the time), outlined to Preetorius the new strategy: he should urge Tietjen to ask Goering for permission to produce the opera. It was, however, important, Preetorius was warned, that Tietjen should know nothing of the "background". Whatever this may have been—one presumes it was Goebbels's part in the affair—everything was already fixed (Strecker told Preetorius), and Tietjen's formal request to Goering should be enough to achieve the desired result.

Who knows whether this complicated plan would have succeeded? Before it was fully ripe, war broke out, and that was an end of it. But it had got far enough to give rise to rumours, and Hindemith's mother wrote in all innocence to Willy Strecker on 22 August 1939: "Is it true that the date for the *Mathis* production in Berlin has been fixed for November? Will Paul be able to come to the rehearsals?" Strecker, who had a tender regard for Hindemith's unassuming mother, felt obliged to reply to her in the most official diplomatic terms: "On account of the current situation no firm decision of any sort has yet been made regarding the Berlin production. The existing rumours concerning it do not accord with the facts." Frau Hindemith had obviously spoken out of turn.

The outbreak of the Second World War, following the German invasion of Poland on 1 September 1939, had no immediate impact on Hindemith in his Swiss mountain retreat. For Willy Strecker, however, whose son Hugo was a British subject working with Schott's in London, it was a severe personal blow, emphasised even more tragically by the death of his German son-in-law at the front only a few days after hostilities began. Since Switzerland was a neutral country and still had postal connections with Britain as well as with Germany, Strecker asked the Hindemiths to get in touch with his son. Gertrud wrote to Hugo on 12 September 1939: "We are still sitting amidst a lustily sprouting vegetation beneath a glorious Valaisan September sky. Everything coming to us from outside seems to us like an evil spirit."

Hindemith shared this feeling of detachment. He was even thankful that war conditions made it virtually impossible for him to go to Amsterdam to conduct the première of his new violin concerto. The German Embassy in Berne was prepared to grant him a pass to travel through Germany, he told Strecker, but he did not wish to be disturbed in the "very private and anonymous existence which has become so dear to me". He was working hard on the music of the Breughel ballet and the text of *Die Harmonie der Welt*, which he described in great detail in a letter dated 25 September 1939:

"I see it as a very large and very serious work . . . a mixture of ordinary domestic life, momentous world events (Reichstag, Thirty Years War) and cosmic matters (astronomical allegory). I hope I can bring it off as I have it in my head. But I shall need time and a continued period of peace—let's hope I shall be granted it."

Koussevitsky had invited him to take a composition class in Tanglewood in the summer of 1940, and he had accepted. Now, in November 1939, came a telegram from Voigt in New York, offering him a course at a university to precede the summer engagement. He was surprised. "It is touching," he wrote to Willy Strecker, "that he takes so much trouble over me, but this offer (which is obviously intended as a sort of sheet anchor) is not quite the right thing. The pay is not good enough, and anyway it starts in February, which seems to me, in spite of everything, too early. Something better will surely turn up to follow on the Boston affair [Tanglewood]. All the same, this offer shows that I can bank on further work over there."

Hindemith did not know the lengths—some of them perhaps not altogether legal—to which Voigt and other friends in America had gone in their attempts to extricate him from what they considered his perilous position in Europe. Nor did the details of the fictitious plan worked out by Voigt in New York, Nabokoff in Wells and Cameron Baird in Buffalo to ensure that Hindemith would be allowed to enter the United States emerge until Professor Crawford R. Thoburn discovered the correspondence in the files of Wells College and published them in 1973 (a copy of Professor Thoburn's Faculty Club lecture is in the Hindemith Collection at Yale).

What the plan amounted to was a number of technical engagements at several universities and colleges, including Cornell, Wells and Buffalo, at fictitious salaries. These would help persuade the American immigration authorities that Hindemith, if allowed into the country, would have enough money to support himself. The work the colleges would expect from him, once he was there, would be much less than the invitations suggested, and he would be free to take other engagements to suit himself.

It would appear from his letter to Nabokoff dated 4 December 1939 that Hindemith did not fully understand what was being offered him. The letter, surprisingly laconic in tone, was written in German, and the translation is Thoburn's:

"I suspect that your offer with respect to Wells and Cornell is born of anxiety for my future. I thank you for being concerned about me, although up until now there exist no grounds for worry. But I do know very well that on the other side of the Atlantic, out of shooting range, they take the European problems more seriously than we here, and that, above all, the nervousness is much greater than it is here, in immediate proximity to all the horrors. To be sure, we are not entirely without anxiety over the future; no man knows what the next day may bring under the present conditions of political opportunism, and it is possible, after all, that by next spring the mess will be general—though I do not believe that. Up until now they have left me alone completely, not out of any excessive civility, but because up till now my age-group hasn't been called up at all—not even the people of higher military rank, to which group my rank as corporal (I was by no means a general) hardly belongs. Throughout the winter things will probably remain as they are, for an acceleration in the war during the cold months is hardly conceivable, and this war seems to be distinguished by overly-limited fronts and a surplus of soldiers. But whatever may come, it is a comfort in any case to know that there is a way out."

Allowing for the fact that this letter was written during the period of the "phoney war" before Hitler began his march west, it still seems a curiously unperceptive analysis of the situation to come from a known critic of Nazism with a half Jewish wife. In the event, Hindemith decided to accept the offers from America, but to travel alone "and to send for my wife when things begin to look up financially or in case the war stretches out into autumn".

Part of the reason for this apparent reluctance to face reality was certainly financial. According to the writer Maurice Zermatten (*Revue Musicale de Suisse Romande*, June 1973), his Swiss friends, who were more alive to the possible dangers than Hindemith, urged him to accept a loan so that he and Gertrud could travel together. He refused. "If I find no work out there," he said, "who will pay it back?" Another reason, of which he himself was perhaps not entirely conscious, was his unwilling-ness, shared by Gertrud, to give up the home in which they had found so much happiness. It was possible in the tranquillity of the Swiss mountains for them to persuade themselves that life was basically unchanged. In a letter to Willy Strecker dated 9 January 1940 Hindemith described their life there:

"Christmas and New Year passed off according to pro-gramme with giving and receiving presents, visits and theatrical performances. In addition there was our landlady's wedding, at which I played on my viola, making theatre decorations for the village, wine-bottling in Sion and sundry other such important occasions. My work was a bit neglected . . . I want first (for financial reasons too) to complete the ballet and then really get down to the opera." In a postscript, signed by Gertrud as well, he spoke of their "fruitful solitariness, which in one year has given us more than twelve years in Berlin".

But then, at the end of January 1940, the time came for

Hindemith to part from Gertrud and his home in Blusch, and it needed considerable effort to keep up the fiction that he was simply going off on his fourth tour of America. Being still of German nationality, he needed special recommendations to ensure safe conduct as a "friendly alien" through British waters. These, secured with the help of Hugo Strecker in London, included a letter from Sir Adrian Boult. Before leaving Blusch, Hindemith wrote Hugo Strecker a letter of thanks:

"The documents you enclosed will certainly be of immense help, and I shall embark with a quiet mind. . . . I am very touched that Sir Adrian Boult should have written such a genuinely warm and convincing testimonial for me. In the past years I have experienced things at home which have shaken my faith in my fellow beings. Except for your father and a few other true friends, absolutely nothing has remained. Here, on the other hand, we have from the very first received nothing but good from people we did not even know before and for whom we brought neither advantages nor disadvantages. And now, at a time when hatred and evil appear to be ruling the world, we have more than once been shown where friends are on whom we can count."

PART THREE

LAND OF LIMITED IMPOSSIBILITIES

Chapter 1

1940:

SETTLING IN

HINDEMITH ARRIVED IN New York on 16 February 1940
after a stormy sea crossing. So loud, he wrote to Gertrud, were
the waves and the ship's orchestra that he could hear nobody
but his immediate table companion, an elderly Chinese who,
on their last evening, asked him who were the most important
living German composers.

After a few days with Voigt in New York he went to Buffalo.
His friend Cameron Baird, head of the music department in the
university there, had been an important confederate in the plan
to get Hindemith to America. "The professorship offered him
at the university," Voigt wrote to Nabokoff, "is in the nature
of pretense . . . as Mr Baird is subscribing the amount of his
salary. He will only be asked to give two lessons or lectures a
week, the rest of the time to be his own, the principal purpose
being to discuss and to set under way the plans for the founding
of the new conservatory in the fall. . . . It would of course be a
wonderful opportunity for Hindemith, as he would be sole
director, untrammelled by traditions and policies he might have
to contend with were he to take over the directorship of an old
school."

Whatever Baird had in mind to offer him for the future, it
seemed unlikely that Hindemith would accept it. He did not
care for Buffalo, and the weather was terrible. "Through all the
eternal making of arrangements I can hardly get down to any
real work," he wrote to Gertrud, who passed this extract from
his letter on to Willy Strecker on 27 February 1940. "And on
top of that this caricature of a town which, apart from a few
quite nice streets, consists of kilometre-long stretches of Siberian
wooden houses devoid of all charm—not exactly enlivening,
especially in slush, ice and snow. And besides, the snow is
black."

His immediate duty was to teach fourteen hours a week in
the university, and he also spent a day each week at Wells

College (where Nabokoff was head of the music department)
and at a girls' school. "A day such as yesterday takes it out of
one quite a bit," he wrote to Gertrud from the Hotel Lenox in
Buffalo which he had made his temporary living quarters. "I
have been talking a solid seven hours, which in view of the
foreign language and the not so easy material is quite enough—
and after the last lecture at about ten in the evening one feels
accordingly. The classes at the other university are still as
deadly as ever—out of sheer despair I give the silly geese, who
are as ignorant as they are untalented, some of the most primitive exercises for beginners. . . . There's no more talk here of
school plans, and I don't think anything will come of it. I'm
glad, for, if I were to become the director of this school, I can
already visualise the classroom in which, after a few years of
working here, I should hang myself."

These are for Hindemith unusually harsh and dejected
words, but they came from a man who was deeply homesick.
Other passages in his letters show that in spite of this his customary optimism and resilience were still alive. He had managed
a lecture at Cornell University before about three hundred
people "quite well", he told his wife, and now Yale was showing
some interest in him, which would be better than Buffalo. The
violin concerto would be given its first performance at Boston
in April (in fact, Mengelberg forestalled him, presenting it in
Amsterdam on 14 March with Ferdinand Helmann as soloist).
There was the prospect of a commission from Friedrich Stock
in Chicago for an orchestral work. He was discussing with
Massine a ballet based on Weber's music. All in all, he reported
confidently, there was plenty of work for him, and he told
Gertrud to give up the house in Switzerland and come to join
him in May. There was no longer any pretence that his stay in
the United States was temporary. As later letters reveal, he
notified the American authorities at the earliest possible opportunity of his intention to apply for naturalisation.

A friend from the early years in Cologne read in the local
newspaper that Hindemith had been engaged to give six
lectures at Yale University, beginning on 30 March, and she at
once wrote to him. The younger Thalheimer sister, Margret
Löwenthal, had left Germany with her husband and daughter
just before the outbreak of war, and they had made their way to
New Haven, where she had some distant relatives. She and her

family were now settled there, and the name Löwenthal had been altered to the more pronounceable one of Lowe.

That she and Hindemith should have come together again in so vast a continent in precisely this one town caused Mrs Lowe to comment in her letter to Hindemith on the surprising ways of fate. Hindemith's reply from Buffalo treated the question from the philosophical angle: "Today," he wrote (in German), "there can be no more surprises. The most one can be surprised at is that ordinary life still keeps going. So your news was unexpected rather than surprising."

They met towards the end of April at a concert in Boston, at a time when at last, as he wrote to Willy Strecker, he was "beginning again to enjoy life and its goings-on". The main reason for this was that his future now looked more settled. Following his preliminary lectures, the Music School at Yale offered him a permanent appointment as Visiting Professor of the Theory of Music. This meant that from September he would no longer have to use up all his time in commuting from one university to another, and would again have time for composition.

In his letter to Strecker, dated 26 April 1940, he listed his musical successes so far: "Koussevitzky has played the *Mathis* symphony seven times with great success. Last Friday Violin Concerto—excellently done, huge success"—and also his setbacks: "I have broken off relations with Massine, for artistic reasons, but shall still deliver the Breughel score as per contract."

It is possible to reconstruct the circumstances of his break with Massine from his letters to Gertrud, passages from which she occasionally passed on to Strecker. At the beginning of April, Massine brought his ballet company to Buffalo, and among the works they performed was the Bacchanale from Wagner's *Tannhäuser*, with décor by Salvador Dali. This, as described by Massine in his autobiography, consisted of "a series of weird hallucinatory images": the stage was dominated by a black swan, and there was also a huge black umbrella decorated with a luminous skull to depict Death. Hindemith found it "quite simply stupid", and was probably not in the best of moods when, immediately after the performance, he visited Massine to discuss their projected ballet on music by Weber. Massine's ideas for this did not impress Hindemith, but he nevertheless sketched out a score based on a theme from

Weber's *Turandot* overture and some of the pieces for piano
duet. He planned it as a paraphrase rather than an arrangement of Weber's music, and Massine criticised the score on the
ground that it was "too personal". When Hindemith then
heard that Massine intended to go to Dali for the décor, he
decided that he had had enough, and cancelled the contract.

However, his work was not wasted. Three years later he used
his sketches as the basis of an orchestral piece, the *Symphonic
Metamorphosis of Themes by Carl Maria von Weber*. As for the
Breughel ballet, of which he had already written a substantial
part, that too was eventually abandoned. It has not been
finally established what became of the completed music, but it
seems possible that some of it may have gone into *The Four
Temperaments*, a ballet which he wrote for George Balanchine.
This, though completed in 1940 and first played as a concert
piece, was not produced on the stage until 1946.

The summer festival at Tanglewood, which had been the
main inducement for Hindemith's fourth trip to the United
States, found him still alone. Gertrud, for all her efforts, was
having difficulty, now that the "phoney war" was over, in
securing a passage to America.

The Berkshire Music Festival, as it was officially called, had
been established in the early Thirties near Stockbridge, Massachusetts, by Henry Hadley, the American composer and conductor. A few years later Serge Koussevitzky took it over and
proceeded to turn the festival, now permanently installed on
the Tanglewood estate with a building instead of the original
marquee, into one of the main events of the American musical
year. In 1940 he extended it to include, besides public concerts,
a summer school for American composers and conductors,
known as the Berkshire Music Center. Koussevitzky himself
directed the conducting class, while for the first composers'
class he engaged both Aaron Copland and Paul Hindemith,
whose official title was Head of the Advanced Composition
Department, Berkshire Academy.

His students were by no means the rank beginners with whom
he had had to concern himself at Buffalo and Wells, but young
musicians who had already made a start on their careers,
among them Lukas Foss, Harold Shapero and Leonard Bernstein. However, this made no difference to Hindemith: he set

them to work on the two-part exercises which he had evolved for the second part, still unpublished, of his book *The Craft of Musical Composition*. He wrote to Gertrud: "My seven composers are beginning very slowly to behave themselves. I have been drilling them so thoroughly that I have had to calm the outbreaks of despair, with occasional shedding of tears, in a number of private sessions. Now they have all come more or less to see what real work means. When the six weeks are up, some of them at least will leave the school as discerning and perhaps quite usable fellows, if not over-endowed with talent."

His classes were not quite as grim as that account might suggest. It was a very hot summer, and some of the sessions were held out of doors at the lakeside. "After an hour and a half of hard work," Lukas Foss told me, "he would take off his clothes and put on his swimming trunks and jump into the water like a frog. He was always the first in the water and the first out. Back to work! Tremendous discipline. Tremendous health."

Besides these composing classes he also worked with the school orchestra and gave lectures to larger groups of students, of whom there were three hundred at the Center. Both activities he enjoyed, though he told Gertrud: "It is sometimes not exactly easy to hold the attention of a hundred people or so in what is after all not my native language." As Foss recalls, his English at that time was fluent but not always correct, and he spoke with a heavy accent. What little free time he had he spent walking the countryside in the intense heat, composing or making plans in his head.

When the time arrived for the public concerts, Koussevitzky was disturbed to find that Hindemith's pupils had nothing tangible to show for their efforts: he had intended to round off the festival with a concert of compositions completed in class. In fact the class *had* produced something, which was subsequently published. It was a four-part setting, with accompaniment by piano, harp or strings, of the Irish folksong "The Harp that once through Tara's Halls". But it lasted only two and a half minutes and was therefore hardly suitable for a concert finale.

Still, Koussevitzky had plenty of compositions by Hindemith himself which he could use. Performances were given of the *Mathis der Maler* Symphony, the little opera *Hin und Zurück* and a number of the recent crop of sonatas. A new organ sonata, his third, was given its first performance on 31 July by E. Power Biggs.

It is evident from his letters written at Tanglewood to Gertrud, Willy Strecker and to Mrs Lowe in New Haven that Hindemith had now overcome his early depression and returned to his usual high spirits. He gave news of the compositions on which he was working. Besides the new organ sonata, there was a cello concerto and a symphony. He was also preparing the two-part exercises with which he had plagued his summer students for publication by Associated Music Publishers in New York. Nevertheless, a hint of homesickness still occasionally showed through. The Berkshire hills, he told Strecker, reminded him of the Black Forest or the woods of Thuringia, and during his lonely rambles he often thought of his old walking companion. But his main concern was Gertrud's delay in joining him. Other refugees from Europe were arriving daily in New York, he told her. Why was she not among them?

Gertrud's delays were not of her own making. "If all goes according to plan," she wrote to Willy Strecker in May, "I shall leave Blusch on the 21st. The *Rex* sails on the 29th." But then the sailing was postponed and finally cancelled, and she had to look for another ship. She did not dare leave Switzerland, since she had no re-entry visa, but she had of course to give up her beloved house in Blusch, since it had been let to new tenants. Zermatten offered her a room in his home, but she refused, preferring to be by herself in what she described to Strecker as a "doll's house" in Sierre. From there she made frequent excursions to Zurich, Lausanne and Geneva in her search for a passage. Georges Haenni writes in his reminiscences in the *Revue Musicale*:

"She went regularly to Saint-Maurice, where she enjoyed the Gregorian chants at the Abbaye royale. She was a very convinced and fervent Catholic convert. When there, she stayed in a hotel opposite the railway station. Some officers of the Tenth Brigade were quartered in the hotel, and her comings and goings attracted the attention of the military police. One day they interrogated her and, seeing her German passport, they became suspicious. She was very upset, and mentioned my name as reference. This brought me a long telephone call from the brigade. I recognised the voice at the other end: it belonged to a former pupil of mine at the training college. I managed to convince him of the innocence of their 'suspect'. On my assurance of her complete trustworthiness she was released. After that, as one can well imagine, she became more prudent and discreet."

Willy Strecker was for some reason still convinced that the war would soon be over, and he advised her to sit it out. Gertrud agreed that this might be the safer course, but what could she do, she asked him, when Paul wrote her a letter of twenty-two pages urging her to come as soon as possible? "And so I throw myself into the adventure," she wrote on 4 August, "that is, if it is possible to get all the necessary visas in time. It is a fine old race, because ships will take nobody who has no visa, but the consulate will only issue a visa when one has a berth! Luggage and Alfi I shall have to reduce or sacrifice entirely. Paul writes that he doesn't give a damn if all the packing-cases and manuscripts sink to the bottom of the sea!!"

To add to her anxieties, her entry visa for the United States, valid for four months, was due to expire in the middle of September, and the whole process of acquiring one would have to be started again. Just in time she managed to secure a passage on a Greek ship. Abandoning Alfi to the care of friends and arranging for the luggage to be sent on afterwards, she hurried to Lisbon, from where on 3 September she sent Willy Strecker a picture postcard: "The first half of the odyssey is done, the ship sails in two hours. May the second part also go safely."

In the middle of September, shortly before Hindemith's work began in Yale, she at last arrived in New York.

In outward appearance Yale University would be more familiar to an Englishman than to a German, for it is built, like Oxford and Cambridge, as a group of separate colleges, each with its lawn-covered quadrangle. Scattered between them are the buildings—libraries, halls, churches—which serve the university as a whole. The architectural style is mainly Gothic— or rather neo-Gothic, for only one building on the Old Campus goes back further than the nineteenth century. If the impression as a whole is vaguely European, the effect is happily modified by the presence, in and on the edges of the college complex, of more modest timber-built dwellings which recall the early

English settlers. Houses of that sort can still be seen in many Kent villages, and the place names of the towns round about—Hartford, Norwich, Bridgeport, Stamford—still further emphasise Connecticut's English origins.

The town of New Haven, in which Yale University is situated, is however a product of America's own industrial expansion—a small reflection, in the rectangular layout of its streets and the blocks of tall buildings between, of New York, only some seventy-odd miles away. Small by those standards, it is nevertheless a town of nearly two hundred thousand inhabitants and, though it lies on the coast within the shelter of Long Island, it is not—and gives no sense of being—a seaside resort. The nearer one comes to the shore, the grimmer the outlook, and the escapes lie either along the coast to the east, away from New York, or north across the gently rolling hills.

This was the direction the Hindemiths chose when they came to seek a home. West Elm Street lies some three or four miles from the university campus on a road running straight out of the town, and the house they chose was a small timbered dwelling standing in a small garden of its own. From there, his "nice little furnished home to the west of the town", Hindemith wrote on 27 October 1940 to Willy Strecker:

"Everything is once more as we wanted it. The position is convenient and pleasant as well. We walk five minutes to the woods and find ourselves then amidst lovely clumps of oak trees with glorious paths stretching for hundreds of miles across the country. When you at last find a chance of coming here you can accompany us again on our wanderings. In the meantime we shall be in training!"

The house, 134 West Elm Street, had the additional advantage (at least in Gertrud's eyes) that it lay on the opposite side of the university from that in which most of the faculty members lived. She was determined from the very start to protect her husband from the sort of automatic sociability, the casual droppings-in and the shop-talk which so easily arise in a community of identical interests, and which she no doubt feared would be more prevalent among the reputedly companionable Americans than the reticent Swiss. Here, surrounded by ordinary middle-class citizens who had nothing to do with the university, they were more likely to remain undisturbed. Her instinct was right. Few of their neighbours knew—or (if they knew) cared—that they were living next door to a famous composer. Locally the Hindemiths were known simply as "that nice German couple".

Hindemith's work as Visiting Professor of the Theory of Music, at a salary of four thousand dollars a year, obliged him to spend three days a week at the university. The other four days were his own. To reach the university he could travel by bus, though more usually Gertrud would take him there in the car which they very soon acquired with the help of one of Hindemith's new faculty colleagues, the organist Frank Bozyan. Though he could drive a car himself, Hindemith preferred to be chauffeured by his wife. Sometimes, if he felt like it, he would walk the whole distance. Gertrud on these days remained at home, not only attending to the housework and resuming her busy secretarial duties in connection with his artistic work, but also striving to improve her English, which at the time of her arrival was almost non-existent.

As for the Music School itself, it looked, Hindemith reported to Strecker, very encouraging. "Not large, but very well equipped (fine library and everything else) and with a good number of talented people. One can work really well here, and the prospects of achieving good results are as good as, if not better than anywhere else." Speaking with all the experience of his three previous American tours, he added: "Altogether musical life here has made tremendous progress in the past four years. The star system has diminished a lot in significance, there are signs everywhere of a striving for the essentials, and the eagerness to learn is unbounded, almost beyond belief. So there is much work to be done, and what I can contribute is obviously regarded as both welcome and useful. I have every reason to believe that I shall continue to enjoy my work here. The peacefulness of Blusch was a good preparation for it."

The School of Music was (as it still is) a graduate school, open only to students who had gained their undergraduate credentials elsewhere. It was not at that time particularly distinguished. It had achieved some eminence at the beginning of the century through the efforts of Horatio Parker, an American composer of solid European training who was quite unable to appreciate the originality of one of his early Yale pupils, Charles Ives, and preferred to pass on the school, when his time came to retire, to another pupil as conservative as himself. David Stanley Smith's favourite contemporary composers were Elgar and Vaughan Williams.

Towards Hindemith Smith's attitude might not have been quite so radical as Parker's towards Ives—he probably did not think him entirely mad—but his resistance to Hindemith's concert at Yale two years earlier was symptomatic of the safe attitude which, as the time for Smith's retirement after twenty years as dean became imminent, some of the younger faculty members were anxious to break. The appointment to the staff in 1938 of another refugee from Germany, the musicologist Leo Schrade, who had taught in Bonn, might be seen as the final manifestation of the Parker-Smith spirit, and the almost simultaneous appointment two years later of Ralph Kirkpatrick, the harpsichord player, and of Hindemith as the first signs of the hoped-for rejuvenation.

The faculty members who were in favour of change can be easily identified, since they later became Hindemith's personal friends. At their head was Richard Donovan, a Professor of Theory who had been assistant dean since 1930 and who, at the time of Hindemith's appointment, was acting dean. Others were Bruce Simonds, a concert pianist as well as a member of the faculty since 1928; the university organist Luther Noss, and his assistant, Frank Bozyan; and Ellsworth Grumman, an assistant professor of pianoforte playing. But there were others on the faculty whose attitude towards Hindemith was more reserved, perhaps even at times hostile. They included Smith (still there, though no longer dean) and Schrade, whose reservations may have owed something to the fact that he was the possessor of solid academic qualifications, whereas Hindemith had none—at least on paper.

Hindemith's impact on the staff and students of the School of Music will be dealt with in the following chapter. As far as social contacts are concerned, one can detect in the reminiscences of his American colleagues an initial feeling of relief that the great man from Germany who had come to live among them was so human, so amusing and so lacking in self-importance. No doubt the more orthodox attitude of Schrade, who was felt to be stiff and rather difficult to get on with, had been responsible for a certain amount of preliminary apprehension, and the feeling of gratitude in the Yale community was all the greater since the newcomer made things so easy for them. Mrs Margaret

Bozyan, for instance, having invited the Hindemiths to her house for dinner, warned her children to be on their best behaviour. "When they arrived, my seven-year-old was seated frog-like before the fire, reading comics. The first thing Hindemith did was to say: 'I wonder if I could do that?' and squat down like a frog himself. So our attempts to impress the children of the importance of our guest failed at the start."

For occasional relaxation the Hindemiths liked to visit the theatre to see performances of Italian operas, or go to the cinemas, where he showed a preference for Westerns. And Ellsworth Grumman recalls in the *Yale Alumni Magazine* of December 1964: "At the time he came to New Haven there was a jigsaw puzzle craze and Hindemith was fascinated by them. We all provided him with the puzzles we had in the family. On occasion he would complain that he had been kept up till three in the morning to finish one. He entered into the more frivolous life of the School with keen relish. At one of the Hallowe'en parties Gertrud appeared dressed as Brünnhilde and he as her steed from *Götterdämmerung*. Later in the evening they gave a dizzy demonstration of the fast Viennese waltz to music by Johann Strauss."

The Hindemiths returned hospitality as well, and their guests were likely to find caricatures of themselves marking their places at the table, drawn by Hindemith himself. Some found Gertrud's German-style cooking on the heavy side, though all agreed she was a good cook. "Their meals were something to remember," Mrs Ellsworth Grumman recalls, thinking in particular of Gertrud's lentil soup and "a wonderful German stew with wine". After the meal the guests would be asked to join in paper games. Hindemith was never content with mere chat, but wanted the entertainment to have some intellectual purpose, however slight. Consequences was a favourite: drawings of figures in the usual way when the company was mixed, but sometimes, if the guests were capable of it, bars of music. Hindemith impressed the wives of his colleagues with his expert knowledge of domestic science. He helped Gertrud with the housework and could discuss the merits of various gadgets, polishes and detergents from personal experience. He enjoyed using the vacuum-cleaner, which he handled like a musical instrument, relishing its hum and the variations of tone and rhythm he could make with it as he cleaned the carpets.

Gertrud had more difficulty than her husband in winning the affection of the Americans. She offended several people in New Haven, not only by standing between him and his visitors, but also by the tactless way in which she on occasions did it. Her harshness may have been due to her lack of command of English (that is the excuse that is generally made for her), but even her closest friends sometimes found her proprietorial attitude towards her husband rather disconcerting. She was by no means the American idea of a typical German *Hausfrau*. Energetic, excitable, forceful, she seemed to have assumed the responsibility of protecting her husband not only from his admirers, but also from his own convivial nature. She watched his drinks and she watched his hours, and it was seldom that he could escape her eagle eye, even if he had wished to. However, they soon noticed that she was not in fact domineering. Aware of his fiercely independent spirit, she knew exactly how far she could go without arousing his anger. Common interests naturally ensured that she was closer to the wives of their mutual friends than to the husbands, but she had no close friends of her own. As a good German she accepted without question her subsidiary role in marriage, and the more independent attitudes of American wives did nothing to alter her outlook. She was utterly loyal to her husband and extended her friendship only to those who were ready to accept, if not her conviction that he was the most important musician in the world, at least her right to believe it.

The other social centre of Hindemith's life in America— what one might call the European one—was the office in New York of Associated Music Publishers. This firm had originally been set up by a consortium of the main European music publishing houses to act as their American agent, but the outbreak of war in Europe and the simultaneous presence in the United States of almost all European composers of note (Stravinsky, Schönberg, Bartók, Milhaud, Krenek, Martinu, Weill—to mention only the best known) obliged them to become publishers in their own right. Already German-orientated from the start, they tended to select the new staff needed for the expansion of their activities from emigrants, and thus their offices became a congenial meeting-place for homesick European musicians.

Hindemith's closest friend in the firm was Carl Bauer, who

was not a refugee. Born in Mannheim, he had come to America in the Twenties for business reasons, and had for many years been in charge of AMP's hiring department. Described by a somewhat critical colleague as "two hundred per cent German", Bauer had a fondness for the good things of life, and Hindemith's visits to his publishers tended to end in lengthy wine-drinking sessions in New York with his friend. Whether Hindemith's nickname for Associated Music Publishers, which was the Pub, had anything to do with this must remain a matter for conjecture, but there is evidence that Gertrud disapproved, if not of Bauer, at any rate of this side of his dealings with her husband, from which she was usually excluded. Mrs Phyllis Bauer, his widow, who before her marriage had been a secretary in the publishing firm, told me that on one occasion Hindemith returned home from New York with such a hangover that he was unable next day to take his class at the School of Music. Gertrud rang up the publishers in great indignation. "What have you been doing to my Paulchen?" she asked.

By arrangement with the parent firm in Mainz, Schott's of London took on the responsibility of publishing Hindemith's works, both old and new, in co-operation with Associated Music Publishers. Hugo Strecker, Willy Strecker's son, was appointed to look after his interests, and in a long letter to him dated 9 November 1940 Hindemith provided a detailed picture of his life, both musical and personal, during his first year in America. He wrote it in English (one assumes as a deliberate demonstration of his new loyalties) and I reproduce it here with all its mistakes:

"My dear Hugo, it is already more than six weeks ago that your kind letter arrived. I did not find the time for an answer—you can imagine how a man is occupated by welcoming his wife, establishing a household (although furnished with foreign goods, it is yet the third one), starting again as a teacher and drinking tea at innumerable receptions in his and in other's honour. Everything is completely settled, we are very happy and even after this more than beautiful time in our peasants-village we like the place and the life here in this nice atmosphere, which is not so far from Europe.

"We hope you are still more or less in the same state as in your most recent descriptions. The conditions of life change so rapidly today, that it is almost completely stupid to write about things, which look for a receiver of a letter like fancy stories about prehistorical facts. However, I try to answer all your questions, even if you will find it more than funny.

"All the reprinted Sonatas are a great help for us. We were rather in sorrows, and I especially did not see any solution of the question, since Voigt could not make up his mind and print —even not on my own expenses! *Mathis* arrived two weeks ago. It is a pity that it was not available in August. There was a performance of the Boston Symphony in the Berkshires with a tremendous success, and everybody asked for miniature-scores. We printed here a third organ-sonata, I hope the Pub sent it to you. Furthermore we copied score and parts of a new Cello-concerto, which will be played by Piatigorsky and the Boston Orchestra after Christmas, and finally I finish for the same orchestra the score of a Symphony. You ask about other pieces to be printed. I don't know whether the number of sold copies are your basis of considerations; in this case I would not express my own opinion too loudly. However, I think it is not necessary to reprint that awful *Suite 1922*, neither with picture nor without. The piece is really not a honrable ornament in the music-history of our time, and it depresses an old man rather seriously to see that just the sins of his youth impress the people more than his better creations. . . . As I see the situation, things like *Let's build a town* are wanted, and some of the school-music (*5 Stücke für Streicher*). And rather important would be to have the piano-score of the Violin-Concerto (the new one from last year). I asked already Voigt to send his last copy to London. The piece has been played in Boston and Cincinnati, and now Koussevitzky takes it in his Musterkoffer on his trips.

"The Theory-book (at least the second part) will be published in two or three weeks. It is rather needed, and will be a great help especially for my own teaching-work."

The final part of this letter requires some preliminary explanation. Hindemith, as a German citizen, was a member of STAGMA, the German equivalent of the Performing Right Society in London, that is to say, an organisation responsible for collecting and passing on to the composer fees earned from the public performance of his works. Now that Hindemith was resident in America, the position had become complicated. If he were still a member of STAGMA, Hugo pointed out, fees earned in England (from the BBC for instance) would be paid to the custodian for enemy property, and Hindemith would get nothing for the moment. If, on the other hand, he had renounced his membership of STAGMA, or STAGMA had cancelled it, the fees could be collected by the Performing Right Society in London and passed direct to him. But this might depend on whether Hindemith had already registered an application for American citizenship. Hindemith's letter continues with an answer on this last point:

"You are right, I asked for my first papers. But I don't believe that this has any influence on my Stagma-membership. I don't believe either that the Stagma would see in such a step a reason to renounce my membership. I don't care for the Stagma at all, since my complete income from this source does not exceed 7.89M or so a year. But I think, your father would be very shocked if he knew I want to renounce. (Even the First paper-story will make him look very sourly! But I can't help, I finally must know where I belong to, and I cannot spend the best part of my life waiting for better times—without the possibility to gain even a very modest income). Of course the BBC cannot pay as long a composer belongs to a hostile organisation. But I think that in the present circumstances the performances in England are not very numerous, and if there comes some money at all, I would be glad to contribute for humanity's sake even with such a few Tropfen auf den heissen Stein, if the sum will be seized . . .

"I hope you are in spite of all the more than scheisslichen circumstances as well as possible. Greetings to all my friends, especially at the BBC. . . ."

For all its disruptions and disturbances 1940 had indeed been musically a prolific year. Hindemith ended it with a song, based on St Luke, Chapter II, Verses 1–14, which describe the journey of Mary and Joseph from Nazareth to Bethlehem on the eve of the Nativity. It was the first of that series of motets which over the following years were intimately connected both with Christmastime and with Gertrud—on this occasion a private song of thanksgiving for her safe arrival in their new home.

Gertrud too seems to have felt the need of a private celebration of her first Christmas away from Europe, and she refused Margret Lowe's invitation to share their Christmas goose in German style. At the same time, in her letter to Mrs Lowe dated 12 December 1940, she hinted pretty clearly between the lines that a renewal of their old close ties was not desired. "We have refused all offers of turkeys or other birds so far," she wrote (in German). "The term was rather strenuous for Paul, and he has been writing a lot of music. In between times there was—since we are no longer sitting on our solitary Swiss mountain—a certain amount of unavoidable 'social life' to deal with, and we have still not returned all our 'duty calls'. Over the holidays we have decided to be by ourselves for once (at last!!) and more or less to shut ourselves away from the world."

Chapter 2

THE TEACHER AND
HIS AMERICAN STUDENTS

IN THE AUTUMN of 1941 the Visiting Professor of the Theory of Music became a fully-fledged professor at an increased salary of six and a half thousand dollars a year—a sum on which he and Gertrud could live, if not sumptuously, at least adequately.

One of his first duties, while he was still visiting professor, was to draw up a scheme for reorganising the whole curriculum of the School of Music. It is more than possible, though nothing was officially said, that this was a test of his suitability for the post of dean, vacant since Smith's retirement in 1940. Hindemith's plan, worked out with his wonted thoroughness, threatened to turn the work of the school so drastically on its head that the faculty rejected it in alarm. Hindemith was disappointed, of course, that this might have cost him the deanship, but to a certain extent he was also relieved: he had no real desire to become involved in administrative duties. He preferred to work directly with his students, and had very clear ideas about how he wished to do it—and also about the label under which he wished to operate. The thought of being called Professor of Composition, as the university had originally suggested, appalled him. Only God, he exclaimed, could teach composition. However, he could not consent to the departmentalisation that the agreed title of Professor of the Theory of Music implied. He protested vigorously when it was proposed that his composition pupils and his theory pupils should have separate periods with him, each once a week. He pointed out that in Berlin he had had all his students continuously with him for eight hours daily on five days of the week, and he pressed for a similar arrangement at Yale.

He got his way—at least to the extent that he was allowed to have his students, whether majoring in composition or theory, all together for continuous periods. But he had to be content with only sixteen hours of class teaching in a week, this being considerably more than other teachers gave. His class became virtually a school within a school. Such an appetite for hard work might have been expected to spoil Hindemith's relations with his easier-going colleagues, but on the contrary it proved infectious. As Luther Noss said: "We all worked a little harder in consequence."

The invigorating new atmosphere in the school owed much certainly to Hindemith's energy and high spirits, but equal credit for it can be given to the man who became dean in 1941: Bruce Simonds. A quiet person of considerable charm and wit, he admired Hindemith both as a composer and a man; they were of the same age; and they had, apart from music, a common love of walking. In the summer vacation of 1941 Hindemith wrote to his new dean from Pittsfield, Massachusetts, where he was on holiday: "Now we are sitting in our nice house in the meadows, far away from all concerts, musicians and similar creatures, and from tomorrow we shall have a long hiking-period through the Green Mountains. If you hear in your dreams resounding 'Yoo-hoos' and other mountainous exclamations: it is the Hindemiths." A man to whom one could write in that style would hardly be upset by his under-ling's occasional disparagement of the academic niceties. The title of Master of Music in particular roused Hindemith to hilarity: "My God, how can anyone ever be a *master* of music?" And he was disdainful of the marking system. Asked in his first year to award marks to his students, he replied: "Give them all sixty." When told that this meant they had all failed, he said: "Well then, give them all ninety." Such behaviour, which might have aroused indignation in other academic circles, was gathered up and passed around with delighted chuckles by Bruce Simonds and his colleagues.

During the years 1940 to 1953 Hindemith taught some 250 graduate students at Yale. Of these 47 emerged with their master's degree. Only in the first year were students (including Lukas Foss and Norman del Joio) permitted to enter his classes under special arrangements. Once Hindemith joined the regular staff he accepted students only under the prevailing rules of the university. He had no private pupils.

As a member of the faculty he had a say in the selection of students, and letters in the Yale Collection show that he took this side of his duties very seriously. He was equally serious about the award of master's degrees at the end of the course: of the 47 approved by him, 12 were in composition and 35 in theory.

Only a few of the Americans who studied with him achieved any wide amount of fame. Leaving Foss and del Joio aside as special cases, one finds the names of Ulysses Kaye, Morris Levine, Frank Lewin, Howard Boatwright and Yehudi Wyner, all of whom have made a mark in one field of composition or another. But in addition to these there are a whole number of former students who later became prominent in teaching, performing, music publishing and so on. It is probably as good a record as any teacher can ever hope to show, and all the more impressive when one considers the wide basis of practical knowledge and skill which all his pupils absorbed, whether they eventually made use of it or not.

As in Berlin, all his pupils, whatever their talents or interests, were expected to join in the class work in a practical way. Whether majoring in composition or theory, all were called on to compose, to sing, to play familiar and unfamiliar instruments, and to concern themselves, in the Saturday morning class, with the history of theory, which involved philosophy and theology as well as music theory from the earliest times. He demanded a lot of them. As long as they did what was required, he was not unduly impatient with the clumsiness of their efforts. What he would not tolerate was any sign of idleness: if a student complained of lack of time, he would reply in all seriousness: "Well, there's always between two and four in the morning."

Not surprisingly, his methods proved daunting to the lesser spirits, who quickly took leave of his classes. Those who remained—and his classes never exceeded a dozen or so—cheerfully accepted the rigours involved for the privilege of belonging to so distinctive a set. This was not snobbery—the demands were far too exacting for that—but pride in being found worthy. It was Hindemith's great gift as a teacher that he could give his students the impression of being on an equal footing with them, of working together as colleagues in tackling and solving problems.

A practical outcome of his first year's teaching was a piece for piano, which was performed by one of the students, Ruth Vinitsky, in Sprague Hall, the concert hall of the School of Music, in May 1941. In a letter dated 14 December 1964 in the Hindemith Collection at Yale, Ruth Vinitsky recalls: "Everybody had some part in the composition of it, because we did it 'live', so to speak, with Hindemith at the blackboard—each one taking turns in supplying the notes needed. At the end of the term, when it was all completed, Hindemith wrote out the whole thing for me and asked me to perform it. Of course it sounds like a Hindemith piece, and came off very well!" The manuscript of this piece, which has not been published, is in the Yale Collection.

The reproach that Hindemith's teaching caused his pupils to write as he himself did might at first sight appear to have some truth in it. However, one can legitimately ask whether the blame for this lay with Hindemith himself or with his students. He had very definite ideas, as all his books from *The Craft of Musical Composition* to *A Composer's World* show. And inevitably, being a practical teacher, he tended to solve the problems he set in his own particular way. This does not mean, however, that he regarded his solutions as the only possible ones. It merely meant, as he once told a student who was worried about the teacher's effect on his own style: "If you study with me, you might as well write like me. If you have anything to say, it will come out."

When Lukas Foss (who told me the above story) applied to join his class at Tanglewood in 1940 Hindemith warned him: "If you study with me, it's like putting yourself in the hands of a doctor. You've got to do what he says." That sounds dogmatic, but in fact Hindemith was simply stating the obvious truth that, if his students wished to learn from his practical experience, the easiest way would be to listen to what he had to say. Whether they eventually accepted or rejected his solutions was a matter for them to decide for themselves: he was not, however, prepared to waste time arguing about it in class.

It was an attitude more suited perhaps to Berlin than to New Haven, for the reason that German students had a solid tradition against which to measure their achievements, whereas in America there was no generally accepted native background. Recognised American composers such as Walter Piston and Roger Sessions were European in outlook, Charles Ives had not yet been recognised, and George Gershwin hardly was to be taken seriously. Young Americans, except for one or two hardy natures such as Foss, were not in a position to accept Hindemith's teaching in any critical spirit, and in consequence the temptation simply to imitate was all the stronger.

The most, therefore, of which one could accuse Hindemith

Vevey, poste restante, June 12th, 1961.

Dear Dame Edith,

I am, as usual, late with this reply to your kind letter. The reason is, that we were again on a concert trip (to Prague and Germany), and with journeys, rehearsals, and performances there was hardly any time left over for other things.

I considered and reconsidered your suggestions of a libretto derived from your splendid account of Carlyle's domestic sufferings, and I hope you will not be too cross with me if I voice some doubts as to the feasibility of this theme. The charming essence of your narrative is, of course, that we know: here is a great man, with whose achievements as a historian and philosopher we are acquainted, and that now we see him in incongruent and unexpectedly awkward situations. This contrast can hardly be shown in a short opera — nothing can be implied; Carlyle would, for instance, have to clear the situations

Hindemith's handwriting: passages from letter to Dame Edith Sitwell

with whom no collaboration is desirable — but with the same fastidiousness I have the faint hope that you will have some further suggestions. If so, please don't think of any music or of acoustical effects, but only of visual action; the musician will find out how music can be amalgamated with it, and for this some very sketchy notes only are necessary at the beginning — the better if in multiple form ... Needless to say that, besides musical considerations, I greatly enjoyed your jotted down scenario.

We found your Shakespeare book when we returned, and what we have read so far (not much, to be true) increased our already existing amazement and admiration. With your friendly assistance we musicians will end up as really erudite people! Many thanks for your thoughtfulness.

Warmest greetings, also from Mrs. H., and heartfelt thanks for the dedication, Sincerely yours

Paul Hindemith

Left: Hindemith conducting, Munich, 1957

Below: Paul and Gertrud Hindemith, 1958

was his failure to temper his teaching approach to the differing circumstances. Yet there is evidence that he did in fact do exactly that. Like Schönberg and Krenek before him, he discovered that American music students were badly grounded in the basic principles. The two volumes of *The Craft of Musical Composition* which were the outcome of his work with his Berlin students assumed too much previous knowledge to be of immediate use to his American ones, so he immediately set about writing a new manual. This, published by Associated Music Publishers in 1943, was entitled *A Concentrated Course in Traditional Harmony*.

"Despite the evident loss of prestige which conventional harmony teaching has suffered," he writes in the preface, "we must still count on it as the most important branch of theory teaching, at least so long as it has not been replaced by any generally recognized, universally adopted, more comprehensive, and altogether better system." It is therefore necessary, he goes on, for students to know it, and his book sets out to provide it in the speediest and most practical form possible. "I am consciously taking this step backwards in full realization of its relative unimportance. Its purpose is not to provide a traditional underpinning for the principles set forth in *The Craft of Musical Composition* (which is not necessary, since for the understanding reader tradition is present on every page of that work), but to facilitate the speedy learning mentioned above, and this in as little scholastic a manner as possible, so that a close connection with living music may be continuously felt. . . . The fact that harmony can be taught along these lines has been proved by the class for which and with whose active participation this brief manual was written. In the Yale Music School we went through the material in this book thoroughly in a few weeks."

A second book, *Elementary Training for Musicians*, appeared from Associated Music Publishers in 1946. Since it, like the first, was based on his class work at Yale, we may take the methods advocated in it as evidence of Hindemith's own teaching practice, and indeed statements by former pupils confirm that assumption. The purpose of the book, says Hindemith in his preface, is to convey knowledge "of all the basic conventions and facts of musical theory and their traditional representation in written form", i.e., notation. And he goes on: "This knowledge is presented through the most intensive kind of work:

G

exercises. The great number of exercises compels the student to
practise seriously. . . . In his very first steps he must be converted from an attentive listener into a working musician. This
can be accomplished only by making him articulate. The
familiar type of theory class, in which one never hears a tone of
music, sung or played, except for the chords pounded out on
the piano by the teacher, must disappear! . . .

"A lazy teacher will always present this excuse: How can a
beginners' class be articulate if the students can neither sing nor
play decently? The answer is that the teacher himself must
make them sing and play—not like singers or advanced players,
but so that they can open their mouths (willingly!) and produce
tones just as any singer in a chorus does. It is quite common to
find excellent instrumentalists (not to mention composers) who
have gone through six or more years of practical and theoretical
studies without ever having opened their mouths for the most
natural of all musical utterances! What is true for singing is
true for playing, too. . . .

"After these observations the aim of this book ought to be
clear: it is *activity*. Activity for the teacher as well as for the
student. Our point of departure is this advice to the teacher:
Never teach anything without demonstrating it by writing or
singing, or playing; check each exercise by a counter-exercise
that uses other means of expression. And for the student:
Don't believe any statement unless you see it demonstrated
and proved; and don't start writing or singing or playing
any exercise before you understand perfectly its theoretical
purpose."

He did not regard his own textbooks as beyond criticism. All
of them were written, rewritten and revised both before and
after publication. As for the intended third volume of *The Craft
of Musical Composition*, dealing with three-part writing, he was
already early in 1940 talking of it. In a letter to Willy Strecker
dated 27 October 1940 he wrote: "I shall begin on the third
book round about Christmas time. I have already done some
preliminary work and the form is now fixed. I shall work it out
with one of my classes here and write it down immediately with
my experiences in class in mind. If all goes well, it should be
finished by the end of the school year."

Nearly a year later however (September 1941) he told
Strecker: "I had already completed three chapters of the third

volume, got then into such unexpected difficulties that I put it aside again. Now I am tackling the new problems very thoroughly with my class and hope to get a good bit of it finally done this season. Am I taking too long for your purposes? For mine too, but there it is." In August 1945, when the war had ended and he could resume contact with Germany, he told Strecker that he hoped to complete his "much revised" third volume by the winter. Even this estimate proved false, and in fact he never completed the book to his satisfaction. (It has since been published posthumously.)

Howard Boatwright, one of the pupils with whom the third volume was worked out, told me that in his classes at Yale Hindemith's theoretical formulations often differed "quite drastically" from those set out in the first volume of *The Craft of Musical Composition*. "He gave his class typed versions of the third volume right up to what would have been practically the last chapter. One thing that held him back from publishing it, however, was the gap that took place between the first concept of his theoretical system and his use of these materials with his students in America. He felt he really had to go back to the beginning again and weave it all in to perhaps one very large volume. He often talked of that: revising the whole thing from beginning to end." Boatwright's conclusions why he never did so are convincing: "I think he felt he needed his energy in his last years for the pieces he still wanted to compose, and he was no longer quite so fired up with the idea of developing a system which would solve everybody's problems. I think he lost a little of that faith which shines so clearly out of the introduction to *The Craft of Musical Composition* and was to me, as a young person at that time, very attractive."

The Hindemith Collection at Yale University includes some reminiscences of former students, spoken or written down in later years:

"A student improvised (sung) a bass line to a printed melody in *Traditional Harmony*. A girl student improvised an alto to add to the bass. Hindemith called on a third student to supply a tenor voice, remembering the bass and the alto. Reply: 'Well, I'll try.' Hindemith: 'Of course! What else?'" (Mrs Joy Crocker in a letter dated 13 August 1973.)

George Jacobsen recalls (on a tape) that the class would

gather around the piano to hear a piece freely composed by one of the students and would, under Hindemith's guidance, discuss technical problems arising from it.

Louis Hemingway, on another tape, remembers an occasion when Hindemith brought the score of *Mathis der Maler* to class and played and sang from it. "You could tell he himself thought this was perhaps one of his greatest works." But in places he would criticise it, remarking: "Oh, I could have done better with that."

Charles Fraker (in a letter dated 11 June 1973) recalls that Hindemith told his students to look at Verdi's scores; he also thought Tchaikovsky "solid and workmanlike". At the end of a class he would sometimes invite a student to play Schubert's marches for piano duet with him. "I wish I had written that," he said after a performance of one of them.

These are of course events recalled after a time-lapse of a quarter of a century—lively enough, but scrappy and relatively unimportant. There is much more solid evidence of Hindemith's teaching methods in a rough diary kept by another student, the late George Lam. In a letter to Luther Noss, dated 20 February 1964, Lam wrote:

"These are reminiscences put on paper right after class or the next day. Essentially it is a journal of the Hindemith composition class 30 September 1941–29 January 1942. It contains a great many remarkable sayings in rough draft. I shall have to make a clean copy of it . . . with misprints corrected. However, for your amusement, I send you a copy of the first two pages. . . . Pages 29–31 are a copy of Hindemith's *Enthusiasm* for Flute and Viola, with my comment: 'Mr Hindemith wrote this piece in about half an hour Thursday morning, 15 January 1942—as a criticism of Louis Hemingway's piece. It was copied by John Dunlap with Mr Hindemith's approval.' PH wrote it on the blackboard, and we saved it before he was ready to wipe it off."

Unfortunately Lam died in 1968 without completing the promised work on his diary, and the 30-page typescript, which he intended to go to the Yale Collection, was not discovered among his papers. Perhaps—as is much to be hoped—Lam's journal will yet come to light, but meanwhile I can at least reproduce the sample pages he enclosed with his letter to Luther Noss. For the sake of clarity I have myself undertaken the editorial work Lam intended to do, though keeping it to the absolute minimum:

"The first class with Hindemith. He began by asking David Holt how he went about composing. Holt hesitated, and then said that he usually had a rhythmical idea first, which eventually assumed a melodic shape, which then may or may not ask for its harmonic consideration. Hindemith asked the class whether they agreed with this. There were assents, and Dunlap suggested that he first would think what form the piece was to be in. Another enlarged on this, only to be demolished by Hindemith asking whether form was something to be filled out. In summary he divided composition into three phases:

"(a) You plan a piece, what instruments you are writing for, who is to perform it, where is it going to be played, how big a hall, how long the piece, slow or fast, a thing in itself, or part of a bigger one. 'Suppose,' he says to me, 'you were to write your piece for oboe, flute, clarinet and bassoon—would you expect four players to come, bringing their instruments, just to play twenty measures of Lam's music? Obviously it might be an interlude: your piece would come, say, after a Mozart symphony. How would your piece compare with the Mozart? So all these things determine what you are going to do.'

"(b) The next step is to decide how your piece is going to be. 'You are writing for flute, clarinet, oboe and bassoon. What clarinet?' 'A.' 'Now what is good on that instrument?' Then he explains the range and the bad notes; so with the other instruments. 'Let us do a slow movement. What form?' I say: 'Two-part.' 'All right, suppose you have a form—first section roughly on a level, next a climax, third something to round it off. Now, let us see: A—what will that be? B—how are you going to get to your highest note? Straight, or in sections? No sequences. We'll get to the top through BABA, and then come to a climax, and without further ado do section C, quiet again.'

"He then drew up the key structure for A: E—C sharp—E; for B: E flat—D, G—F sharp, B—B flat; and for section C: E—A—E. Then he made all his class (we are seven) go to the blackboard and said: 'Now invent a theme.' Everybody writing. 'Now invent another one; now a third. That's enough.' Then he began criticising Levine's theme, first singing, then criticising the number of notes in it, and correcting.

"(c) 'Now,' he says, 'your free invention might begin. You

write one theme, then another—twenty, fifty—until you find that they fall into groups, and that some of them are better than others. So pick the ones most suited for your purpose and your instrument. I don't ever begin at the beginning; after I have my plan I can work on any section—even begin a fugue in the middle.'

"Before we reached this stage, he discussed his musical aesthetics and asked if we thought music expressed anything. He said it did not, but that music was capable of evoking different reactions in different people. Then he mentioned Schönberg, and said a composer should know what he is doing and why he is doing it, but Schönberg confesses he does not understand what he writes, and at times does not understand what his students write. 'We are full of tradition, and the first step in composition is to attain technique—only to be freed from it and invent freely—be free as a child—and *then* develop a technique. This might come from a reaction to all that went before, but that is not necessarily good, though some good might come from not doing what had been done before. So in a sense composition is like a big arch: it begins with unconsciously inventing and then adding technique, and then forgetting technique and inventing consciously, developing the technique almost unconsciously.' He said that Beethoven could never have invented the theme of the first movement of the Fifth Symphony without having the whole in mind, because you just don't invent such an inane thing—and that the sketch books prove it."

Reading this, one may suspect that some of the lesson was at the time somewhat over young Lam's head, since his description is not entirely consequential. However, the description does vividly convey Hindemith's craftsmanlike approach to the job of writing music, while supplying a useful reminder that his approach was not *only* craftsmanlike. Hindemith regarded inspiration, not as unimportant, but as a private matter between the artist and his muse. The fact that he gave it little consideration in his classes was probably due to his feeling that young composers—and young American composers in particular—were only too ready to believe that inspiration was everything. His duty as a teacher, as he conceived it, was to provide his pupils with the tools to develop their inspiration (if they had any) in the most practical—and therefore the best possible—way. It was beyond all doubt Hindemith's delight in tackling problems (both musical and otherwise) for their own sake that enabled him to make them as fascinating to his students as they were to himself. His lessons, we are constantly assured, were never dry.

They were, however (as Lam's account has hinted) very taxing. Louis Hemingway, the involuntary begetter of the *Enthusiasm* for Flute and Viola (still preserved in the Hindemith Collection at Yale), has confided his feelings to a tape:

"I thought in the beginning he was extremely demanding and extremely meticulous: that it must be done almost in his particular style or he wasn't going to be interested in it—if you got off the track into something that might have been a little more *your* style. Often in the beginning I was very frustrated. Then, as the year progressed, he without telling us was giving us more and more latitude to go off in our own direction. It was a very subtle thing, the way his moulding of ideas that he was imposing on us suddenly became—I won't say our own ideas, but we felt we were going off on our own much more perhaps than we really were."

Hemingway was one of the students who eventually decided that music was not his métier. When he returned from military service after the war he worked in a bank in New Haven. During one of their occasional chats over the counter, Hindemith said to him: "I've always been so disappointed that you didn't stick with it." Hemingway remarks: "In other words, he was telling me—perhaps a little too late—that he thought I had some promise in the creative field, and maybe he was right. And I'll never know. So it is always a sort of frustration. I wonder whether he realised perhaps that he could have sold me on coming back if he had worked at it a little more or encouraged me a little more."

It is true that Hindemith was not generous with spoken encouragement, though he would reward students now and again for good solutions in class with a dime out of his own pocket. Being himself not susceptible to flattery, he probably thought acceptance into his class was encouragement enough and did not need to be emphasised by patronising words. He flattered his students in less direct ways, such as for example knowing them all by name after only a single class, or by crediting them with his own inexhaustible capacity for hard work.

In a quite literal sense Hindemith was a friend to his students. Critical in class of their efforts, he was never deliberately harsh or wounding in his remarks. The feelings of inadequacy he frequently aroused in them were not due to censure, but to their own despair at being unable to match the facility, ingenuity and dogged determination of their master. "He could write a fugue for you in front of your eyes," Lukas Foss remarked in a conversation with me. How disheartening such complete musicianship must have been to his struggling students was revealed to me by one of them, Carl Miller, who confessed that for years after completing his studies at Yale Hindemith continued to figure in his nightmares.

But another, the film composer Frank Lewin, in a letter in the Yale Collection written on 5 December 1964, pays tribute to the lasting effect which Hindemith's teaching methods had on his American pupils: "If I were to adduce Hindemith's most memorable impression on me, I would cite his remark in a class in which we chewed on the three-part writing material, to the effect that in writing music *everything* must be made conscious: melodic material, harmony, harmonic rhythm, texture, instruments—everything. At the time this seemed (to a green student) a hazardous piece of advice. Might it not stifle imagination? The more I write, the more I find that what he said is absolutely true . . . I have found that in writing music for films every note has to count—there are no fillers or unnecessary voices. I may not have attained the aim of 'making everything conscious', but I am aiming for it, for in that direction lies that elusive factor called 'control', without which writing music remains a game and does not become a skill."

Chapter 3

1941–45:

MUSICAL ACTIVITIES IN AMERICA

FROM THE TIME of his appointment in Yale a marked change took place in the pattern of Hindemith's musical life. Hitherto active in roughly equal proportions as composer, performer and teacher, he now dropped his performing work almost entirely, except in so far as it played a role in his teaching activities. And during the first two years even composition—at least as far as the issue of new works was concerned—occupied a subsidiary place. In the year 1941, in which the Symphony in E flat and the cello concerto (both written the previous year) received their first performances, he brought out only two sonatas (for English horn and for trombone) and a little set of variations for cello and piano. However, he did early in that year complete his revision of the *Marienleben* song cycle. "Now at last it has its final shape," he wrote to Willy Strecker on 27 September 1941.

His preoccupation with this, the most introspective of his earlier works, can perhaps be taken as evidence of his state of mind at the time, when the contemplative side of his character seemed to gain the ascendancy over the more active and outward-looking. The change was clearly connected with his exile from Germany. It had begun in the tranquillity of Blusch but, whereas there he was surrounded by a community that, if not German, was sufficiently closely related to give him a sense of belonging, here in America he was far more conscious of his rootlessness. His sense of isolation is always discernible in the long letters he and Gertrud continued to write to Willy Strecker in Germany. Sometimes it betrayed itself only by a disparaging tone: "On my rare visits to the big cities I encounter the usual sample of old acquaintances: Igor [Stravinsky] with spouse, the gigantic Otto [Klemperer] and the remaining horde of concert givers or goers." At others the nostalgia was more openly expressed: "The Pub offices in New York are a kind of substitute for the Weihergarten [the Schott building in Mainz] . . . But there is nothing to replace the original."

Gertrud shared his feelings. "You have no idea how often we sit here in the evenings in our practical, motorised living-room-kitchen and think dismally of you," she wrote to Strecker on 16 February 1941, "or how often I have to try to damp down Paul's fury when the publishers' copies and proofs arrive. You spoiled him terribly with all the consideration and loving care you lavished on his compositions. A good thing probably to see and learn how things are done abroad: it will then be a double pleasure when the lovely real things begin once again to arrive freshly-baked from Mainz."

Hindemith's contacts with his fellow composers from Europe seem in spite of his nostalgic feelings to have been rare. Now and again he wrote in his letters of encounters with Stravinsky in New York, and in 1943 Milhaud and his wife visited them in New Haven. But both these old friends, to whom he was nearest in spirit, were the farthest away in terms of geographical distance, since they lived in California.

For Hindemith there were, however, always two saving factors to protect him from the ravages of nostalgia: his love of hard work and his delight in his natural surroundings, both of them characteristics which Gertrud shared. After his second course in Tanglewood, he wrote to Willy Strecker on 27 September 1941 from New Haven:

"The summer went by in a flash and, although I often intended to write to you, nothing ever came of it. First there was so much work to do during the whole of July and August that with the best will in the world I could find no time for writing. And after that holiday idleness set in, with a resumption in full glory of all-day rambles, badminton matches and lazy baskings in the Berkshire sun. We had a very pretty house there, in a sprawling village far away from all noise, music and musicians. It had formerly been a sculptor's studio, and for that reason the whole north wall was one gigantic window. . . . The summer school, in which I was again this year very busily engaged, was about ten miles away, and that was of course a great advantage with our new little car, which is a great success.

"I had a lot of work with my composition class, but more still with a history course, in which my group of about 150 people wended its way singing and playing through the music of the twelfth to the sixteenth centuries. It was a very fine effort, never done on this scale before, and it proved a very valuable experience for all concerned. Every Saturday (for six weeks) we had a concert in which all the participating groups performed what they had learnt during the week. The whole programme comprised about two hundred pieces, of which most had never before (except at the time they were written) been sung or played. Each of the participants had a full score of all his pieces and, since you are more or less familiar with the process of manufacturing musical material, you can imagine how much preparatory work that meant for me, on top of the school and my own work. Beginning in March we copied and duplicated every note of it here [at Yale], and on the whole thing I spent no more than six hundred dollars. Can't you find me a job with Schott's sons doing something similar?

"After the very exhausting summer school, made even more exhausting through the Boston orchestra's festival concerts (audiences of 10,000 to 13,000 each time!) which are loosely tied up with it, we missed you very much, for we drove up to Vermont for rambles in the Green Mountains. This is an almost totally unspoilt area—so untouched that you are more or less lost if you leave the trails—and unusually beautiful. Woods of a variety, denseness and naturalness which you can find nowhere in Europe, and mountains with wonderful views. One of them, Mount Mansfield, has perhaps one of the finest panoramic views in the whole world: far away towards Canada, across the huge Lake Champlain to the Adirondack Mountains of New York State, and in the east the mountains of New Hampshire. In spite of most of the hotels being teetotal (Vermont is very puritanical) we often said: 'If only Willy were with us.' We were sure you would have enjoyed it all as much as we did and would have reckoned it among the finest of our rambles together.

"Last week from our house in the meadows we enjoyed the northern lights against the gently yellowing autumn landscape. We returned here five days ago. Everything is just as we left it, except that the family has been increased by two newborn kittens (the remains of a litter of three) which did the journey from the Berkshires, before their eyes opened, with their mother in the back of the car."

This letter, the last he was able to write to Strecker until the conclusion of the war, ends on a final nostalgic note: "What will the wine be like this year?"

With the American entry into the war in December 1941 the Hindemiths, who still had German nationality, officially became enemy aliens, and as such had to report at regular intervals to the police. The war also brought changes at the School of Music: semesters were lengthened and vacations curtailed so that courses might be completed in a shorter time. Both had the effect, by no means unwelcome to him, of narrowing the scope of Hindemith's activities, which for the next three years were centred on his home and the university in New Haven. He settled down, in both the literal and the figurative sense, to cultivate his garden. His music was being played with increasing frequency throughout America, but only rarely could he be persuaded to attend performances. His own appearances as a practising musician were confined to occasional concerts in New Haven. One of the most striking of these was a recital at the large Woolsey Hall, where in February 1942 he played the eight violin sonatas by the seventeenth-century German composer Heinrich Biber. He was accompanied on the harpsichord by his faculty colleague, Ralph Kirkpatrick. "It was an extraordinary feat," Ellsworth Grumman recalled in the *Yale Alumni Magazine* of December 1964. "Each sonata . . . was performed on a violin tuned differently, none in the regular tuning in fifths. A student was kept very busy off stage tuning a violin for the next sonata."

Gertrud contributed to the war effort by putting in several hours a week as a ward secretary at the local hospital. She also began to improve her French with Henri Peyre, a professor at the university, and by 1945 had progressed so far that she was able to graduate at Yale in French philology.

Their social life was confined to a small circle of close friends —the Simonds, the Donovans, the Nosses and the Grummans. Once a year, in summer, they would cut themselves off even from those and go off alone for a holiday, usually spent in some remote cottage on the North Atlantic coast, where they would have a quiet time walking and painting. On one of these holidays they built a complete Indian village out of driftwood and other materials picked up on the beach. They took it back home at the end of the holiday and set it out on the veranda.

The students too were occasional visitors to their home. As Mrs Ellsworth Grumman recalls on a tape in the Hindemith Collection at Yale: "He would have his students in class, and they would all get so interested that he would go on and on, whatever the time. And then they would go down to Pepe's on Wooster Square and eat pizzas and go on discussing, and then perhaps after that go out to his house till late at night, still talking music." One can assume that this last part of the day's programme did not happen too often, for the students were as much aware as anyone else of the jealousy with which Gertrud guarded her husband's privacy.

When one or the other of the male students was called up for military service, either she or Hindemith himself would keep the contact alive with a series of chatty letters, full of parental concern and encouragement. "Dear General," Hindemith wrote (in English) to one of them, the clarinet player Leonard Berkowitz, soon after he was drafted. "Thanks for your letter, which reminded me very much of the time when I had my military training. I was also No. 81, and I was no good starter, either. Anyhow I think it is good for everybody to be thrown out of his regular trade for a while, and to see other people, live under other conditions and hear other opinions. Music must not necessarily suffer under such conditions, one can construct and solve musical problems without writing one note. I developed quite a kind of virtuosity of this kind and was able to compose while marching or being surrounded by noisy comrades and later by the still noisier shells and bombs."

The compositions of 1942, as few as in the previous year, reflect the narrowing of the boundaries to which he had, with the American entry into the war, deliberately subjected his life. The setting of a number of poems in English (by Blake, Shelley, Moore, Thompson and others) for voice and piano can be seen as an exercise in the musical handling of his adopted language. The other two completed works, the Sonata for Two Pianos and the *Ludus Tonalis*, are essays in pure counterpoint. The *Ludus Tonalis*, subtitled by the composer "Studies in Counterpoint, Tonal Organization and Piano Playing", represents the farthest Hindemith had so far gone in that direction. It was, as he himself said, a work in the style and spirit of J. S. Bach's *Wohltemperiertes Klavier* and *Die Kunst der Fuge*, "though without the qualities of either". Cast as a cycle of twelve fugues, separated by interludes, it makes use of all known fugal variations, but differs radically from its models in its arrangement. Hindemith follows the tonal relationships which he set out in his *Craft of Musical Composition* as the natural order, and uses the interludes between to lead from one to the other. The cycle is thus a self-contained whole rather than a series of pieces which can be played independently of each other. Its importance as an epitome of Hindemith's musical thinking, expressed in its plainest and purest form, is beyond dispute, though its outward austerity will perhaps always prevent it from winning wide recognition in the concert hall.

Both these works for piano were given their first performances outside New Haven: the sonata by the two-piano team Dougherty and Ruzitska on 20 November 1942 in New York and the *Ludus Tonalis* by Willard McGregor on 15 February 1943 in Chicago.

In addition to a well-stocked music library, the Yale School of Music possessed a small collection of old musical instruments, and not long after his arrival Hindemith began, as previously in Berlin, to think of ways of putting these to practical use. He early endeared himself to Miss E. J. O'Meara, the librarian, who was a faculty colleague, by the delight with which he pounced on rare old texts on her shelves and by his readiness to make do with what was there rather than press for additions (all she could recall having acquired at his suggestion was *Der Kanon* by Fritz Jöde). He won her favour still further by his attention to the somewhat neglected collection of instruments. "There was a monochord made by Lotta van Buren, which had been lying about for years and was coming to pieces," she recalls on a tape in the Yale Collection. "Hindemith took it home, repaired it and provided it with a scale. When he brought it back, he had a screw and a screwdriver in his pocket, and he put up a hook, so that it could be hung up on the wall. When I thanked him, he said: 'No thanks: you do for me, I do for you.'"

Another colleague whom he persuaded to "do" for him in the same sort of way was Marshall Bartholomew, director of the Yale Glee Club Associates, whom Hindemith invited in 1941 to start a course of vocal composition in the School of Music. One of Hindemith's grumbles in his *Elementary Training for*

Musicians was, as we have already seen, that students were reluctant to open their mouths "for the most natural of all musical utterances", namely singing. Certainly there was no lack of interest in glee singing: indeed, one of his students, Louis Hemingway, was a member of the Whiffenpoofs (glee clubs at Yale tend to adopt such picturesque names) and in addition, as he states on a tape in the Yale Collection, he did "some choral arranging and some sort of barber-shop, informal things" in his spare time. But the reluctance with which Hemingway admitted to his teacher what he was doing sufficiently demonstrates the attitude of Americans towards glee singing. Enjoyable enough in itself, it was hardly to be identified with real music. Hemingway was surprised when Hindemith showed great interest in his activities. He probably would not have been if he had known more about Hindemith's European background and his efforts to persuade people to make music rather than merely to listen to it. It was natural that, in a country in which the division between performers and listeners had been elevated almost to the level of a doctrine, Hindemith should be delighted to find individual persons at any level willing to join in actively, and he immediately set about putting their talents to a higher use.

Together with Leo Schrade he inaugurated a Collegium Musicum at Yale to study the works of composers of the pre-Bachian era. The performances at Tanglewood, described in his letter to Strecker, were the first try-out of a plan later to be successfully developed over a number of years at Yale University. Whereas at Tanglewood the period covered was large and the pieces mainly vocal, at Yale the approach was more specialised, and included instrumental pieces played on old instruments from the university's collection and from museums in the vicinity.

The first concert took place at the Sprague Hall on 26 April 1943 and was devoted to music of the early seventeenth century. As the programme shows, members of the staff and their relatives appeared in unaccustomed roles. The conducting was shared by Bartholomew, Noss and Donovan, while Hindemith himself played a bassoon and a viola da gamba. His students played other instruments or sang in the chorus, which also included Gertrud Hindemith and Rosalind Simonds, the wife of the dean, herself (like her husband) a concert pianist.

It is noticeable that Schrade's name is missing from the programme. In general, his contribution to the Collegium Musicum concerts, which continued (though not at regular intervals) until 1953, has received less than its due, the whole credit going to Hindemith, who conducted all the concerts after the first. Perhaps Schrade would not have objected. His great historical knowledge was undoubtedly important in raising preliminary interest in the university for early music, but of the accuracy of Hindemith's efforts to interpret it in sound he himself was highly critical. All the same, as Howard Boatwright told me, "even Schrade had to admit that no one he had ever heard conduct sixteenth-century choral music gave it such a sense of structure". Boatwright added: "The Collegium Musicum concerts turned out to be more or less a fountainhead for the performance of old music in the United States. I don't know anyone who actually copies Hindemith's methods of performing the music, but the love for it, and a knowledge of the sources, and the sense of excitement one could get from that music—that certainly derived directly from Hindemith. The leading groups in the United States today nearly all contained at the start one or more people who were in the Collegium Musicum."

The year 1943 ended with two premières within a space of ten days. On 29 October the Philadelphia Orchestra, conducted by Eugene Ormandy, gave the first performance of the *Cupid and Psyche* Overture, and on 7 November the Fifth String Quartet was performed in Washington by the Budapest String Quartet, for whom it was written. This work, Hindemith's first composition in this form for twenty years, was composed in May and belongs in form and essence rather to the foregoing *Ludus Tonalis* than the virtuosic overture.

The orchestral work that can confidently be described as Hindemith's most popular, the *Symphonic Metamorphosis of Themes by Carl Maria von Weber*, was given its first performance in New York on 20 January 1944 by the Philharmonic Orchestra under its musical director Artur Rodzinsky. Basically, as we have seen, it had already been composed in 1940 as a ballet for Massine, and the work Hindemith did on it was more a matter of rearrangement and orchestration than new creation. Like the *Cupid and Psyche* Overture it probably owed its existence more to the desire of his publishers for new works appealing to the prevailing American taste (that is to say, colourful orchestral music) than to his current musical preoccupations.

It seems to have been a matter of complete indifference to Hindemith which of America's star conductors, if any, presided over the launching of his new orchestral works, and it can be assumed that the succession of eminent names connected with them—Koussevitzky, Mitropoulos, Ormandy, Rodzinsky—gave his publishers more gratification than the composer himself. None of these men ever became personal friends in the way that in Europe Furtwängler and Scherchen, Sacher and Rosbaud had been. No doubt his early years as an orchestral player had something to do with this. Orchestral players notoriously view conductors in a different way from audiences, and the qualities they despise in a conductor are very often those in which the public takes the most delight. It is always evident in Hindemith's assessment of conductors that those with star reputations aroused both suspicion and resistance in him, and only one—Furtwängler—ever enjoyed his undiluted approval. With the others—and they included even so loyal a champion of his music as Otto Klemperer—he preferred to keep his distance.

In America he was dependent on the famous names to a far greater extent than in Europe, since they were the virtual dictators of music life. If he wished his works to be widely heard there, he was obliged to cultivate their favours—or allow his publishers to do so on his behalf, which was the course he preferred. He was quite willing to carry out the commissions they gave him: this was after all a tribute to his ability as well as a welcome source of income. But it may be doubted whether these works—from whose performances he so frequently stayed away—were as important to him as the less ostentatious ones such as the *Ludus Tonalis* and the motets, of which he wrote one virtually each Christmas time. It was in these that he really got to grips with his current musical problems.

In any assessment of the influence his stay in America had on him it is necessary to separate the obvious external features—among others, the increased output of large orchestral works—from the traces of a growing urge for refinement of expression. He was now in his forties, the age of experimentation past. It was the time, not to forge a new musical language, but to clarify his existing one. Evidence of his growing conviction that truth lies closer to simplicity than to complication can be found in a letter which he wrote on 2 March 1944 to his young faculty colleague Luther Noss, who was now on active service with the American armed forces. Hindemith was commenting in his not quite correct English on two compositions by Noss (who had studied in Vienna with Alban Berg) which happened to come to his attention:

"I am sure you came in that strain of forced exaggeration and unnecessary complication (everybody does!), which in itself is not condemnable, especially as it is one of the best ways to collect useful technical material and to get rid of many emotional things, but you should have taken these works as a starting point and should have tried to bring clarity and adequacy of appearance and means in the heap of material. What I cannot understand is that a man with so great a gift for composition (I wished our other composers here had only a quarter of it!) can live without always working and trying to become more and more perfect. Self-criticism is certainly a good thing but it loses all its sense when it prevents fertile and healthy seeds from becoming sturdy flowers. Wait till you come back! I'll see to it that you get to work."

In May 1944 Hindemith's contract as Professor of the Theory of Music at Yale was renewed for a further three years and the annual salary increased to 7,500 dollars. This was certainly intended to be a fractional compensation for his rejection of an invitation from Chicago University to assume a professorship there at almost double his previous salary at Yale. He gave his reasons for refusing the offer in the letter to Noss already quoted: "Everything is too hectic there, there are no trees, and I don't want to be interested in developing new schools. I have my own problems that I want to develop."

Characteristically he did not mention another reason for remaining at Yale: that he felt an affection both for the university and for his friends there. A little episode that occurred in 1944 illustrates the happy atmosphere of the place. It concerns the composition of a song, "The Frog", which is not mentioned in any list of his works, though it is to be found in manuscript, along with L. P. Curtis's account of its creation, in the Hindemith Collection at Yale:

"Paul Hindemith's 'The Frog' was first performed at Jonathan Edwards College in 1944 by Carl Lohmann, Secretary of the University, and Ralph Kirkpatrick, both fellows of this College.

"At that time the Master and Fellows of Jonathan Edwards were planning another of their Grand Gala Gaslight Concerts, familiarly known as Victorian Evenings.... To invite Paul Hindemith to compose something for the occasion seemed fitting, since he had burst into the Fellowship in 1940 with vivacity, laughter and wit. Accordingly, I tried.

"I had been lucky enough to hear Dickens' 'Ode to an Expiring Frog' turned into a duet in Nigel Playfair's immensely comic production of George Lillo's *The London Merchant*. I took the verses to Paul and let him read them....

"Paul, enraptured, instantly agreed to set the verses to music and promised to bring his composition to the Fellows' Dinner on the following Thursday evening. He came, armed with a sketch for an aria and staff paper. There in front of the Fellows he inked in the score, including the dynamics, with the hand of a master. Suddenly, he stopped. 'But,' he said, 'we have no recitative. Bring me the *Encyclopedia*.' I asked, 'The letter F?' 'Yes,' he replied.

"And so it happened that the 'Recitative e aria ranatica' combines both Dickens' verses and part of the opening paragraph on Frog in the *Encyclopedia Britannica*."

The main composition of 1944 was the problematical *Hérodiade*, subtitled "Récitation orchestrale, after the poem by Stéphane Mallarmé". It was commissioned by Mrs Coolidge as a vehicle for the dancer Martha Graham, who first performed it (with scant success) at the Library of Congress in Washington on 30 October 1944. Martha Graham has described (in *Opernwelt*, February 1964) a meeting with the composer on 19 June 1944, when he played the music to her. According to one of his students, Carl Miller, they did subsequently exchange ideas on the staging of the work but, after mutually rejecting each other's suggestions, Hindemith told her to do with it as she pleased. And the impression that their work together was anything but close is reinforced by Miss Graham's uncertainty whether the composer even saw her performance.

Hérodiade has remained an intractable work. It is untypical both in its subject—Hindemith never before nor since gave such free expression to sensuous feelings—and in its treatment. In a programme note written for a later performance Hindemith maintained that his reason for giving the vocal line of Mallarmé's poem to a number of instruments rather than to singers was to avoid diverting attention from the dancers. This had the advantage, he asserts, of allowing him to increase the expressiveness of the melodic line, since he did not have to consider the limitations of physical voices—an unexpected argument from a composer who had always maintained and was progressively to act on the belief that the most expressive of musical instruments *is* the human voice. It is interesting, incidentally, to note that he had used a similar technique in the Sonata for Two Pianos of 1942, in which the movement entitled *Rezitativ* is an exact setting of an (unsung) medieval English poem "This World's Joy".

In *Hérodiade*, as in the sonata, he did not intend the poem to be spoken over the music. As he later explained in a letter to Willy Strecker dated 22 February 1948: "The melodic lines in the orchestra are the recitation, which follows the poem word by word." By this time the work had of course had several performances both as a ballet and as a concert piece, and Hindemith knew by experience where its difficulties lay. "As a ballet (only two dancers) it will probably suffer the sad fate of being done only in an idiotic way, for what nowadays hops around on the stage is for the most part too limited to cope with a work demanding the highest degree of concentration and dedication. It *is* a very esoteric work. Even for the experienced connoisseur it is impossible to read the text and hear the music at the same time: one cannot expect the ordinary listener to appreciate the two separate factors and the way they interact. So you will not get very much joy out of this particular article, since nobody can really discover what it is about—though I myself believe it is something out of the top drawer."

In view of his quite definite disapproval, it is very surprising that Hindemith later gave Vera Zorina permission to make a recording of the work in which she recites the poem over the music. But, as he told Miller: "These people are my friends. What can I say to them? Let them do it."

It was not a sign of pusillanimity—a weakness of which Hindemith can on no account be accused—but rather the result of the distinction he had come to make between the composer's function and the performer's. When he was active in both capacities he was always uncompromising, but now that he had virtually withdrawn from the performing side (at least as an instrumentalist), he came increasingly to believe that his compositions must be allowed to stand on their own feet. His reluctance to attend performances of his works, old or new, was to a great extent due to his feeling that it was merely a waste of his time: the compositions were complete, now let the performers make what they could of them.

Kurt Stone, who worked closely with him on the preparation of his scores for publication in America, has seen in Hindemith's attitude to the performer an explanation why his printed music contains so few expression marks, dynamics and other interpretative signs and instructions. Writing in the *American Choral Review* of April 1964, Stone observes: "He considered such detailed markings condescending, and he refused to talk down to performers by telling them through fussy markings what any accomplished musician who takes his profession seriously would know anyway. (Unfortunately, his views were somewhat unrealistic in this particular area.) Not that he demanded perfection at first try. As long as there was serious and honest effort . . . he not only radiated pleasure (though never ostentatiously— eyes only!), but he also was ready to laugh at occasional . . . imperfections."

From the American entry into the war until its conclusion in Europe in April 1945 the Hindemiths were cut off from direct contact with Germany. Messages occasionally got through with the help of intermediaries in Switzerland and Portugal, and Willy Strecker even received some of the less bulky scores published in America. But news from Germany was obviously scanty and much delayed.

Musically Hindemith was not entirely forgotten there. Schott's kept all his works in print, and a few brave spirits continued to play his music in public here and there, though the unofficial ban was still in force. The Nazis remained as unpredictable and disorganised as ever in their attitude towards him. In August 1943 Schott's received a letter from the authorities in the Sudetenland, addressed to Hindemith at the Kuhhirtenturm in Frankfurt. The letter, passed on to the publishers by Hindemith's mother, who was still living there, stated that a series of concerts was being organised in Reichenberg to overcome the existing prejudice against modern music:

would Hindemith be interested in submitting a work for performance? Another letter, from Goebbels's Propaganda Ministry, arrived at Schott's about the same time. In this the publishers were requested to forward a copy of Hindemith's *Unterweisung im Tonsatz* to a firm in Italy, which was interested in bringing it out in translation. Willy Strecker was provoked into a spirited reply: "It would be better if the work were first of all to be officially recognised in Germany, thus offering a basis on which it could be promoted abroad."

In October 1943 both the Kuhhirtenturm and the house of the Lübbeckes nearby were damaged by bombs. Nobody was injured, but the roof of the tower was destroyed in the subsequent fire, leaving Hindemith's still furnished music room open to the skies. Some manuscripts which he had left there perished in the fire, though his sister Toni and Emma Lübbecke-Job managed to rescue a few. In the following March bombs struck again, and Hindemith's mother and sister, who had taken refuge with a neighbour after the damage to the Kuhhirtenturm, were once again made homeless. Frau Hindemith, as indomitably independent as her son, refused the hospitality offered them by the Streckers and the Lübbeckes and moved to Butzbach, a small town to the north of Frankfurt. Three days later the Lübbeckes' home was totally destroyed by bombs, and some of Hindemith's manuscripts disappeared with it. Emma Lübbecke-Job and her husband moved to Bad Homburg. Hindemith's brother Rudolf spent the war as conductor of an orchestra in Krakau and emerged from it unscathed.

Gertrud's relatives were less fortunate. Her mother was caught up, in the last months of the war, in the air-raid which destroyed a third of Wiesbaden. Ill with arthritis, she was evacuated to the mountains outside Frankfurt in an open lorry. The rigours of the journey proved too much for her and she died shortly after arrival. Hans Flesch was working in a military hospital outside Berlin when the Russians closed in. He vanished without trace. His wife, Gertrud's sister Gabriele, and their daughter Margot eventually, with the help of the Hindemiths, emigrated to the United States.

Chapter 4

1945-47:

HARMLESS NEW ENGLANDER

BY THE TIME Hindemith became eligible for American citizenship, five years after his arrival there on 2 February 1940, the war was already in its final stages. Gertrud would not become eligible for a further five months, by which time the war might be over and the way open for a return to Europe. Hindemith, however, set the wheels in motion for his own naturalisation right away.

According to Osea Noss, whose friendship with the Hindemiths had grown very close during her husband's absence on active service, he took his application very seriously and spent hours studying the booklet on the American constitution and way of life which is presented in advance to all candidates for citizenship. He learned it off by heart and invited Gertrud to question him on it. It was wasted labour, for Judge Carroll Hinks, who conducted the official hearing, considered Hindemith too eminent to be examined in public, and invited him and his two sponsors (Robert French, the Master of Jonathan Edwards College, and Ellsworth Grumman) into a private room. As for questions on the constitution, there were none, and Hindemith was granted American citizenship without having his knowledge of its ways put to the test at all. That, as Osea Noss has recorded on tape in the Yale Collection, made him "mad as a red hen". However, as a courteous gesture of gratitude for the consideration shown him, Hindemith gave Judge Hinks the manuscript of his song "Sing on there in the Swamp". The judge, wary (one supposes) of possible charges of bribery, sent the manuscript to a friend at Yale, who in turn presented it to the university.

Shortly afterwards the Philadelphia Musical Academy offered Hindemith an honorary degree. His lack of official academic qualifications, European or American, had never hindered his professional activities, any more than the lack of American citizenship had restricted his life in that country, but

it is possible that his acquisition of the one led to his interest in
the other. There was also an element of competition involved,
since his own wife was on the verge of becoming a Yale graduate
in French philology. He consulted his colleagues at Yale, who
were able to tell him that the Philadelphia Musical Academy
(of which he had never heard) was a modest but worthy institution, and acceptance of its honorary degree could do no harm.
It involved no duties for him (though no doubt brought the
academy some useful publicity). Thus reassured, Hindemith
accepted the doctorate of music on 4 June 1945.

"From Europe we start getting news," Gertrud had written
to Luther Noss on 14 April 1945, when the war with Germany
still had a few days to go. But, she added, "we don't know yet
whether our mothers live." Only some weeks later did she hear
through the Red Cross of her mother's death.

Hindemith's first letter to Willy Strecker was written on 29
August from Petit Manau, Maine, where he and Gertrud were
spending their annual holiday "in a lonely farm on the coast
near the Canadian border". In it he brought Strecker up to
date on the musical news since they were last in contact, and
revealed that he was now writing a concerto for the pianist
Jesus Sanroma. He gave the address of the house in New Haven
into which they would shortly be moving, requesting Strecker
not to pass it on.

That Hindemith, at a time when the possibility of a triumphant return to Germany lay open before him, should not only
have moved into a new house, but actually bought it, seems
rather surprising. In fact, the decision was to a certain extent
forced on him, since the owner of the rented house in New Elm
Street had decided to sell all his properties in the district. A
move was therefore inevitable, unless the Hindemiths themselves were prepared to buy the house. Not wishing to leave
that part of New Haven, which they both liked, they agreed to
buy, but preferred to invest in a larger house belonging to the
same owner just round the corner.

This, 127 Alden Avenue, is a typical Connecticut two-storey
timber-frame house with a portico in front and a covered
veranda behind. They moved in on 1 October 1945 and
immediately started making it their own, knocking down a wall
between two bedrooms upstairs to provide a spacious music

room, stripping the inner woodwork of its dark varnish to restore the beautiful natural grain, and setting to work in the garden, which was much larger than that in New Elm Street. With its trees at the back and its surrounding hedge of lilac bushes, it soon gave the impression of a small country estate.

It was the first house in their whole lives which was entirely their own, and Luther and Osea Noss, who helped with the removal, were surprised to see that the furniture they chose to install in it, though tasteful in appearance, was of cheap quality. Whether, as Luther Noss assumed, this was due to the fact that the Hindemiths had not got over the loss of the beautiful furniture they had stored when they left Berlin and which, as far as they knew, was now lost for ever; or whether (as Osea Noss more practically felt) it was due to a shortage of money cannot of course be established for sure. There is yet another possible reason, no less speculative: it is that, though to all intents they had decided to make America their permanent home, subconsciously they might have felt they would one day be returning to Europe.

They could have been in no doubt that Germany was eager to have them back. On 16 November 1945 Hindemith reached his fiftieth birthday. In a letter dated 19 November Willy Strecker wrote from Mainz an account of what had been done, in spite of all the difficulties in a defeated country not yet emerging from the post-war material and spiritual chaos. In Nauheim, where Frankfurt's radio station was at present functioning, the *Mathis der Maler* Symphony and the violin concerto had been played, and were shortly to be repeated at a public concert in which *The Four Temperaments* would also be played, with Emma Lübbecke-Job as soloist. Hamburg was also bringing out the symphony and the violin concerto. In smaller gatherings both the *Ludus Tonalis* and the harp sonata were being performed for the first time. The newspapers were full of adulatory articles, and all sorts of rumours were flying around of Hindemith's impending return to Germany. Meanwhile, failing his presence, his mother was being pressed into service to represent him at various concerts. She looked proud and happy, and Strecker was overjoyed that she had lived to experience her son's rehabilitation.

Among the congratulatory messages Hindemith received was one signed by seven orchestral players in Wiesbaden: "After having given the successful first performance of your wonderful violin concerto, we take the liberty in the name of both orchestras in Wiesbaden to offer you our best wishes on your fiftieth birthday and to express the hope that we shall very soon see you back among us in Germany."

In America too the fiftieth birthday was celebrated with a two-day recital at the Juilliard School of Music in New York, in which works ranging from the song cycle of 1922, *Die junge Magd*, to his latest compositions were played. The final concert, which Hindemith himself conducted, included *In Praise of Music*, a revised version of his early *Frau Musica*, which he had made in 1943 with an English text, and in which, as he happily told Strecker, the audience joined lustily. The soloists included the singer Enid Szantho, the violinist Isaac Stern and the pianist Bruce Simonds, who played the *Ludus Tonalis* and, together with his wife Rosalind, the sonata for two pianos.

To acknowledge the many good wishes he received on his birthday, Hindemith composed a four-part canon, which he had printed on a card, surrounding it with an elaborate border of his own design, consisting of mathematical signs and symbols. The rather melancholy text of the canon he took from the *Rubaiyat* of Omar Khayyam:

Oh, threats of hell and hopes of Paradise!
One thing at least is certain: this life flies;
One thing is certain and the rest is lies;
The flower that once has blown for ever dies.

His more personal thanks to his dean for the large and very active part he had played in the birthday celebrations was conveyed on a card which Bruce Simonds showed me when I visited him in his home in New Haven. It depicts two grand pianos, one being played by a crab (Simonds's zodiacal sign) and the other by a long-haired maiden in flowing robes (Rosalind Simonds was born under the sign of Virgo). Listening to them are Gertrud, in her familiar form of a lion, and a scorpion. In all his other caricatures Hindemith depicted himself as a small, bald-headed man. The card for Simonds is one of the few occasions on which he drew himself in his zodiacal guise.

There was certainly something of the scorpion in Hindemith's reply to the adulation now being lavished on him, particularly in Germany. "I think it is being overdone," he wrote to Willy Strecker on 26 December 1945, "and the only outcome will be a violent reaction." In the same letter he gave a first indication of his feelings on the subject of returning to Europe:

"The 'calls' for my return came in for a while daily and with increasing urgency. But since they were almost exclusively the expression of their writers' purely personal feelings, and one can hardly undertake yet another change of existence on such a basis, I think it is better to leave things for the moment as they are. So far I have had no official enquiries, and I do not expect any, since the people who have come to the top through favourable circumstances are no more inclined now than they were before to give up what they have got, and will certainly resist violently the advent of an 'outsider'. Besides, whoever is given the power to try and clean out the pigsty will simply be and remain the pigsty-cleaner, and the really constructive work can only be done by his successor. I cannot imagine anything that would interest me less! I feel that the best thing I can do, during the few years in which I shall still be in possession of my full faculties, is to write as much and as well as I possibly can. That would of course not exclude occasional visits to Europe, which we both dearly want—whether private, for concerts or temporary teaching jobs. But it is certainly too early yet to decide that."

Hindemith's most direct tribute to the nation which had given him refuge and to which he felt he now belonged was composed in the following months, when his normal college routine was disturbed by nothing more onerous than a quick trip to Toronto and Montreal to deliver lectures. *When Lilacs Last in the Door-Yard Bloom'd* is described as "A Requiem for Those We Love" and is dedicated to the memory of Franklin Delano Roosevelt and the American Fallen in World War Two. The death of America's great wartime president, on 12 April 1945, had affected him deeply and into this work, a setting of Walt Whitman's poem on the death of another president (Abraham Lincoln), he projected more overt emotional feeling than was discernible in any other of his American works. Hindemith saw Whitman's words as an ode to peace, heralding the reconciliation of enemies and the awakening of a new spirit of brotherly love. As such, they were the expression of his own

unwavering belief in the power of music to unite and reconcile
—a conviction which first came to him, as he has told us, when
as a young man of twenty-two he heard the news of Debussy's
death.

The Requiem was first performed in New York on 5 May
1946 by the Robert Shaw Choral—"far and away the best
choir in the world," Hindemith wrote to Strecker, "and the
success was corresponding. Last week it was broadcast on all
Columbia networks throughout the land." Other reports
suggest that the work was not quite so enthusiastically received
as he imagined. His own emotional identification with it may
have blinded him to the reactions of others. Nevertheless, it
always remained one of the works closest to his heart, and in the
ensuing years he conducted it many times all over the world.

The offers from Germany eventually began to assume a more
official form. Among them were invitations to become director
of the Hochschule in Berlin and to establish a new music
school in Frankfurt. Another offer arrived one day when Luther
Noss was with him, and Hindemith showed the letter to his
colleague: it was an invitation to conduct the Berlin Philharmonic Orchestra. That, Hindemith remarked, was the sort of
letter he had dreamed of receiving as a boy. But, like all the
others, he turned it down.

His fears that all this European adulation would lead to a
reaction showed no signs yet of coming true. In Germany, in
the first five months of 1946, the *Mathis der Maler* Symphony
was performed fifty times, the *Four Temperaments* twenty times
and the violin concerto fifteen times. In May the ballet *Nobilissima Visione* was produced in Hamburg, and the competition
among German opera houses for *Mathis der Maler* was so great
that the publishers were considering giving it to four of the
leading ones—Berlin, Düsseldorf, Hamburg and Stuttgart—for
simultaneous production. During the war, Willy Strecker
wrote, he had "made a sport" of publishing the new compositions of Hindemith which reached him in spite of the Nazi
ban, "and luckily we were not caught". His action in keeping
everything in print was now reaping its reward. "Hardly any
of the other publishers can meet the demand, and in consequence Krenek, Schönberg, Bartók, Weill, Berg etc. have been.
consigned to virtual oblivion. You and Stravinsky are the only
ones of the whole former group still left."

All the same, Hindemith firmly resisted Strecker's request for the scores of his most recent works. There were several older works still to be performed in Germany—among them the *Symphonic Dances*, the Symphony in E flat and the cello concerto —and these should be done first, he said. As for the revised *Marienleben*, "I would quite frankly prefer not to give it out yet, though it is completed. Or if I eventually do, then first in the States and, only when it is sufficiently known there, in Germany. My reasons for this may sound rather strange to you, but I have no doubt that you will understand and agree with them."

There follows, over three and a half large and closely hand-written pages, a remarkable description of his present feelings, compounded of bitterness, resentment and disappointment towards his fellow countrymen. The whole letter, nine pages long, was written on 15 July 1946 from the Hotel Guardiola in Mexico, where he had gone to conduct two concerts of his own works. The passage in which he attempted to explain these feelings to an old and trusted friend gives the impression of having been written at top speed in a mood of emotional agitation mounting at times almost to incoherence:

"As you rightly suspect, I have since the end of the war received hundreds of letters, and the stream shows no signs of drying up. After all the years of separation we awaited even the smallest scrap of news with suspense and longing. The very detailed newspaper stories had prepared us for all the tales of misfortune, destruction and misery, but all the same we were deeply moved by the sad individual destinies we saw spread out before us. Our immediate impulse was to go over and do what we could to help. More and more news arrived and, once the descriptions of past or present situations had lost some of their topicality, the gist of almost all the letters began to show through. It was: we want this, help us with that, you can surely do this and do that, we expect the following. . . . Well, that is understandable, though, so long as it is a matter of purely material things, a small teacher's salary with only rare additional earnings soon puts a limit on what one is able to do. (The publishing rights of the few things that sell well, like the harmony book for instance, belong to Mainz or London and consequently are under the jurisdiction of the Alien Property Custodian, who won't release a penny of it.)

"The constant requests for confirmations that the writers

were never Nazis can also be dealt with, though anyone can see how worthless such testimonials must be when they are based on complete personal ignorance of what might have happened during the last critical eight years. To these can be added numerous requests for affidavits, for travel expenses, for finding jobs, etc., etc.—but those, thank goodness, settle themselves on account of the financial situation already described. As I said, it is all understandable and, though there is not much I can do, has my fullest sympathy.

"But where my sympathies unfortunately refuse to function properly, that is in the sphere of music. What the letters bring to light there is quite simply disgusting. I have always regarded myself as a private musical person, and what the public does with the music I write has nothing to do with my private life, any more than I have the desire, through my music, to affect the private lives of others. But now I am gradually beginning to feel like a cornerstone on which every passerby can pass the water of his artistic opinion. Even that one could put up with, for it is after all the usual consequence of being well-known and successful. What I cannot put up with, however, is when even one's best friends—indeed especially those—publish to the whole world what they know of me. It is done in the name of 'advancement of art', of 'reconciliation' or 'ancient loyalties', but it is clear, even at the first glance, that what everyone is really trying to do is to make as much as he can for himself out of the present opportunity. Time and time again, till I am sick of it, I am being told that such and such is going to perform this or that, and always with the undisguised aim of winning praise, of involving the composer, even of putting him under an obligation. (The same thing happens over here too, but without so much yelling, nobody pushes himself forward quite so much, yet probably—to judge by the various recordings sent me from over there—the performances here are very much better.)

"And then everybody knows exactly what I ought to do. The present musical needs in Germany are all that matters and must at once be obeyed! It never seems to occur to anybody that perspectives change, that people who have been thrown out neither can nor wish to build up a new life for themselves every few years, that there might be other things to do than to set about restoring a ruined musical framework—however big and fascinating a task that might be—and finally that the person who is being asked to do these things might have opinions of his own based of necessity on very different physical and spiritual considerations. For all of them one is simply a toy brick which they are trying in their egoism to force into the position which suits them best in order to get the most favourable results for themselves.

"And all that in the name of artistic ideals! *I* must be idealistic enough to give up at once all I have laboriously built up here, simply to help the machinations of *others*. God, when I think how I have considered starting again over there, how much thought and anxiety and love I have expended on the possibility of helping to restore order again! But it is only too obvious that an idealism that is all on one side can be of only very little use. One must just wait until the waves of artistic egoism which are apparently breaking with particular violence over my head die down and give way to the clearer currents of a more sensible musical atmosphere.

"Now you will surely understand how much I should loathe throwing a piece like the *Marienleben*, which has grown particularly close to my heart, into this puddle. It will without doubt flourish much better in the healthier (if also not ideal) climate over here."

Hindemith did not in fact release the revised *Marienleben* yet to anyone, but put it away to await a more favourable climate, and settled down to write the symphony which had been commissioned by Antal Dorati for performance by the Dallas Symphony Orchestra. In November he was in New York for the long-delayed first stage presentation of *The Four Temperaments*.

Since Balanchine first commissioned that work in 1940, the American Ballet had undergone a change of form. In 1946, together with Lincoln Kirstein, Balanchine founded the Ballet Society, a club organisation which staged performances for members only. Its aim was "to present a completely new repertory, each with the collaboration of independent painters, progressive choreographers and musicians, employing the full use of *avant garde* ideas, methods and materials. There will be no touring nor attempt at a continuous run."

The first offering of the Ballet Society, which had no theatre of its own, was staged in the Central High School of Needle

Trades in New York on 20 November 1946. It consisted of *The Spellbound Child* (to Ravel's *L'Enfant et les Sortilèges*) and Hindemith's *The Four Temperaments*, for which scenery and costumes were designed by Kurt Seligmann. In spite of the theatre, which was as inhospitable as its name (Anatole Chujoy in his book *The New York City Ballet* describes it as "a huge, barn-like hall . . . as impersonal as a railroad station") *The Four Temperaments*, a theme with variations describing natures melancholy, sanguine, phlegmatic and choleric, was a success both with the public and the critics. Nevertheless the Ballet Society, true to its principles, performed it only once. However, when it acquired a permanent home at the New York City Center in the following year, Balanchine staged *The Four Temperaments* again with some revision in the choreography, and the work went on to become one of the most successful items in the repertory of the New York City Ballet, which eventually emerged from the Ballet Society.

Willy Strecker, after responding sympathetically to Hindemith's outburst from Mexico, tactfully refrained from pushing him further. He concentrated rather on reporting the increase in what he described as the "genuine understanding and interest" in Hindemith's music in Germany. He had been very impressed, he wrote in October 1946, by the production of *Nobilissima Visione* in Hamburg under Hans Schmidt-Isserstedt, with choreography by Helga Svedlund. And on 17 December he wrote that *Mathis der Maler* at the Stuttgart Opera had been better done than in Zurich and was a big success.

"In me personally," he observed, "the work aroused once again profound regret for the circumstances preventing you from writing the Kepler opera, which could by now long have been completed. But a work such as *Mathis* could never have been created on the banks of the Mississippi or in Massachusetts, Texas, etc., any more than *Der Freischütz* or *Fidelio* could. I found myself thinking of our tour in the Black Forest, our visits to Grünewald and to Hölderlin's 'Main', and hope a time will come when we shall be given the Kepler after all—and many other homegrown things."

If he had hoped with his subtle reference to his German roots to break down Hindemith's resistance against a return to Germany, Strecker must have been disappointed with the reply. But probably he knew his friend well enough to recognise to what extent Hindemith in his letter of 20 January 1947 was in fact arguing against his own real inclinations. He was glad, Hindemith wrote, that at the performances Strecker described, he himself had not had to experience "all the expressions of sympathy, the outbreaks of enthusiasm and the just as strong feelings of resentment which, however well concealed or not yet clearly defined, were probably also there". As for the argument that a creative artist is dependent on his native roots:

"At the beginning I came to much the same conclusions as you, but today I think quite differently about it. In one's younger years landscape, atmosphere, schooling and personal identification with objects and events may provide an important stimulus to one's artistic work; but now I find that the chronicle of people, events and experiences and their interpretation and portrayal through art is really not so very closely connected with these external matters. More important than collecting new ones on the spot is how one uses the experiences one has already had. If that were not so, I would in the course of the past twelve years have entirely lost the desire to make use of a German subject. At a maturer stage of life the Rhine seems no more important for the working out of deep-felt plans than the Mississippi, the Connecticut Valley or the Gobi Desert. So the Kepler, put off again and again, will some time see the light of day. That it hasn't yet done so, any more than the theory book I've been working on for the past ten years, is due in the first place to the persistent hope of achieving greater maturity, knowledge and powers of expression, and in the second to that curse of human existence, a permanent lack of time."

The letter is full of references to his American ties and plans, both present and future. The first performance of his new symphony for Dorati, the *Symphonia Serena*, was to be broadcast throughout the country; for a symposium at Harvard University he was writing a choral work *Apparebit repentina dies*, "an early medieval account of the Day of Judgment"; he had promised to write a clarinet concerto (for Benny Goodman) as well as another ballet. But nevertheless he divulged that he had now decided to make a limited concert tour of Europe in the coming spring, starting with a concert in Rome on 14 April:

"But please keep all this secret. I have no desire to be sacrificed to the whole pack of 'friends', nor to take part in any musical or

H

other official events in Germany. Even on the completely private and unpublicised basis I have planned there will probably be more fuss and hubbub than is congenial to a harmless New Englander."

This was not by any means a capitulation or even a partial change of mind. He had already, in his letter to Strecker from Mexico in May 1946, spoken of his hope of paying a quick visit to Europe "in order at least to see my mother". And the concert and teaching engagements he had accepted in order to finance the trip were all outside Germany: in Italy, Belgium, England, Austria and Switzerland.

There was plenty of work to be done before his departure. He completed the composition of *Apparebit Repentina Dies*, and at the end of February was in Cleveland for the first performance of his new piano concerto. Back in Yale, he set about preparing the fourth Collegium Musicum concert, devoted to compositions of the fifteenth century. This, like the two previous (and the subsequent) ones, was repeated, after the first performance in New Haven, at the Metropolitan Museum in New York, where Emanuel Winternitz, a friend and active collaborator, was curator of the musical instruments section.

In view of all these tasks, which were additional to his teaching duties, he decided not to attend the first performance of the *Symphonia Serena* in Dallas on 1 February 1947. "Why should I go to hear my own works?" he asked Bruce Simonds. However, in the end he did consent to go, though only because he had a certain musical problem on his mind and thought that he could best work it out in the train, where he would be undisturbed. Carl Miller, who gave me the clearest account of this episode which is one of the favourite and most widely recalled ones at Yale, said that his students were amazed when he came into the classroom, grinning from ear to ear. "Why aren't you in Dallas?" they asked. "Because I had solved my problem by the time I got to New York," he said. "So I got out of the train and came back home."

On 2 April 1947 he and Gertrud set sail from New York on a Greek ship bound for Genoa. They left as Americans on tour, confident of their return. Four weeks earlier Hindemith had been voted to full membership of the National Institute of Art and Letters, a by no means negligible honour, since the Institute's membership was limited to 250 American citizens "qualified by notable achievements in art, music or literature". It is true that he had since 1943 been one of the twenty-five "similarly distinguished foreign citizens" who were admitted as honorary associates of the Institute, but admission to full membership was a comforting confirmation of his full American identity. And, though the official announcement was dated 19 April 1947—after his departure—Hindemith certainly already knew that Yale University was about to appoint him Battell Professor of the Theory of Music with effect from 1 July and to raise his annual salary by a further thousand dollars.

PART FOUR

DUAL NATIONALITY

Chapter 1

1947–53:

A VISITOR TO EUROPE

THEY ARRIVED IN Genoa on 19 April 1947 and Hindemith immediately started on his concert tour of Italy. From Trieste Gertrud wrote on 22 April to Willy Strecker: "We are infinitely happy to be here again, and it is terribly moving being so affectionately welcomed everywhere."

In spite of their attempts to ensure secrecy, the news of their trip to Europe had leaked out. It prompted Wilhelm Furt-wängler to write him a letter from Switzerland, where he was now living in a clinic while fighting for his own rehabilitation in Germany—this time not against the Nazis, but against their conquerors:

"I have often during the last months and years considered writing to you, but in the end always decided against it. I did not want, until my case was settled, to 'place a burden' on you. Such inhibitions may be baseless, but in certain situations they are stronger than one thinks, and it would be difficult from outside to imagine how unpleasant my personal position has long been.

"But that has not prevented me from following everything to do with yourself and your work with great attention and sympathy. However different our starting points, I have always had the greatest regard for your talent and of course for the person behind it. Recently I had the opportunity . . . of making the acquaintance of your latest compositions . . . and formed the impression that the encounter with America has done the composer no harm (a theory that is frequently advanced here), but that, on the contrary, the works are more accomplished and mature than ever before. . . ."

In fact Furtwängler's "inhibitions" once more got the better of him and he did not send the letter, which would certainly have pleased Hindemith with its comment on his compositions in America. In place of that letter, Furtwängler sent on 15 April only a short note from Florence, where he was conducting, regretting that, though they were both in Italy, their engagements would prevent them from meeting. "To see you again after all this time would be a very great pleasure," he said. "The passage of time clarifies and explains much: an article from me about Hindemith would today be very different from what I once wrote in Nazi Germany."

They met a little later in Switzerland and resumed their old friendship. Other old acquaintances were renewed too when in May, after concerts in Amsterdam and Brussels, the Hindemiths at last went to Frankfurt. The first few days were spent privately with the Streckers and with his mother and sister. He did not see his brother Rudolf, who was teaching in Munich, though it appears (from a letter written by Willy Strecker to Preussner on 7 March 1956) that at some stage Rudolf's wife, the pianist Maria Landes, paid him a visit. If this was an attempt to effect a reconciliation between the two brothers, she received no encouragement. The reason for the estrangement is not known.

The presence of the Hindemiths in Frankfurt was soon discovered, and he was obliged to attend a concert at which, among other of his works, Walter Gieseking played the solo part in *The Four Temperaments*. He saw a performance of *Mathis der Maler* at the Frankfurt Opera (temporarily housed in another theatre following the destruction in an air raid of the building in which he had so often played). Interviewed on the radio, he gave Heinz Schröter, his interviewer, little joy. Asked to describe his feelings on being back on German soil after ten years, he merely said: "It is wonderful. One comes back and finds much as it was before, the faces are the same, one exchanges greetings as before. One has no feeling of having been away so long."

He was less circumspect in the letter he had duplicated for despatch to the many unknown correspondents who bombarded him with requests and with musical manuscripts. He was already sending from the United States as many CARE parcels as he could afford, he said. He could give no useful advice about emigration to the United States or on how to gain entry to an American university. He could give no help in denazification proceedings, having been absent from Germany for ten years. And finally he expressed his surprise at the number of people named Hindemith who wrote to him. "I can scarcely regard these newly awakened family feelings as a basis for answering other questions, since at a time when this name was despised in Germany no such expression of family solidarity was in evidence even among near relations."

Examples of the sort of letters he was receiving are contained in the files of his publishers, to whom he sent them for a formal, off-putting reply. On them, in his or Gertrud's handwriting, are frequently scribbled scathing or sarcastic remarks. These were of course intended only for Strecker's private consumption, but they do suggest that Hindemith's suspicions that his fellow countrymen were trying to exploit him for their own purposes were still very much alive. Long-winded as some of these letters are, they are for the most part inoffensive, and one gets the impression that he often detected self-interest where none was intended.

Symptoms of strain also marred his first appearance in Vienna, to which he went in the latter part of June after a concert in London. He endured the choral greeting at his hotel, the flowers and the solemn reading of a sonnet especially written for the occasion with a good grace, but at rehearsals he antagonised some of the players by having little to say, and at the end of the concert alienated the audience by cutting short their enthusiastic and prolonged applause with the remark: "Thank you, but now let's go home."

After a concert and lecture in Salzburg, he and Gertrud left for Switzerland, and there Hindemith went down with an attack of gout, caused perhaps, as Gertrud wrote from Sierre, by a too enthusiastic reunion with the local wine. On 23 August he conducted a concert at the festival in Lucerne, and for the first time in Europe his programme contained works other than his own (a Bach suite and a Mozart piano concerto, with Dinu Lipatti as soloist). From Lisbon they returned to New York on the ship on which Gertrud had sailed seven years earlier to rejoin her husband.

Hindemith's reappearance in Germany intensified interest in his works, among them those written in pre-Nazi days. The opera house in Essen had a sensational success with *Cardillac* in November 1947, and in February 1948 Wiesbaden revived *Neues vom Tage*, though a morally minded city councillor tried unsuccessfully to prevent it. Hindemith's mother, who attended the first performance, wrote to Willy Strecker: "The papers published good reviews, but the ghost of Goebbels is still stalking lustily about: that cannot be so quickly laid."

Hindemith himself was not very interested in these revivals. Of the production of *Neues vom Tage* he wrote: "It is like reminding an old sea captain of how he used once with such youthful intrepidity to sail his fivemaster round Cape Hatteras." He settled back comfortably into his New Haven routine, teaching his students and composing a new cello sonata for Piatigorsky. To help out Arthur Mendel, of Associated Music Publishers, he played the viola d'amore at an amateur performance of Bach's *St John Passion* in New York. He clung to his American life with an almost demonstrative obstinacy. The news that in his absence he had been awarded an honorary doctorate by Frankfurt University elicited from him only the remark: "*Mer werd halt alt (und bleed)*." (We're getting old—and dotty.) A similar award from Columbia University, on the other hand, gratified him. He received it at the hands of General Eisenhower, the university's president, and afterwards he wrote to Strecker: "I had a long talk with him about his experiences in Germany."

He was reluctant to undertake another European tour. They had returned from the first trip penniless, he claimed. His letters to Willy Strecker during these months are dominated by financial worries. He complained that, owing to the complicated arrangements between Schott's in London and Associated Music Publishers in New York, he was receiving too small a share of the money earned with his compositions. Once Strecker had sorted matters out, he decided, after toying with the idea of a summer teaching post in California, after all to undertake a second European tour. But again he asked Strecker to keep his plans secret. "I am constantly being plagued by old friends," he wrote, "by those who want to become so and others who claim they once were, and I have no taste for any of them, being overworked and not anxious always to be the sucker for others." It is another echo of that irritable and suspicious note which had begun, since the end of the war, to creep into his dealings with other people.

There is no need to register in detail his activities during the first part of his tour, which began in August 1948 in England with a teaching engagement at the Bryanston summer school, and continued with conducting engagements in Switzerland, Italy, Germany and Austria. The Hindemiths established a base at Sierre in Switzerland and invited his mother to join them there.

In Venice they saw a production of *Cardillac*, on which Hindemith reported to Willy Strecker on 16 September: "The music holds up quite well. Most of the pieces are still enjoyable, so that the score could be rescued musically with a few relatively minor alterations. On the other hand, the libretto is unfortunately so idiotic that, if the piece is to survive, the whole action will have to be completely changed. It could be done and I know how—but where can one find time to carry out all one's plans?" He found it only two months later during a two-weeks' holiday at Taormina in Sicily.

Cardillac was the second of his major works which he felt obliged in later years virtually to rewrite. The first, *Das Marienleben*, was given its first performance in its revised form on 3 November 1948 in Hanover by the singer Annelies Kupper and the pianist Carl Seemann. In a long introduction completed in the summer before he left America, Hindemith explained why he had felt the revision to be necessary:

"The strong impression which the first performance made on the audience—I had expected nothing of the sort—made me aware for the first time in my musical existence of the ethical qualities of music and the moral obligations of a composer: though I had given of my best in the *Marienleben*, it was, in spite of all my good intentions, not good enough for the work to be laid aside for ever as the best that could be done. I began to perceive the ideal of a music, noble and consummate, which I should one day be capable of realising, and I knew that from this time on the *Marienleben* would lead me along this path and act as a standard from which to approach my ideal. This attitude, partly sentimental and partly aggressive, towards an already completed work led me very soon to make tentative efforts towards improving it. They were followed by more radical changes of a technical and intellectual nature, and at length the new *Marienleben* emerged, still basically the same, yet technically and spiritually renewed. It is the result of a continuing process of experimenting and correcting."

The old version, he observed, was "essentially a series of songs, held together by the text and the action as it developed from that, but otherwise following no overall musical plan". In its new form he uses tonality in a symbolic way, centred on the tonic of E, which represents the figure of Christ. The Virgin Mary is represented by its dominant B; the divine by A; eternity by C; and so on. The tonal relationships are derived from the theories which he expounded in *The Craft of Musical Composition*. Their employment, he claimed, enabled him to give the work a coherent musical structure leading, at different points, to a dynamic and to an expressive climax. It was not necessary, he added, for the listener to know the technical processes involved in order to understand the songs. As for their effect on him, "this kind of tonal construction never seemed a burden—on the contrary, I always found in it a welcome additional source of musical inspiration".

Hindemith was not the first composer to look back in later years on his youthful works and decide that he was now technically equipped to do them better. And, having turned himself in the meantime from a composer content to rely on his instinct alone to a highly conscious musical thinker, it was inevitable perhaps that he should attempt retrospectively to give the best of his early works the benefit of his later conclusions. But it might be asked whether a composer is in fact ever wise to "improve" on a work which has already, whatever its imperfections, gained public approval. Works of this kind quickly assume an identity of their own, independent of the composer. Only too often in such cases the public, uncertain which of the two versions to accept as authentic, tends to ignore both. This fate seems (though perhaps only temporarily) to have overtaken both *Das Marienleben* and the opera *Neues vom Tage*, which he revised in 1953.

If *Cardillac* is proving more resilient, it is the original version with the text of Ferdinand Lion which shows signs of surviving rather than the radically reshaped second. The new libretto, which Hindemith wrote himself, can scarcely be considered an improvement on Lion's work, so strangely condemned by Hindemith as "idiotic". Admittedly it is closer to the original tale by E. T. A. Hoffmann, in that it reintroduces the character of Cardillac's apprentice, who was eliminated by Lion entirely. As a result, however, the action not only becomes much more diffuse, but the character of Cardillac himself is weakened. From the sublimely obsessed figure, convinced that his work is too good for humanity, he descends to a self-questioning schemer who momentarily seeks Wagnerian "redemption" in the arms of an opera singer, a scene played against the background of an opera by Lully. This scene, however ingenious musically, does not help to make the action clearer. One feels that Hindemith, in attempting to examine the moral issues involved in the story, has only succeeded in obscuring them.

As on his previous tour, Hindemith had planned to keep appearances in Germany to the minimum: he made a short private visit to Frankfurt at the beginning of October and conducted a concert in Baden-Baden immediately afterwards. In November, however, he was approached by the American military government with an invitation to tour the American zones of occupation in Germany and help as conductor and lecturer in their "reorientation programme". He seized the opportunity eagerly. To appear in Germany as an official cultural ambassador for the country of his adoption was far more acceptable to his pride than returning as an emigrant ostensibly seeking re-acceptance. In the lectures he gave in Munich, Nuremberg, Frankfurt, Wiesbaden and Berlin during the first few weeks of 1949 he made no secret of his American loyalties, and in consequence came in for a considerable amount of criticism from his audiences, who consisted for the most part of musical colleagues and students.

His reception was most cordial in Berlin, where he lectured to packed audiences at the Free University and the Hochschule. As one Berlin reporter (Elisabeth Mahlke) put it in the *Neue Zeitung* of 19 February 1949, framing her report in the form of an open letter: "Let's admit it, that all of us who knew you in former times were somewhat concerned as to how this reunion after the Thousand Years would work out. But just hearing you speak—at your first lecture in the beloved, now so badly damaged Hochschule in the Fasanenstrasse—was enough to sweep away these concerns and the Thousand Years. For what you said—still with a light Frankfurt accent—about 'Music History as an Educational Factor of the Composer' was spoken in the same room in which you once introduced your pupils to living musical history through performances on the old instruments from the State Collection. That you replied with a regretful 'No' to the question whether we might win you back to this city, we understood and at the same time deeply regretted. Your informative descriptions of the opportunities for work and of your obligations in your new country are for us reason enough."

This demonstrative show of affection—something which Hindemith seldom encountered and never encouraged—certainly owed something to the fact that Berlin at the time was a beleaguered city, grateful to the Americans for keeping it supplied by the so-called air lift. But even in this city where past memories were strongest there were some who saw Hindemith's identification with America as a betrayal of his German origins. As one of his critics put it in a sublimely brazen letter in the Soviet-licensed newspaper *Nationalzeitung*: "It is a pity that Hindemith does not feel a higher obligation to Germany, which gave him his education and training, as well as the hardships which matured him."

The controversy continued after his return to the United States in April 1949. He was interviewed by the press on arrival in New York, and a report appeared in the *New York Times* under the heading "Music in Germany is Seen on Decline". Among the points Hindemith was alleged to have made were that Germany's receptivity to contemporary music had been set back beyond the point it had reached in the Twenties, and he had met no new composers there whom he would call real composers. "When asked if there was any insurgent, creative musical urge in the country, as there had been after the First World War, he replied: 'Absolutely nothing'."

The *New York Times* report was reproduced in the German press and aroused much indignation. On Willy Strecker's urgent advice Hindemith wrote a piece for publication in Germany to assuage wounded feelings. In his interview, he declared, his intention had been to point out the difficulties in Germany and to praise the efforts being made there to restore musical standards. It was inevitable that after a gap of fifteen years there should be a lack of young musicians, but he was confident that they would eventually emerge. "To help to smooth the path in that direction through practical musical work, through understanding, advice and productive criticism," he concluded, "I have always seen and still see as my natural duty."

A fuller account of the same interview, published in New

York on 10 April 1949 in the German-speaking *Sonntagsblatt Staats-Zeitung und Herold*, does suggest that Hindemith had been misrepresented in the *New York Times*: the fuller account shows his estimate of the state of music in Germany at that time to have been both moderate and sensible. There is no need to reproduce his views here: they refer to a period which is as long forgotten as the controversy he unwittingly aroused concerning it. But the affair has been worth recalling in some detail since it does illustrate the uneasiness created by divided loyalties. The very obstinacy with which Hindemith advertised his American allegiance was to a large extent an act of self-persuasion, aimed against those intangible instincts at which Gertrud hinted in a letter to Ludwig Strecker when the second tour in Europe was over:

"The days in Germany were wonderful. To you of course it seems odd that contact with one's old home can be so lovely in spite of all the misery. But an afternoon like that at your house, with the *Krapfen* and the cosy coffee table, is something that through all these years one has been pining for."

The year 1949 was a busy one creatively. It began with the Concerto for Horn and Orchestra, which he completed while still in Europe. On his return to America he wrote the Concerto for Woodwinds, Harp and Orchestra, which he himself described as "a harmless little bit of music". In it he celebrated his silver wedding by bringing in snatches of Mendelssohn's Wedding March. He also wrote two scenes of the libretto of the Kepler opera.

In July he and Gertrud set off by car on an extended tour of the United States, taking a roundabout route to Colorado Springs, where he spent a week teaching, lecturing and conducting. After that they went to New Mexico, returning to New Haven in September. He brought back with him two new compositions: the Concerto for Trumpet, Bassoon and Strings and the Sonata for Double Bass and Piano.

They remained in New Haven only long enough to prepare for a temporary move to Harvard University, where Hindemith was to begin a year's residence as Norton Professor. An invitation to deliver the Charles Eliot Norton lectures is considered a high academic honour, and the Music School at Yale felt obliged, however reluctantly, to give Hindemith leave of absence for a full year. The six lectures he gave at Harvard form the basis of his book *A Composer's World*, which will be dealt with in detail in the following chapter.

While he was at Harvard, the Hindemiths lived in the Hotel Fensgate in Boston and returned to their home in New Haven only at weekends. It was during this time that he received the news that his mother had died on 23 November 1949 at the age of eighty-one.

"Poor Paul has had a dreadful week," Gertrud wrote to Willy Strecker on 29 November. "The sad news came right in the middle of the very tense days before his last lecture. It was admirable the way he finished off his highly concentrated work in spite of everything, tearing himself with all his strength out of a sort of daze. We drove to Boston yesterday on snow-covered, rather slippery roads in silence, he scribbling away until the last moment. This final lecture was in consequence particularly impressive and profound. The audience sat spell-bound to the very last word and then broke out into long applause. . . . But a big stone has today been lifted from our hearts, and we are enjoying it like children not having to get ourselves armed for another Monday."

Hindemith did not go to Germany for the funeral: it would have been difficult to postpone his final lecture. For a woman of his mother's unpretentious character it was a lavish ceremony which Willy Strecker arranged in Frankfurt. Her son's *Trauermusik*, composed for King George V, was played by members of the radio orchestra in Frankfurt, Fried Lübbecke delivered a funeral oration, and wreaths were laid by representatives from the towns of Frankfurt, Hanau and Butzbach, where her life had been spent.

Thanking Strecker for all the trouble he had taken, Hindemith wrote: "It must all have been very moving, and the last echo of so-called fame which this world has to offer and which she in her own way accepted whimsically [he used the English word] but not without a certain amount of pleasure, was well-meant and certainly no more than she deserved." An out-pouring of emotion was not to be expected: it was not Hindemith's way. But one can detect something of the genuine devotion that had underlain the undemonstrative relationship between him and his mother in the simple words he wrote to Strecker: "Fortunately it was possible to ensure that her last years were relatively comfortable, thus compensating her for many earlier hardships."

Before the end of that remarkably creative year Hindemith completed the first movement of his Sinfonietta in E, commissioned by the Louisville Symphony Orchestra and first performed on 1 March 1950 in Louisville, Kentucky, with Hindemith himself conducting. In the following month, after the completion of the composition class that had followed his lectures at Harvard, he and Gertrud set out on their third visit to Europe. This time he appeared as a viola player as well as a conductor, in Mozart's Sinfonia Concertante in Berlin and in Bach's Third and Sixth Brandenburg Concertos in Vienna. He also conducted the first performance of his Concerto for Horn and Orchestra in Baden-Baden on 8 June, with Dennis Brain as soloist, having held it back until he could conduct it himself. As he wrote to Willy Strecker: "Ninety-nine per cent of conductors are so devoid of wits that it is better to show them first how it should be done." The final highlight of the tour was a visit to Hamburg, where he took part in the Bach bicentenary celebrations, conducting the Magnificat and delivering a lecture which he eventually published. It is an interesting and revealing comment both on the composer he most revered and on himself, and I shall deal with it in detail in the following chapter.

Between these musical events he paid a visit to Zurich to discuss the offer he had received of a teaching post at the university there. As he had told Professor Heinrich Straumann, who made the first approaches, in a letter written from Boston on 30 November 1949: "If the decision were dependent on my personal inclinations alone you would very soon see me arriving to take over the chair you have so cordially offered. For me Zurich would be the ideal centre of operations as far as my European commitments are concerned."

These were far from merely polite words. From the very start of his musical career Switzerland had played an important and invariably happy role in his life. All his doubts on the wisdom of returning to Europe centred, whether he acknowledged it or not, on his conflicting emotions concerning Germany. Here was a chance to be close to, yet not part of, the land in which his true roots lay. Yet he was reluctant to break his connections with Yale. What he hoped for—and was indeed

able on this visit to achieve—was an arrangement which enabled
him to retain both posts, spending a year in one, to be followed
by a year in the other. Thus, when in September 1950 he and
Gertrud took ship for America, they knew that a year later they
would be returning to Europe on a more settled basis.

We can pass shortly over the events of the next two years,
divided equally between Yale and Zurich. Hindemith had now
reached that period in the life of a successful artist when there
is little to do but sit back and enjoy the world's adulation.
There was no lack of marks of distinction. Another honorary
doctorate had been conferred on him in 1950—this time by the
Free University in Berlin. In 1951 the city of Hamburg awarded
him its Bach Prize; in 1952 he was elected a member of the
order *Pour le mérite*, the highest cultural honour Germany can
offer, since it is limited to only thirty living persons distinguished in the arts and sciences; and early in 1953 his Septet
for Wind Instruments was chosen by the New York music
critics as the best chamber work of the year (rather belatedly,
one might add, since it had been written in Taormina and first
performed in Milan in 1948). "The septet is suddenly on the
lips of all grocers and fishmongers, who have now put us in the
ranks of their more important customers," Gertrud wrote to
the Strecker brothers.

Hindemith tended to conceal his feelings about such signs of
recognition behind a straight face in public and a few facetious
remarks in private. But the letter of thanks he wrote in 1951 to
the Hamburg Senate following the award of the Bach Prize is
more revealing. In it he recalled that famous headline which
had been splashed across the front page of Goebbels's newspaper *Der Angriff* at the height of the showdown with the Nazis
in 1934: *Warum Vorschusslorbeeren für Konjunktur-Musiker Hindemith?* (Why Advance Laurels for Musical Opportunist Hindemith?) And he commented: "The honours being awarded me
at the present time are indeed, in a different sense, 'advance
laurels'. Perhaps one should regard such prizes only as an
acknowledgement of good intentions and not as a reward for
achievement. As such they would be due to all who genuinely
strive to reach beyond themselves, and it is only more or less by
chance that they fall on the one whom a variable fate has
momentarily placed in a more glaring light."

So highly self-critical and self-deprecating an artist as Hindemith cannot easily assume the role of a Grand Old Man, even less so when he is aware, as Hindemith so acutely was, that the crowning achievement of his life had still to be written. The Kepler opera, which had been conceived as an expression of all his beliefs, artistic, social and religious, had not yet progressed beyond a general outline, two scenes in text and a few musical themes, which (as with *Mathis der Maler*) he worked out in the form of a symphony. This was done to please an old friend, Paul Sacher, to whom the *Harmonie der Welt* Symphony is dedicated. It was first performed by the Basle Chamber Orchestra under Sacher on 25 January 1952.

But it was surely in part the nagging pressure of this unwritten opera which, together with a commission from UNESCO to write a choral work on a text by Paul Claudel (that truly Grand Old Man), finally persuaded Hindemith at the beginning of 1953 that he must give up part of his teaching load in order to gain more time for composition. That decision made, he had to choose which part to give up: Yale or Zurich. And in his resolve to sacrifice Yale one can equally suspect the influence of that nostalgia for Europe which he had always been at such pains to deny.

The farewell party was held in the Hindemith home in Alden Avenue on 2 May 1953. Its unexpected lavishness was such that it has become almost a part of Yale's history, and even today one has the feeling that to have been among the invited guests confers a treasured mark of distinction. One of the favoured ones, Margaret Bozyan, typed out at the time, for the benefit of her children, a detailed description. With the help of this I am able to reconstruct it now.

Hindemith himself was responsible for the decorations which filled the whole of the house. On large sheets of paper he drew and painted scenery which transformed the modest hallway into a marble palace, the kitchen into a crypt and the dining-room into a spacious park. "At extreme right a white picket gate leading to a peaceful greensward dotted with trees. At center was a long path through the park, the most important figure being that of a statue of a lion playing a cello."

The "program of overwhelming attractions" consisted of several of Hindemith's party pieces which we have met before, though they were probably new to his American guests.

"Minimax, a recital given by the Band of the 358th Infantry Regiment" goes back to Donaueschingen: it consisted here of a string quartet (Hindemith and three of his colleagues) playing parodies of German *Lieder*, Viennese waltzes and Italian operetta. The same quartet played his version of the *Flying Dutchman* overture, which "includes all the mistakes ever made by any orchestra" and swings off into a waltz "when things got too bad". Between these a male quartet (Noss, Donovan, Simonds and Boatwright) sang "Songs of Pomp, Circumstances and Fire Prevention", Boatwright's wife Helen, who had sung solo parts in many of the Collegium Musicum concerts, performed an eighteenth-century musical farce; and Emanuel Winternitz, of the Metropolitan Museum in New York, did some conjuring tricks.

At the centre of the entertainment was an academic discussion about a mysterious figure which Hindemith had fashioned out of "driftwood or a root". It wore painted shorts and had two faces, one at the front and one at the back. Four professors, including Leo Schrade and Henri Peyre (Gertrud's French teacher) solemnly discussed this "recent archaeological find" and came to the conclusion after much clowning that it was "a creature interested in games and athletics, especially interested in Society, heavy in the middle, light in the head, with some fish-like traits: in short, an example of Homo Yalensis."

The food, buffet style, included a whole ham, a whole turkey and "two huge trays of tiny, all-colored 'petits fours', each one decorated with a musical symbol, or even a staff with a couple of notes." At the end of her graphic account Mrs Bozyan wrote in pencil: "I snitched 4 tiny cakes. They may become dehydrated—immortalized soon!"

The house in Alden Avenue was put up for sale. On 14 May Hindemith conducted a Collegium Musicum concert covering the complete period previously explored in the series, from the twelfth to the seventeenth centuries. The final piece, certainly not by accident, was a Bach motet, *Singet dem Herrn ein neues Lied* (Sing unto the Lord a New Song). The concert was repeated, as had now become customary, in the Metropolitan Museum in New York.

On 2 June, shortly before embarking for Europe, Hindemith wrote from the Hotel Biltmore to his lawyer Oscar Cox in Washington: "The ending school year with its exams and concerts, our dissolving of the household combined with the constant flow of buyers, sellers and farewell-wishers—and on top of all the obligation to finish the Claudel piece—it was just too much. Today we are leaving, and the next six days will be spent in plain laziness. I decided to actually do nothing at all, which will be a novum in my life."

Chapter 2

A COMPOSER'S WORLD

A Composer's World: Horizons and Limitations was the title
Hindemith chose for the book he made out of the six Charles
Eliot Norton lectures delivered at Harvard University in the
winter of 1949–50. He gave the lectures extempore in English
and had them recorded on tape as he spoke them. According to
Luther Noss, he was none too pleased when he read the trans-
cripts of the tapes, and he spent a considerable time improving
his texts before releasing them for publication. There are frequent
complaints in his correspondence in 1950 and 1951 of the time-
consuming nature of this editorial work, and he was somewhat
discouraged when Arthur Mendel, the translator of his previous
book *The Craft of Musical Composition*, criticised his English after
reading the first few chapters and suggested that he should rewrite the text in German and then have it translated. Fortunately both for him and us, the Harvard University Press
decided that Hindemith's English style had a flavour of its own
which was worth retaining and brought the book out in 1952 as
prepared by him. The author pays his publishers a grateful
tribute in his preface: "They unflaggingly encouraged a side-
line literate who rather preferred writing music; they were
patient with an author whose only reliability was his never
being on time with his instalments; and they had a most
generous understanding for his literary and linguistic weaknesses." We can share his feelings of gratitude for, whatever his
"literary and linguistic weaknesses" in English may be, they in
no way inhibit his ability to express himself on profound subjects
with all his wonted clarity and vigour, free from all traces of
academic dryness.

A *Composer's World* covers a far wider field than *The Craft of
Musical Composition* and consequently provides even more
evidence of the man behind the music. The earlier book is
concerned mainly with his technical ideas. Here, in *A Composer's
World*, we are shown what the irrational, inspirational aspects
of music meant to him. If he seldom spoke of these aspects to
his pupils or his friends, it was not because he was indifferent
to them, but because they were firstly (as he supposed) self-

evident and, secondly, difficult to put into words. He starts off by describing his point of departure, which he calls "the typical artistic way of understanding the world":

"To the scientist our method—or, in his eyes, nonmethod—of looking at everything without ever fundamentally comprehending it must seem utterly amateurish. In fact, the artistic approach *is* essentially and inevitably amateurish, its distinction from the amateur's point of view being merely a considerably wider panorama. We must be grateful that with our art we have been placed halfway between science and religion, enjoying equally the advantages of exactitude in thinking—so far as the technical aspects of music are concerned—and of the unlimited world of faith."

Hindemith here uses the word religion in a literal sense, though in no strictly doctrinal one. He proclaims his belief in music as a moral force in the world by quoting both St Augustine (*De musica libri sex*) and Boethius (*De institutione musica*). He summarises St Augustine thus: "Musical order, as recognised and evaluated by our mind, is not an end in itself. It is an image of a higher order which we are permitted to perceive . . . if we put our enjoyment of such knowledge . . . into the side of the balance that tends towards the order of the heavens and towards the unification of our soul with the divine principle." And Boethius: "Music is a part of our human nature; it has the power either to improve or to debase our character."

There is, in Hindemith's view, a radical difference between the two approaches. According to St Augustine, "music has to be converted into moral power. We receive its sounds and forms, but they remain meaningless unless we include them in our own mental activity and use their fermenting quality to turn our souls towards everything noble, superhuman and ideal. It is our mind that brings about this conversion; music is but a catalytic agent to this end. The betterment of our soul must be our own achievement, although music is one of those factors which, like religious belief, creates in us most easily a state of willingness towards this betterment. In short, we have to be active; music, like humus in a garden soil, must be dug under in order to become fertile." In Boethius, on the other hand, "music has become the active partner; our mind is a passive receiver and is impressed and influenced by the power music exerts."

It is obvious, from all that has gone before in this book, which of these approaches enjoys the greater share of Hindemith's approval, though his ideal, he claims, lies in a synthesis of the two. In the manner in which he formulates his preference for the active over the passive as a means of achieving his ideal, he indirectly throws light on that period of his life which was devoted to writing his *Music to Sing and Play*. This, as we now see, was no side-step, but an essential and vital part of his artistic development.

The composer's main objective, he writes, should be "to lift the consumer to a higher level by convincing him of the harm a constant yearning for entertainment produces; and as a means to this end the writing of suitable music for the amateur was recommended. Certainly, writing such music will not be the only means, but it will be the form in which the desire for replacing external brilliancy with genuine musical values finds its clearest expression. Once a writer's technique and style is organised in this direction, so that music which satisfies the amateur's wishes can be created, his approach to his entire work will inevitably undergo a radical change: the emphasis on moral aspects will now become recognisable also in his works written for the concertising professional, and now he will talk with a different spirit to the general audience, which, in its basic benevolence, will be ready to accept his leadership towards better goals."

This is of course the Augustinian approach. The Boethian, in contrast, tends to force the listener "into such a state of passivity that his faculty of musical perception will crave only pieces which ... in every respect satisfy his basest instincts—music which is nothing but a cheap and trashy amenity, an opiate always and everywhere available. Our present era, in which the majority of listeners is constantly subject to this kind of music, has, in my opinion, reached a point below which a further degeneration of the Boethian attitude is impossible."

This view, when transferred from the general to the particular, produces from Hindemith a scathing attack—saved, however, by its grim humour from mere peevishness—on the musical life of America with its crack orchestras and star conductors, its mindless virtuosos, its commercial radios and its Muzak. "Musical industrialism", "relentlessly running music-faucets", "sewage system of sound"—these are just a few of the epithets.

"It is said that one of the most horrid tortures inflicted on captured political enemies of Nazidom's tyrant was the incessant gramophone playing of patriotic songs; this drove the victims to the verge of insanity. Compare this fact with the answer given by the owner of a delightful little hotel when asked why the otherwise pleasant atmosphere of his lobby had to be marred by a daily and nightly groaning loudspeaker. He said: 'Have you ever felt how horrifying silence is?' Silence, one of the most merciful gifts of heaven in this noisy world! Silence, the horizon against which alone music assumes contour and meaning!

"It is our era that has had the privilege of adding to those old disgraceful blemishes on mankind's record—political dictatorship, slave labour, prostitution, racial prejudice—the modern complement, the 'captive audience'. We may have some hope that this plague of bastard music, like others that scourged the human race, such as cholera and scurvy, will wane and be reduced to a bearable minimum, simply because there has been too much of it."

In the chapter devoted to education the autobiographical flavour is particularly strong. It can be seen, for instance, in Hindemith's approving description of earlier methods of training the young:

"If a boy was found to be gifted for music, he was given as an apprentice into the care of a practical musician. With him he had to get acquainted with many branches of music. Singing was the foundation of all musical work. Thus singing, mostly in the form of group singing, was one of the most important fields of instruction. The practical knowledge of more or less all instruments was a *sine qua non*. Specialisation was almost unknown. Frequently a musician may have been better on the keyboard than with the bow and with woodwinds or brass, but that would not have absolved him from playing as many other instruments as possible. And all this playing was done with one aim in mind: to prepare the musician for collective work; it was always the community that came first. Soloistic training was nothing but a preliminary and preparatory exercise for this purpose. Hand in hand with this daily all-round routine in instrumental training went a solid instruction in the theory of music—not only what we call theory in our modern curricula, namely harmony, counterpoint and other branches of practical instruction, but true theory, or if you prefer another name, the scientific background of music.

"This vast stock of general musical knowledge was the hotbed in which the germs of composing grew. If a musician had any talent for composition, he could always draw on this tremendous accumulation of practical experience, once he wanted to convert his ideas into audible structures. Composing was not a special branch of knowledge that had to be taught to those gifted or interested enough. It simply was the logical outgrowth of a healthy and stable system of education, the ideal of which was not an instrumental, vocal or tone-arranging specialist, but a musician with a universal musical knowledge—a knowledge which, if necessary, could easily be used as a basis for a more specialised development of peculiar talents. This system, although it provided for the composer the best preparation possible, did not guarantee him any success. Only posterity decided whether he was to be counted among the few extraordinary creative musical figures each country had produced throughout the world, or among the many preparers and pioneers who had to blast the way for those great fulfillers, or finally among those who generalise, smooth out, and popularise the more original work of the genius."

This corresponds very closely with the teaching method Hindemith himself tried to follow, in Germany and the United States and briefly in Switzerland. But for the organised musical academy—a modern development—he had little but abuse, castigating it for its "schedule tyranny" and its unrealistic "teaching of teachers who in turn teach teachers". In his attitude to composition Hindemith was unashamedly aristocratic: he did not believe that composition could be taught in "the democratic way" to every student who felt the ambition to become a composer. "Artistic creation is individualistic, because it is as private as your dreams, nobody can interfere with your artistic phantasms, and although physical powers may prevent a work of art from coming into structural existence, the individualistic act of creation in the artist's mind can never be touched."

The whole basis of Hindemith's belief—and it is the recurring theme throughout his book—is that composition is a divine gift which comes and goes as it pleases, and the most a musician can hope to do is to equip himself as thoroughly as possible to grasp it when it comes. "Teaching according to these maxims, I never found vanity or frustration as a result. How can you be conceited if the overwhelming number of musical facts you can learn makes you conscious of your smallness every moment of your musical existence? And how can you be frustrated, if you know composing is not necessary unless the creative talent shows up unexpectedly?"

At this point Hindemith makes another short excursion into the directly autobiographical:

"Once I had a discussion on this subject with a well-known composer. He said: 'I think your system of teaching composers is all wrong. It discourages young people, to face an almost un-surmountable heap of knowledge and technique. When I studied with a famous teacher in Europe, every student in the class had the feeling that he was the elected genius of the future, that the piece he was writing right now was superb, and that it was merely a question of time and practice before his fate as a successful composer was confirmed.' The response to this re-proval is: If one cannot face the obstacles lying before a com-poser's career he should not be permitted to embark on it at all. Why must an apprentice composer be wrapped in cotton, when instrumentalist students come in touch with those obstacles from the very first day in obvious and mostly discouraging forms? Certainly it is not necessary to emphasise obstacles, but an honest teacher can never hide them. And what else is the result of a constantly flattering instruction but a pampered egotist who to the end of his life will be the only one convinced of his greatness, when everyone else ceased to share this opinion shortly after the performance of his first composition? There is but one conclusion that can be drawn from these statements: Don't teach composition the way it is usually done. Teach musicians. If once in a long while one of your students shows creative talent, let nature have its course. A fellow educated in the way here described will use all his manifold experiences to the right purpose, and what you can teach him beyond all this is more valuable than the teacher's instructing a pupil: it is the united effort of two equals in the search of perfection, in which the one participant is mostly but not always leading, for his is the greater experience."

With regard to Hindemith's own creative methods, the most self-revealing chapter in *A Composer's World* is that dealing with

musical inspiration. As we have already seen, he regarded
inspiration as a heaven-sent gift, over whose coming and going
the recipient had no control. In describing in his book what
he means by inspiration, Hindemith uses the German word
Einfall:

"*Einfall*, from the verb *einfallen*, to drop in, describes beautifully the strange spontaneity that we associate with artistic
ideas in general and with musical creation in particular. Something—you know not what—drops into your mind—you know
not whence—and there it grows—you know not how—into
some form—you know not why." But this, as he observes, is not
the end, but only the very beginning of composition—in fact,
not even that, for even people with no training at all can occasionally receive such musical ideas, and "who can be sure that
the inner singing and ringing that any Mr or Mrs X feels
bubbling up in a musically uncultivated mind . . . is not, in its
unshaped authenticity, at least as beautiful and satisfactory as—
and perhaps even better than—the greatest composer's unshaped inner singing and ringing?

"It is exciting to know how primitive, commonplace, colour-
less, and insignificant the first ideas, the primordial *Einfälle*, of
even extraordinary musical masters are. But it seems almost
more exciting to recognise the specific talent with which those
masters keep their ideas fresh and, despite all mutations, basically intact, during the sometimes considerably long interval of
time required for the treatment of these ideas. In this they are
led by tradition, by the presumptive conditions of performance
of the future piece, by its purpose and style, and, to a minor
degree, by personal whims and fancies that may add certain
flavours to the final form."

Hindemith draws attention to the sketch books of Beethoven
as visual proof of a composer seen wrestling with his initial
Einfälle. "To watch the plodding through those many stages of
development is oftentimes rather depressing: if that is the way
a genius works, chiselling and moulding desperately in order to
produce a convincing form, what then is the fate of the smaller
fellows? Perhaps it is always true that in working from the
tiniest and almost imperceptible spark of structural invention
up to an intelligible musical form, a petty composer is very
much like Beethoven. If only the work involved in reaching this
goal really counted, there would be many a genius."

But there is a quality which distinguishes the genius from the petty composer, and that is "musical vision":

"We all know the impression of a very heavy flash of lightning in the night. Within a second's time we see a broad landscape, not only in its general outlines but with every detail. Although we could never describe each single component of the picture, we feel that not even the smallest leaf of grass escapes our attention. . . .

"Compositions must be conceived the same way. If we cannot, in the flash of a single moment, see a composition in its absolute entirety, with every pertinent detail in its proper place, we are not genuine creators. The musical creator, like any other creative individual, is permitted to share with the demiurge the possession of vitalising visions; but it is the privilege of the demiurge to transform them into concrete existence without any interfering technical obstacle, whereas the creative musician, by reason of his earthly heritage, has to overcome many hurdles between them and their realisation. If he is a genuine creator he will not feel disturbed or discouraged by this fact. Not only will he have the gift of seeing—illuminated in his mind's eye as if by a flash of lightning—a complete musical form (though its subsequent realisation in a performance may take three hours or more); he will have the energy, persistence and skill to bring this envisioned form into existence, so that even after months of work not one of its details will be lost or fail to fit into his photomental picture. This does not mean that any F sharp in the six hundred and twelfth measure of the final piece would have been determined in the very first flash of cognition. If the seer should in this first flash concentrate his attention on any particular detail of the whole, he would never conceive the totality; but if the conception of this totality strikes his mind like lightning, this F sharp and all the other thousands of notes and other means of expression will fall into line almost without his knowing it. In working out his material he will always have before his mental eye the entire picture. In writing melodies or harmonic progressions he does not have to select them arbitrarily, he merely has to fulfil what the conceived totality demands. This is the true reason for Beethoven's apparently more than philistine bickering with his material: a desire not to improve or to change any *Einfall* but to accommodate it to the unalterable necessities of an envisioned totality, even if with all his technical skill and experience he has to press it through five or more versions that distort it past recognition."

As a contribution to the unsolved (and perhaps insoluble) question of the nature of artistic inspiration, Hindemith's metaphor of the lightning-illuminated landscape is valuable. One is immediately reminded of Wagner's account in his autobiography of the conception of the overture to *Die Meistersinger*, which he claimed to have heard "sounding in my inner ear with the utmost distinctness" during a rail journey from Venice to Vienna, before even the text of the opera was written. If, as Wagner tells us, he was able to write it down a few months later "exactly as it appears in the score today", this did not prevent him from having, like Beethoven, to do some philistine bickering both with it and others parts of his score written afterwards. Hindemith himself seems, like Mozart, to have had the ability to write his music down even in the company of others, oblivious of all outward distractions, but this of course implies only that both were able to work out their problems in their minds without recourse to paper: the process was in fact the same as that of Beethoven with his sketch books or Wagner with his copious use of the piano: to recapture the details of the "envisioned totality".

"It is obvious," Hindemith continues, "that a composer, during the long period the notation of his work requires, is always in danger of losing the original vision of it. The flashlike picture may fade out, the outlines may dissolve, many details may disappear in darkness. One of the characteristics of the talent of a creative genius seems to be the ability to retain the keenness of the first vision until its embodiment in the finished piece is achieved. There is no doubt that this embodiment, if it is to appear as a true realisation of the vision, can come to life only with the assistance of a great amount of technical skill. Skill can never make up for lack of vision, but on the other hand a vision will never receive its true materialisation if a composer's technique does not provide every means towards this end."

Here is Hindemith again harping on his favourite theme of the necessity of technical competence—a habit which once provoked from an intending student the protest: "But, Mr Hindemith, there must be some short cut." Hindemith, who tells this story himself, insists that not only is there no short cut, but an efficient technique is not in itself enough to realise the final vision:

"You may manage the few basic rules of construction with all their combinative possibilities pretty well, and yet the highest degree of subtlety, in which each technical item is in congruence with the respective part of the vision, again may be attained by no one but the genius. There are relatively few masterworks in which this ultimate congruence can be felt. Even in our stockpile of classical music which by common agreement consists of works written by superior composers not many pieces fulfil those highest requirements. True, there are many other great and excellent works, which in their artistic value are by no means less important. They may in their ability to speak as human creations to human beings be closest to our hearts, but it is in those few uncontested masterpieces that we feel the breath of universality and eternity, because their particular kind of perfection, the absolute coincidence of intention and realisation, is almost superhuman.

"The fact that very few masterworks display this congruence of vision and materialisation shows us that even the individual possessing the greatest gift and the highest technical skill is not always able to reach this goal. A tremendous effort is necessary in order to work towards it; not merely a technical effort, but moral effort, too—the effort to subject all considerations of technique, style and purpose to this one ideal: congruence. Again, it is the aspiration towards the ideal unity of the Augustinian and the Boethian attitude towards music which must ennoble our endeavours and which on the other hand pushes, as we know, the final goal into an utter remoteness close to inaccessibility."

I have quoted at particular length from the chapter on musical inspiration because it seems to me to go so far towards explaining the apparent contradictions in Hindemith's convictions and activities which have been the cause of so much misunderstanding about his music. His reasons for revising major early works such as *Das Marienleben* and *Cardillac*, for instance, can be seen not as an inner uncertainty, but as its very opposite when we are aware of the total vision from which they sprang and which he hoped in maturity to recapture more faithfully. His insistence on technical skill, combined with his contempt for mere virtuosity (which included the musicological approach as well as the practical), was the outcome of humility, not of envy. His rejection of methods such as the twelve-tone system lay in his belief that these ignored basic natural laws. Music itself, he asserts in his book, is a fact of existence—"the only earthly form of expression which in the properties of its constructive material permits us to have sensations that are a very faint allusion to the feeling of beings to whom the universal concept of the relativity and interchangeability of time and space is an ordinary experience"—and the need for it is present in us all. The composer is no isolated being, but a member of the human community, and it is his moral duty to use his skill to communicate with his fellow beings.

It is his feeling that this sense of communication has been lost—replaced on the one side by the composer's self-isolation and on the other by the listener's capitulation to the passive acceptance of mere sensual sound—that leads Hindemith again and again to insist on the importance of active communal music-making: "Amateur's music is essentially community music. . . . Once you join an amateur group, you are a member of a great fraternity, whose purpose is the most dignified one you can imagine: to inspire one another and unite in building up a creation that is greater than one individual's needs."

This faith in the moral power of music even leads Hindemith to suggest—if facetiously, nevertheless with a serious undertone —how it might be usefully extended to the field of politics: "A German proverb says: *Böse Menschen haben keine Lieder* (bad men don't sing). It is not impossible that out of a tremendous movement of amateur community music a peace movement could spread over the world. Could it not be supported by our high dignitaries? Instead of the president of the United States solitarily playing the piano in Washington and the ruler of the Russians strumming his balalaika (or whatever he strums) in Moscow, could they not, together with their respective governments, join once a week in an orchestra or chorus, thus giving the world an example of common enterprises towards a lofty goal? People who make music together cannot be enemies, at least not while the music lasts."

It has not been my intention in this chapter to supply a complete summary of *A Composer's World*, a book so full of good sense, invigorating if sometimes exasperating argument and sheer enjoyment that I recommend all who care for Hindemith and his music to read it for themselves. My main purpose has been to extract from it evidence of character and outlook that has not been in very generous supply from other sources. The book is as near to an autobiography as Hindemith ever got. Careful as he is to avoid the use of the first person or to draw too copiously on personal anecdotes, he leaves the reader with the impression that every word in this "guide through the little universe which is the working place of the man who writes music" (to quote from his preface) is based on a philosophy rooted in his own character and experience. The last words of the book are certainly as near as he ever came to a direct statement of his religious beliefs:

"This life in and with music, being essentially a victory over external forces and a final allegiance to spiritual sovereignty, can only be a life of humility, of giving one's best to one's fellow men. This gift will not be like the alms passed on to the beggar: it will be the sharing of a man's every possession with his friend.

"The ultimate reason for his humility will be the musician's conviction that beyond all the rational knowledge he has amassed and all his dexterity as a craftsman there is a region of visionary irrationality in which the veiled secrets of art dwell, sensed but not understood, implored but not commanded, imparting but not yielding. He cannot enter this region, he can only pray to be elected one of its messengers. If his prayers are granted and he, armed with wisdom and gifted with reverence for the unknowable, is the man whom heaven has blessed with the genius of creation, we may see in him the donor of the precious present we all long for: the great music of our time."

The lecture on Bach, written within a year of the Charles Eliot Norton lectures, is equally a semi-autobiographical statement, and Hindemith considered incorporating it in *A Composer's World*. Two factors induced him to change his mind: the feeling, both of himself and others, that the Harvard lectures were complete in themselves, and Willy Strecker's request for permission to print a few hundred copies of the Hamburg lecture, to be sent to friends and colleagues as a Christmas gift. Hindemith was attracted by this idea, and himself took a number of copies for personal distribution. He later translated his lecture into English, in which version it was published by the

I

Yale University Press in 1952 under the title *Johann Sebastian Bach—Heritage and Obligation*. A German re-issue for public consumption came out in 1953 from the Insel-Verlag under the title *Johann Sebastian Bach—Ein verpflichtendes Erbe*.

The Bach Hindemith portrays is a man very like himself: "a tolerant and hospitable man, not averse to the little amenities of life. A good provider, he is out to do well for himself, especially in the matter of financial advantage. . . . He argues vehemently, in endless letters to his superiors, on behalf of his opinions. . . . Sometimes he must have been rather malevolent, or else the Duke of Weimar, his employer, who was by no means hostile to him, would not have imprisoned him for one month in 1717." In his professional function too there are resemblances: "As a teacher he apparently worked with all the advantages and handicaps of an impulsive artist bursting with music, who opens to the student an uninhibited view into the realm of musical inspiration and lets him participate in the process of creation, but who also feels the creative impatience of the genius frustrate the perseverance indispensable in all education." Another resemblance was "his almost exclusive devotion to questions of practical music".

But of course there are important differences as well. "To the theoretical aspects of his art he shows indifference. . . . To be sure, he used the newest advance in musical science, twelve-tone equal temperament, but obviously merely as a welcome aid in realising his wide-ranging tonal visions. The effective basis of his technique remains the old thorough bass." And (most important of all when it comes to comparisons): "Any musician, even the most gifted, takes a place second to Bach's at the very start."

Having spent the first part of his lecture transforming Bach from the statue into which history has frozen him into a real human being rather like himself, Hindemith proceeds to speculate on the slowing down of Bach's creative output during the last ten years of his life. And here, if we do to Hindemith what he himself did to Bach, we can perhaps come closer to the feelings of a man who experiences what Hindemith calls "the melancholy of capacity, of artistic potency". He defines this as "the grief at having been bereft of all former imperfections and with them of the possibility of proceeding further".

What is such a man to do when he becomes conscious of

having reached this point, as Bach did in 1740? He was then fifty-five, which was Hindemith's own age in 1950, when his lecture was written. "Is he," Hindemith asks, "serenely to continue his former work, forcing it by mere rearrangement into apparently new forms? In the course of his ascent he has acquired such a sense of responsibility that this sort of thing must seem to him nothing but primitive reiteration and squandering. Why should he not simply relax now, and enjoy what he has achieved? He had never known idleness, he was born without such knowledge and never acquired it."

Bach took the only step that in Hindemith's opinion was open to him, which was "to apply the means he is wont to use in serenely enhancing, serenely adorning his steepest, narrowest, humblest abode on the outermost plateau. With this his creative work turns into sublime creativity, his craftsman's proficiency into philosophic vision." Hindemith is thinking here of such works as the *Art of Fugue* and the choral preludes, in which the composer "has defeated the realm of substance and penetrated the unlimited region of thought".

It is surely not mere speculation to suggest that in his lecture Hindemith was in fact conducting an essay in self-analysis, for he himself ends it by exhorting others to follow Bach's example:

"Recognition of human excellence in its highest form, knowledge of the path that leads to it, the necessary done with dutifulness and driven to that point of perfection where it out-grows all necessity—this knowledge is the most precious inheri-tance given us with Bach's music. . . . To be resolved to seek the same road to perfection, more than that no one can do. He may proceed some stumbling paces, or fate may permit him to press far ahead. . . . We have beheld the summit of musical greatness. . . . This summit is, as we know, unattainable to us, but since we have beheld it we must not lose it from sight. It must always serve us as a supreme beacon. Like all other artistic issues this summit is a symbol, a symbol for everything noble towards which we strive with the better part of our being."

A glance at Hindemith's creative work in the last ten years of his life shows beyond all doubt that he himself followed the path he there indicated. In his much diminished output, leaving aside a few works written for special occasions (the Pittsburgh Symphony and the Organ Concerto among them), the empha-sis is on the introspective, the philosophical and the spiritual,

Chapter 3

1953–57:

A NEW CAREER AS CONDUCTOR

HINDEMITH'S FIRST ENGAGEMENT in Europe was the performance in Brussels on 9 July 1953 of the work commissioned by UNESCO (United Nations Educational, Scientific and Cultural Organisation). The *Cantique de l'espérance* (English title: *Canticle to Hope*) had already been written, though not finally scored, before he left America. He told Willy Strecker in his letter of 6 April 1953 that it was to be "a kind of *Lehrstück* with a cast of ten to a thousand and with the audience joining in the singing". The reversion to the early *Music to Sing and Play* formula was dictated by the nature of the occasion: the UNESCO conference concerned "the role of music in the education of young people and adults".

In the first letter he wrote to Hindemith on 6 March 1953 after agreeing to co-operate with him on the UNESCO commission (the full correspondence is published in an article by Andres Briner in the *Revue Musicale de Suisse Romande* of June 1973), Paul Claudel mentioned that he was interested in writing an oratorio in three parts. The first part would be a song of triumph based on Psalm 17 (18 in the Authorised Version); the second, based on a private experience, would concern "the spreading of the joyful feeling of Eastertide over a large modern city"; and the last would be a song of hope. Claudel sent Hindemith the text of this last, to be used for the UNESCO commission, and suggested that the other two movements might be completed later.

On their arrival in Europe in June 1953 Hindemith and Gertrud at once went to Claudel's country home on the river Isère in the French Alps, and there during their short visit Claudel related to them the personal experience which he saw as the centre of his projected oratorio, entitled simply *Suite lyrique*. After an operation for cataract he had spent two complete days of blindness, dependent on his aural sense alone. In that state he had experienced in the sounds of the surrounding city a mystical vision, the expression of which he felt to be beyond the reach of words alone.

Claudel himself had no compositional talent, but he was remarkably sensitive to the expressive potentialities of music, according to Arthur Honegger, with whom in 1936 he wrote the stage oratorio *Jeanne d'Arc au Bûcher* (Joan of Arc at the Stake). "He forced me to penetrate the atmosphere, feel the density, the melodic contour, which he wanted," Honegger wrote in *I Am a Composer*. Hindemith too fell under the spell of this rarefied spirit whose long life (Claudel was now eighty-five) had been divided between the worldly sphere of diplomacy and the spiritual realms of religious thought. After their visit Gertrud wrote to him (in French): "Paul would like to compose the complete *Suite lyrique*. . . . He tells me to ask you at once to put down on paper the experiences you expressed so movingly during our visit. He feels that this human interlude of the poet enclosed in night would provide a superb link between the two canticles."

They met again in Brussels at the first performance of the *Cantique de l'espérance*, after which Claudel wrote in his diary: "The music of Paul Hindemith is excellent. Dynamism, excellent dramatic deployment, handling of masses. The hall rose and resounded with cheers." There followed a number of letters and a last meeting in Switzerland at the end of 1953, but the *Suite lyrique*, eventually given the title *Ite, angeli veloces*, was not finally completed until after Claudel's death in February 1955 at the age of eighty-seven. The work, its three movements composed out of order and for very differing occasions, may not perhaps for that very reason figure among Hindemith's very greatest, but as the first expression of his final creative phase, aptly undertaken in the company of a poet who had already long been dwelling in those remote spiritual regions, it clearly has a biographical significance.

During his previous visits to Europe Hindemith had been active as an orchestral conductor not only of his own works, but increasingly of those of other composers. The fact that European countries showed more willingness than America to accept him in this capacity was, as we shall later see, a consideration in his decision to make his permanent home in Switzerland.

He was, it is said, in the middle of a class at Yale when he was handed a telegram from Wagner's grandsons, Wieland and Wolfgang, inviting him to conduct a performance of Beethoven's Ninth Symphony at the third post-war festival in Bayreuth in the summer of 1953. Hindemith, having read the telegram, asked his pupils to guess the two very important people who had asked him to visit them. The students suggested all the names they could think of up to and including the president of the United States. At each name Hindemith shook his head, until one of the students said in exasperation: "God Almighty." "You're getting nearer," Hindemith replied, and showed them the telegram from Bayreuth.

With his sensitivity about being used by others for their own purposes, he would surely have refused the invitation if he had known that Wieland Wagner had deliberately chosen him because he was a non-Wagnerian whose appearance at the shrine would shock the opponents of the new production style he had introduced there. However, if a scandal was intended, none ensued. I myself saw Hindemith at the customary press conference in the theatre during that festival. A small, thickset figure with a pink complexion and remarkably blue eyes, he sat in patient silence between the two provocative young Wagner grandsons. To the best of my recollection he was asked no questions and spoke hardly a word throughout.

From Bayreuth the Hindemiths went to Switzerland to establish themselves in their new home. Maurice Zermatten recalls in the *Revue Musicale de Suisse Romande* of June 1973: "They had not forgotten the Valais region, which had been their first refuge. They dreamed now of owning a house there, where they could be by themselves, very quiet, very comfortable, with plenty of surrounding acres. . . . All their Valaisan friends went looking for a place which must be at one and the same time on a main road, in the vicinity of an airport, if possible within easy reach of a church or cathedral (for Gertrud), and utterly silent, isolated among woods, not far from a lake. Such a place could be found, could it not?"

For all Zermatten's affectionate irony, it was in fact found very soon at Blonay, near Vévey on the Lake of Geneva. A large and not very handsome villa, it stood in a large garden on a steep wooded slope, with magnificent views across the village to the lake and the mountains beyond. In a letter to Osea Noss in New Haven, dated 14 December 1953, Gertrud described the

move, which took place during the summer, after they had made
the joyful discovery that their possessions, stored in Berlin since
1937 and given up for lost, had survived virtually intact.
Gertrud wrote in English, and the occasional mistakes and mis-
spellings are her own:

"On moving day trucks started coming up the hill from all
corners of the earth. The trucks containing our old Berlin things
were first, and things were unloaded which made me burn with
shame and frustration. From huge linoleum-ruins and old
water-pipes to ruined and half-broken kitchen-furniture, it
came out in an avalanche of surprises. But then came some nice
things too and—strange enough—all our antique furniture,
some allready 300 years old, had kept best of all. We had so
many men in and around the house that day, that we could not
count them! At 10 the American Express came with the Ship-
ment from Alden Ave. All in all, it will give you an idea, if I
tell you that 85 bottles of beer (the bottles here are double size!)
were consumated that great day.

"The next days were spent unearthing a long-forgotten past.
We tried to recognize people and ourselves on pictures or to
identify entirely forgotten objects!

"We unpacked cases for weeks. The Villa, which I thought
much too big for us, is filled to the roof! I have not seen half of
all the books and music in the library.

"We had barely made the house liveable, when time came to
go to Zurich and find an apartment there. Again advertising
and round-trips to view all sorts of city-dwellings. We decided
to take a tiny sort of a doll-house, belonging to an American
couple of Swiss descent, which comes here every year and rents
for the winter-months. So now I am sitting here in that 3-room
dwelling, feeling like snowwhite in the dwarf's house. . . ."

Hindemith's comment on their new home at Blonay, given
in a letter to Willy Strecker dated 7 October 1953, is less
dramatic but equally contented: "It is a real pleasure to have
all one's things around one again after so many long years. Of
course there is still a lot of work to be done until everything is in
good order, but it is fun too doing that."

They saw the villa at Blonay as a place of retreat where they
would be out of reach of the world at large. They insisted, even
to their closest friends, that all letters should be addressed
simply *Vévey*, *poste restante*. And when Oscar Cox unthinkingly

passed on the house address to a gramophone company, he received a very sharp reproach from Gertrud, who instructed Cox to inform the gramophone company that they had since moved away from the address he had given. The few friends who were invited there often had difficulty in finding the house: it was screened from the road by a line of trees, and even the entrance gate was all but invisible.

However, the pattern of their life was such that for long periods each year the house remained empty. When he was working at Zurich University, where as in Berlin and Yale he held continuous classes with his students, they lived in the little apartment in Zurich (Resedastrasse 20). And now, as she had seldom done in their younger days, Gertrud accompanied her husband when he travelled to fulfil his concert engagements.

Hindemith's first weeks of solitude in the new house were devoted to *A Composer's World*, which he was himself translating into German. His main musical task was the revision of *Neues vom Tage* for a production at the Teatro San Carlo in Naples. In undertaking it, he was yielding to the opera house's insistence and to Gertrud's persuasions: his own inclination was to refuse to allow the work to be revived. Having now given in, he resolved to remove the notorious bath scene, thus goading Willy Strecker into vigorous protest: "It made the work famous. It would be like *Lohengrin* without the swan."

Since Schiffer was now dead, Hindemith commissioned another librettist (Hans Weigel) to rewrite the text, but dissatisfied with the result (in which Gertrud claimed to have had a hand), he then decided to do it himself. As he told the Strecker brothers, it was not only the text which required revision: "It is clear from the start that the vocal line would have to be altered entirely (though the orchestral part can remain unchanged), for the exaggerated floridity of the old version was one of the main reasons why the opera has never been more than a moderate success: it was stylistically at odds with the light-hearted story."

Neither with the production in Naples on 7 April 1954 (conducted by himself) nor with the revisions he made for it was he finally content, and before he released the revised score for publication (the vocal line simplified as promised) he made further alterations. His work on *Neues vom Tage* can, however, hardly be placed in the same category as his previous revisions of *Das Marienleben* or *Cardillac*. Those had been attempts to get closer, with the help of his improved technical skill, to the lightning flash vision of his first conception. His alterations to *Neues vom Tage* were simply efforts to improve the stage-worthiness of a work which he once described to Cox as "a harmless and funny comedy".

In his final revision Hindemith did not eliminate the famous bath, but merely changed its occupant. It is Hermann, the professional co-respondent, who is now discovered there, and not Laura, the heroine. Since the outcome is the same, there seems little point in the change, except the personal satisfaction Hindemith may have felt in killing a bogy that had so painfully influenced the course of his life. A more important change was his decision to allow his married couple, Eduard and Laura, who in the original version had kept their desire for a divorce alive to the very end, to repent half-way through. This gave him the opportunity to inject some genuine emotion into the brittle story and to demonstrate that human love can persist in a world of cheap sensationalism. The new ending, as Eduard and Laura depart together, leaving the press reporters and showmen to re-enact their legend with a substitute married couple, gives the work more body and a clearer moral message. But, since so much of Schiffer's text and all the original music is retained, the revised *Neues vom Tage* remains a fragile work.

Visits in June 1954 to Vienna to supervise a production of Monteverdi's *Orfeo* in an arrangement of his own and to Oxford in July to receive an honorary degree were other engagements which kept him away from his home before in August he set off to South America on an extensive conducting tour which lasted almost to the end of the year. Somehow he found time before leaving to take some lessons in Spanish. Gertrud, who travelled with him, wrote a lively account of the highlights of their tour in a letter to Osea Noss from Lisbon on 1 December 1954:

"We landed here last week, after a nice trip on a British ship, the *Alcantara* of Royal Mail. The boat old-fashioned and no crazy luxury like on the italian liners. But social life very friendly and even amusing. We were again listed as Mr and Mrs Paul and had a wonderful rest from music-talkers and concert-goers. . . .

"He had great success, wherever he went, and the musicians of the orchestras seemed always happy to work with him. In

Bogota first, discipline was entirely absent, he scolded them like a furious papa his children and all sorts of things came out— that they were underpaid, had not enough light to see, etc., etc., so Paul went with some of them to the government-officer in charge and plans were made for improvement. At the last concert they presented to Paul a wonderful 'Poncho', a shepherd's wool-coat, to be thrown over the head. They earnestly suggested he should walk out on the stage with it to bow!

"The last weeks we spent in Sao Paolo and Rio, concerts with the orquestta brasileira, it was highly worth while to go through all those experiences and see this new mighty world. Now we are tired of noise—and spitting. You have no idea what and how people are spitting around all day, wherever you go and stand. Even the nicest looking people spit over your shoulders without so much as saying hola! Out of taxi windows and house-fronts it goes criss cross and you have to be mighty virtuoso not to get hit. . . ."

They were shocked on their return from South America to read in a Portuguese newspaper of the death of Wilhelm Furt-wängler, which had occurred in Baden-Baden on 30 November 1954. "Although we did not see each other often," Gertrud wrote in her letter to Osea Noss, "we had lived almost 30 years of dramatic life together and he was a great man and friend, nothing can replace him."

The sympathy that had existed between these outwardly so dissimilar men had survived all occasional difficulties and differences of opinion. On Furtwängler's side that is reflected in a letter he wrote to Hindemith on 5 May 1952 after reading the Hamburg lecture on Bach and a newspaper account of the lecture on musical inspiration (similar to that described in the chapter on *A Composer's World*), which he had given in Zurich. "The writer and thinker has now come to join the composer," Furtwängler wrote, "and has given me the joyous sense of perfect understanding and agreement, of starting out from the same or at least very similar principles in regard to the most essential matters." A few months later, on 11 December 1952, he wrote again after conducting the *Harmonie der Welt* Symphony in Berlin: "I think you would have been satisfied with the performance. The longer we worked on it, the more pleasure

the orchestra and I myself in particular derived from it. To me
it seems to be the best of all your orchestral works so far, even if
on account of its length it makes great demands on the
audience."

Hindemith's view of Furtwängler was expressed in his
contribution to the memorial volume published in 1955
(*Wilhelm Furtwängler im Urteil seiner Zeit*):

"What distinguished him from all the rest was the utter
integrity of his approach to music, an integrity of Brucknerian
proportions. Even his critics knew that, from the moment he
raised his baton, it was the soul of the music alone which spoke
to us—through him, its medium. . . . He possessed the great
secret of proportion. Just as he was able to present phrases,
themes, sections, movements, whole symphonies and programmes as artistic unities, so too was his whole musical being
dominated by this feeling for harmonious relations. I got to
know him early—in 1919—and, even though he sometimes
chided me in a friendly way for getting too much involved in
compositional experiments (or what he then considered to be
such), I nevertheless was always aware of his sense of the proportions of a work and its potentialities in performance. This
was often enough in later years to stand me in good stead, even
if I sometimes tended to dismiss as a conductor's foibles things
which were in reality proof of his genuine and deep concern for
music.

"This same concern, this same sense of proportion, were
later, in the Hitler period, to lead him into fighting on behalf of
persecuted musicians at a time when everybody else had given
up the fight as hopeless and he stood in danger of becoming a
Don Quixote. It must surely have been this quality of caring
that drove him to embrace the outwardly successful but still
ephemeral career of a conductor, instead of devoting himself
entirely to composition, which was his more cherished ambition...

"The urge that possessed him . . . was a deep faith in the
essential truth of beauty, which enabled him to transform musical experiences into divine revelations. A man who can do that
is more than a conductor, more than a composer and more than
a pianist—he is quite simply a truly great musician and human
being."

It was true, as Hindemith here remarks, that Furtwängler had
longed to achieve recognition as a composer. He once showed

the score of his Symphonic Concerto for Piano and Orchestra (first performed in 1937) to Hindemith, who told him: "It is a great work. But no one will believe it if you don't stop conducting."

It was an accurate observation which, in reverse order, Hindemith now saw applied to himself. In taking up what was virtually a new career as a conductor, he found a marked reluctance to take him seriously. If by sheer persistence (and with the help of his agents, Walter Schulthess in Europe and Arthur Judson in America) he managed in the ensuing years to secure frequent engagements to conduct Bach or Mozart or Bruckner (even Max Reger), he never quite overcame the scepticism of the critics. He was not a conductor of Furt-wängler's inspirational sort. He was mainly concerned with establishing that the notes were in the right place and allowing the music to speak for itself. However much orchestral players might profess to loathe conductors who lecture them (as Hinde-mith himself in his younger days had loathed Mengelberg), they tend to distrust even more a conductor who says little in rehearsal.

One may well wonder why Hindemith so late in life took up this new activity which used up so much of the time he had hoped to devote to composing. One reason may have been his dislike of star conductors (with the exception of Furtwängler) and a desire to show them how things should be done. Another reason (the one he himself usually gave) was the need to earn money.

The true reason was certainly much more complex and had very much to do with his dual nationality. It emerges clearly from his correspondence with his American friends (and particularly with Oscar Cox, a poet as well as his lawyer) that he saw conducting as a way of keeping a foot in both Europe and America simultaneously. His decision to use Europe rather than America as a base from which to work was based on practical financial considerations. But, as the rather depressed tone of his letter to Cox, written (in English) at Blonay on 13 April 1955, shows, he was conscious that things were not working out quite as he had envisaged them:

"There is no doubt that I have to be in Europe. My two main activities are composing and concertizing (I hope to get rid of any university duties after the current term), both of which I cannot do in the States: for composing there would not be any time left over, as for making a living one is obliged to have a college job—and this, as I had amply time to find out, is practically the end of composing, not to mention the rather hopeless situation of a music teacher whose only obligation seems to be to produce hundreds of mediocre students, write again hundreds of recommendations for them each year and as for highlights in his career waits for a Guggenheim or other fellowship every second or third year. As for conducting, the situation is more than hopeless, as the conductors in the USA more than anywhere else are a kind of brotherhood worse than those of the locomotive engineers': they prevent any outsider to come into their realm.

"Here in Europe with the cost of living still reasonably low and travel distances short, I have plenty of concerts (next year's season is already taken care of) and once I have no more university work I can finally come down and write all those things I wanted to write since years. I hate travelling around, but here I can keep travelling a relatively minor affair and concentrate on the main business. Another point is artistical reputation. Here I am a famous man (whatever that means— but it is part of a musician's existence) while in America in spite of the many students scattered all over the country I was just one of many teachers and nothing else. That beside that I did some composing as a side line, was recognised, to be sure, but what does that mean in face of all the native talent that has to be taken care of and pampered—there is hardly such a thing as free competition, except in a very small way, as far as solo or chamber music playing goes. The best proof for this statement are your clippings which you sent on so kindly. What do they show? Mostly performances of minor importance, never an opera, almost never a symphonic piece—of course one may think they are not worthy of being performed, but over here one thinks differently and I think a musician cannot be blamed if he grasps one of the few chances that life can possibly give him.

"How this American non-reputation works in other countries I told you many times when I wrote you about the situation in South America. Here in Europe it is no better. In Cologne the other day the Bundes President came over from Bonn (as I wrote you); pleasant as it was to have him there it was rather embarrassing not to see any of the Americans, not even a third-rate cultural attaché, and it would have been a fine and cheap opportunity to show some interest, and claim that the successful conductor was something American. Same in London: I had an extremely spectacular concert with the Royal Philharmonics in the new Festival Hall—nobody showed up (besides the sold-out hall!). I am sure you understand: I do not complain, and basically I am glad if beyond concert duties I do not have additional social obligations. I mention these things just as further illustration to my statement that I am forced to do my work here in Europe.

"When I left the States I thought it would be easy to have four or five concerts each year to make annual returns worth while. Last year not even two of them showed up so that the travel expenses would have been higher than the income. Now with the AMP's proposition for next year (I wrote you about), which I thought would be a basis for a trip overseas, it seems to have faded out like McArthur's old generals: nothing any more after the first fanfare."

Clearly Hindemith felt himself rejected by his American compatriots, and the pain that caused him was to sour his out-look on life for quite a while to come, as we shall see. It is perhaps not too speculative to assume that the persistence with which he pursued his conducting career in Europe, to the possible detriment of his creative work, was due to the hope that his success in Europe would eventually shame the American "brotherhood" of conductors into offering him engagements.

His financial situation was not really such as to cause him concern. Royalties from sales and performances of his existing works brought him a substantial income, and there was an eager market for anything new he might write. Yet curiously it never seemed to occur to him that time spent on composing was always likely to bring him in as much money as the same time spent on conducting or teaching. Even the award of Finland's Sibelius Prize ("after the Nobel one the highest available one," he wrote to Cox on 23 April 1955, "and for the poor musicians the only one of greatest international fame") could not convince him that his financial worries were ground-less. The prize was worth something like 30,000 dollars tax-free —a sum equivalent to more than three years' salary at Yale or Zurich. The only conclusion one can draw is that Hindemith and his wife were so scarred by the very real poverty of their earlier years that they had become permanently suspicious of the workings of Fate.

Whatever the truth of the matter, the fact remained that two years after his return to Europe Hindemith had still made no progress with his Kepler opera. As far as compositions were concerned, the year 1955 brought only the completion of the Claudel cantata, *Ite, angeli veloces* (first performed in Wuppertal on 4 June under the composer's direction); the final revisions of *Neues vom Tage*; a sonata for tuba and piano, with which he filled in the last gap in his series; and two little songs to words by Cox, a friendly expression of gratitude for his lawyer's indefatigable aid in sorting out his income tax problems.

On 16 November of that year Hindemith reached his sixtieth birthday. In a letter to Luther and Osea Noss dated 31 December 1955, Gertrud described it as "a really harassing experience, although we fled everything and refused all official festivities. We were haunted in our mountains by hundreds of telegrams and letters and greetings of all kinds. I decorated all our walls with them."

His publishers used the occasion to prepare a little book, *Zeugnis in Bildern* (English title: *Testimony in Pictures*), recording his whole life in a series of photographs, documents, press cuttings and musical quotations. The book can scarcely be called a biography—the Strecker brothers were too well aware of Hindemith's attitude towards that to make any such attempt —but it certainly revealed more about his private and public life than anything so far published. Well meant as it was, it eventually caused its editors (who included Gertrud) more pain than pleasure, with Hindemith in his present touchy mood. During the preparation he raised objections, complained of negligence on the part of the editorial staff at Schott's and ultimately, confronted with the final proofs, forbade its publication. Willy Strecker had to plead with him, pointing out that, if the book had flaws, he should remember that nothing in this world was perfect. "I am truly sorry," he added, "that so nice a thought should cause such difficulties." Only then did Hindemith's better nature prevail, and he allowed the book to appear, though not without a last sour jibe: he did not wish, he said, to have it said of him that he was a "grouchy old man" (he used the English words) trying to hinder "the deeds of talented youth". There must really have been some irrational element in

Hindemith's attitude to the circumstances of his life so to make him forget his sense of humour.

Hindemith had always been remarkably healthy, his occasional ailments being of only a minor nature. The possibility of something more serious arose when during a conducting engagement in Frankfurt in February 1956 he was laid low by internal pains. However, an X-ray examination failed to reveal the suspected appendicitis or kidney-stones. He would gladly, Gertrud wrote to Cox, have cancelled his tour of Japan with the Vienna Philharmonic Orchestra in April, but was unwilling to let them down. A plan to record the opera *Mathis der Maler* under the composer's direction, for which Walter Legge had already engaged soloists and orchestra, had however to be cancelled.

During the tour of Japan, which occupied the whole of April, Hindemith conducted works of other composers as well as his own. It was a successful tour, Gertrud told Cox on their return to Blonay, their only complaint being that the American Embassy there had ignored them entirely. "Paul's health is very good, in Japan I was worried, but the change of clima[te] did wonders and he overcame it all very well. . . . Now gardening and composing fill his time to the brim, and I am playing dragon to chase away the 37248000 visitors from all lands who want to 'look us up'. We plan to have a drawbridge built soon, over a deep, deep moat."

Hindemith was at last working on his opera based on the life of Johannes Kepler, the seventeenth-century German astronomer from whose book *De harmonia mundi* he took his title, *Die Harmonie der Welt*. Possibly his illness earlier in the year may have helped to remind him that time was running out. At his request Zurich University freed him from his class commitments, and he temporarily cut down his conducting engagements.

As during the writing of *Mathis der Maler*, he immersed himself entirely in his work and left the daily correspondence to Gertrud. On 28 May she wrote to Willy Strecker that he was working hard on the text and hoped in fourteen days to start the music. But then, dissatisfied with the text, he decided to try it out on his publishers before beginning composition. He read it out to the assembled staff in the handsome room in the

Schott building in Mainz in which Wagner had once read his
text of *Die Meistersinger* to their predecessors. Afterwards Willy
Strecker made a few tactful criticisms, directed mainly towards
introducing more human warmth into the action. Gertrud
replied that her husband had himself become conscious during
the reading of several weaknesses and was now busy rewriting.

On 13 August she reported: "Paul has not allowed himself a
single day of leisure and has been working without pause on the
revision of the draft. . . . The characters have emerged from
their sometimes rather stereotyped form and are now living,
convincing, humanly interesting. The work has been difficult
because he has had at times to write scenes to fit the existing
Harmonie music [i.e. the symphony]. But this has the advantage
that a lot of the music is already written." He was going to
Lucerne in a few days to conduct a concert. "After the concert
we have reserved September and October exclusively for the
work, so that NOTHING will disturb him and he will certainly
make great progress with the composition. He is so looking
forward to writing the notes!!"

By the end of October, however, he had completed only half
the opera, having been held up for a while by illness. In November he conducted a concert in Hanover and then went to
London to make some gramophone recordings. On their return
Gertrud wrote to Strecker: "Thank God we now have a week
free before going to Vienna. The music he can do anywhere
without difficulty—it's only when he has to work on the text
that he needs complete peace."

The exhausting round continued well into 1957 with a radio
recording of *Cardillac* in Vienna, a performance of *Das Unaufhörliche* in Berlin and concerts in Germany and Italy. "Paul is
working non-stop on the Wallenstein act," wrote Gertrud from
Osnabrück in February 1957. "I am downright glad when
rehearsals intervene, for they force him to take at least a bit of
exercise." Only at the end of May, ten weeks before the
scheduled first performance in Munich, was the opera at last
completed.

Perhaps part of the blame for the lukewarm reception of
Die Harmonie der Welt at that first performance in the Prinz-
regententheater on 11 August 1957 could be ascribed to the
scenery by Helmut Jürgens which Gertrud, in a letter to Ludwig
Strecker, held to be responsible for a certain lack of clarity. But

it seems unfair to ascribe the failure to one ingredient alone. It was a factor of at least equal importance that Hindemith had left Rudolf Hartmann as producer and himself as conductor far too little time to prepare adequately a work of this complexity. That it was overlong he himself acknowledged by making cuts. Whether much of the music is uninteresting, as even some of Hindemith's supporters claim, is of course a matter of opinion, but the circumstances under which a good deal of it was written, in hotels and dressing-rooms, suggest that it would not be surprising if this were so. Hindemith may indeed have relied on his technical facility more than was perhaps wise for a work of this importance. Whatever the cause, the publishers found themselves in the unusual and distressing position of having to comfort the composer. Ludwig Strecker wrote: "In point of fact a work like this should only be done at a festival like Bayreuth before a relaxed audience." Willy Strecker pinned his hopes on the second production in Bremen: "For the success of *Cardillac* too Wiesbaden was the deciding factor, not Dresden."

Hindemith himself took the disappointment calmly and indeed claimed in a letter to Cox that the work had been a great success with the audience. "To the German press the whole thing was rather an unexpected affair, and consequently they were baffled."

Happily the production in Bremen, which took place in November, and with which Hindemith himself had nothing to do, was indeed a success. There were fifty curtain calls at the first performance, and after that a succession of sold-out houses. Nonetheless, *Die Harmonie der Welt* cannot be said to have established itself, and the reason is easy to see: it has neither the dramatic economy of *Cardillac* (first version) nor the human appeal of *Mathis der Maler*. Yet in its much more remote way it is as personal a statement as either of these.

In Johannes Kepler Hindemith found a historical figure with whom he could identify himself on a philosophical level in the same way that he identified himself on an artistic level with Matthias Grünewald. Kepler's belief in the existence of an over-all cosmic harmony was, like Hindemith's own, based on musical conceptions. Hindemith shows him striving against the turbulent background of the Thirty Years War to put his beliefs to the task of rescuing humanity from its miseries. He dies, disillusioned. The final scene of the opera brings together all the

Chapter 4

1958–62:

DISCORD AND RECONCILIATION

In the winter of 1957–58 Hindemith paid a visit to England, where he took part in the Hallé Orchestra's centenary celebrations in Manchester and neighbouring towns. "The concerts were very pleasant," he wrote to Cox, "but with snow storms, dirt and general English winter conditions we got all H.R.M.'s Mid England coal dust, bleakness, and grippe bacilli into our lungs, brains and stomachs, so that on the way back we came down with a pretty nice sickness."

In January 1958 he went to Kassel to prepare a new production of the revised *Cardillac* (in his opinion the only *Cardillac*: he gave instructions to his publishers to tell all enquirers that the earlier version no longer existed). And on 24 February he sent Willy Strecker the manuscript of his new Octet. "A useful piece," he wrote, "though on account of its nature and form no world-shattering event. Still, there has been no piece since Schubert's Octet which the many existing more-than-quartet chamber music ensembles might like to put in their programmes."

A few days later Willy Strecker died suddenly at the age of seventy-four. At the funeral ceremony in Mainz Hindemith played the viola. "It was some slight consolation to me," he wrote to Ludwig Strecker on 9 March, "that you all found my poor playing appropriate for Willy's burial. If it had only not been for such a sad occasion!" To Cox in Washington he wrote: "His death was a great shock for us. I knew him since 39 years and my collaboration with him and Schott's was always pleasant and fruitful. He was a real friend who even in adverse circumstances (and we had plenty of those at one time!) acted as such. We miss him. . . ."

It was a typically restrained tribute to the man who had undoubtedly been the greatest friend of his whole life. If anybody ever took Willy Strecker's place as a confidant it was Oscar Cox. All Hindemith's friendships were based to a greater or lesser extent on his professional interests, and what Willy Strecker had been with regard to his activities in Europe, Cox had now become, though in his different capacity as lawyer, in connection with the United States. He attended not only to publishing contracts and taxation affairs, but also the far more vital question of Hindemith's American citizenship. Regulations laid down that a naturalised American had to spend a certain amount of time in the United States. Should he be continuously absent for a period of five years, citizenship would lapse.

The danger point was now coming perilously close: in June 1958 the Hindemiths would have been five years without setting foot in America. Opportunities had not been entirely lacking: Noss, who became dean of the Yale School of Music a year after their departure, was anxious to have him back on any terms, but Hindemith persistently refused to entertain the idea of a return to teaching (he had finally given up his appointment at Zurich in 1956). Isolated offers to conduct (from William Steinberg in Pittsburgh and Leonard Bernstein in New York) were refused—either as "insulting", because they were restricted to his own works, or as insufficiently rewarding financially. Hindemith was quite aware that he was being difficult, but his pride would not allow him to shape his activities to suit bureaucratic requirements. Having steadfastly and at great cost to himself resisted the Nazis, he had no intention now of seeking to ingratiate himself with the Americans.

"I was fourteen years in America and did my best to collaborate in the development of American music," he wrote to Cox. "Nobody ever bothered to call me an American musician, I always remained for them a foreigner, although I even wrote the piece that in due time . . . may well become one of the few musical treasures of the nation (*When Lilacs* . . .) . . . I am afraid I shall never change my mind, and if stubbornness of this kind prevents me from being regarded an asset for American culture, I cannot help it and must prefer to travel with a stateless passport, as do so many other artists."

Fortunately for him, Cox was not only a resourceful friend, but a very influential lawyer in Washington, and he cut through all the emotional and bureaucratic difficulties by going straight to the American Secretary of State, John Foster Dulles. Enumerating the great services Hindemith had rendered their nation, both at home and abroad, he suggested to Dulles that so eminent and deserving a citizen ought not to be lost to the United States on a mere technicality. Dulles took the point and immediately arranged for Hindemith to be granted honorary citizenship, which freed him from the domiciliary regulations.

Even this rare honour did not finally persuade the Hindemiths that their acceptance by the Americans was complete. He had been commissioned by Steinberg to write a symphony for Pittsburgh's bicentennial celebrations early in 1959 and had agreed to conduct the first performance. It was to be his first appearance in America for five years, yet apart from the Pittsburgh engagement there was nothing in prospect beyond a concert in Waterville, Maine (on the invitation of a former pupil).

He was particularly upset to find that New Haven had nothing to offer him. Luther and Osea Noss came to Switzerland on holiday in the summer of 1958 and looked forward to visiting their old friends in their home at Blonay. Instead, they found a box of chocolates awaiting them at their hotel and attached to it a note from Gertrud, regretting that she and her husband were too busy to see them. And in her usual Christmas letter that year Gertrud was decidedly chilly:

"The fact that we will return without Yale in our program might lead to a misleading interpretation. It has been already said, that Paul 'did not want to go back' or had no 'interest any more to see his old school again'. This is all very silly and embarrassing. You would both do us great justice and favour, if you could answer possible questions with the truth: that Paul was willing, but that nothing could be arranged. . . . We will be passing through New Haven for a few hours, I guess, we might meet, if you are not too busy. But any social affair Paul will decline, you know he hates them . . ."

The autumn of 1958 was filled with concert engagements in Europe. On 23 September the Octet was given its first performance at the Berlin festival, and Hindemith played one of the viola parts himself. On 18 October his newest work, the *Twelve Madrigals* on texts by Josef Weinheber for five unaccompanied voices, was performed in Vienna under the composer's direction, and in November he conducted a performance of *Die Harmonie der Welt* at the Munich Opera. After that he went to London to conduct a performance of Beethoven's Ninth

Symphony. "There was a positive outcry against Hindemith's Beethoven," Rayner Heppenstall wrote in his autobiography. On the other hand his former pupil, Arnold Cooke, thought the performance quite effective. He described it as "an early eighteenth-century view of the work, practical and without apocalyptical climaxes".

By the time the Hindemiths took ship for America (travelling incognito as usual) his programme looked a little fuller, with concerts in New York and Washington to add to Pittsburgh and Waterville. There was obvious curiosity there whether his prolonged absence had changed him, and Kurt Stone found him a very different person. "He seemed to want to be treated as a great man," he told me. As far as the general public was concerned, Stone added, Hindemith was now virtually forgotten, and the press reviews of his concerts were frequently critical.

Relations were not much better in Pittsburgh. The city dignitaries and their wives who assembled on 31 January 1959 to hear the new symphony were joined, at Hindemith's express request, by a group of Pennsylvanian Dutch dressed in their ancient folk costumes. In his symphony (a work which belongs in character more to the extrovert compositions of his American period than to the introspective style of his final years) he had included variations on an old Pennsylvanian Dutch folksong, and in his programme note he remarked that this ethnological group spoke a German dialect rather similar to his own and shared habits and customs with which he was familiar in Germany. The work, he suggested, might help to remind Pennsylvanians of the significant part played in the early pioneer days of their state by Germans. This well-meant attempt to improve German–American relations came probably a little too soon after the war, and the symphony had hardly more than a polite reception.

With Gertrud, Hindemith paid a short private visit to New Haven, where neither the Nosses nor the Donovans proved too busy to see them. There was no explicit reconciliation, Osea Noss told me, and the absence of a concert in New Haven was not even mentioned. But Luther Noss was quick to make amends for the town's failure on this occasion by offering an engagement on behalf of the university in the following year.

That, though it restored their good relations personally, did not entirely dispel Hindemith's suspicion that America had not yet really accepted them back. From Blonay Gertrud wrote to Osea Noss on 17 April 1959 that he was determined to find "something really special" for the Yale concert next year. "But: he also begs Luther to give up the whole plan, if ever he would feel anything like a resistance or opposition within the younger (!) faculty." The same touchiness is evident in Gertrud's response only a few days later (30 April) to Cox's proposal of a ceremonial performance of the Requiem in Washington: "Oscar, do not force this idea of 'Congress' for the Requiem. So many American composers have written similar things (American Creed, Gettysburg Address, etc., etc.), the jealousy would be terrible."

During 1959 Hindemith began to widen his conducting repertoire by including a number of contemporary works in his programmes, among them compositions by Bartók, Berg and Petrassi. He himself composed little in this year, only adding four more to the series of motets for solo voice and piano which he had begun in America in 1940.

During a strenuous tour of Scandinavia in the late summer and autumn of 1959 he experienced a sudden mental collapse. During a rehearsal in Oslo he turned to the leader of the orchestra with the remark: "I don't know where I am." Gertrud, who had not been at the rehearsal, found him in his room at the hotel when she returned for lunch, a doctor in attendance. "He was sitting in an armchair like a child with wide open enormous blue eyes and tried to find out where he was and what he was doing," she told Cox in a letter dated 28 September. "Fortunately he recognized me and was happy when I came. So I threw them all out, doctor inclusive, and tried to bring him to bed and give him to eat. But these two hours I shall never forget. He kept asking me and slowly he reconstructed the pattern." But he was never able to remember the rehearsal at which the collapse took place.

The doctors could find no organic disorders, so it was put down simply to overwork.

The second tour of the United States began in February 1960 with the concert in New Haven. The programme, chosen by himself, included Gabrieli's *Symphoniae Sacrae*, some of his own madrigals and Stravinsky's *Symphonie des Psaumes*, which (as Gertrud told Noss) "Paul thinks is an inspiring work to study for an intelligent student body".

Still cautious of their reception, they refused all invitations to live with their friends and booked rooms at the large Hotel Taft in New Haven. They soon found that their fears were baseless. Yale welcomed them with sincere warmth. From New York Gertrud wrote gratefully to the Nosses: "We had a glorious week in every respect—humanly, musically, spiritually, emotionally—and it was good to be back. I never would have thought that grim old Taft Hotel could be a magic place of delight!"

Among the people Hindemith met during that visit to Yale was Thornton Wilder, the novelist and dramatist. It was not their first meeting, for Wilder had been living in New Haven for many years. However, they had not been close friends. Hindemith seized the opportunity (as he usually did when he met a writer of note) to ask Wilder to suggest ideas for an opera. Wilder, who told me how much he had been impressed by Hindemith's wide knowledge of literature, could not recall whether the idea of using his own play *The Long Christmas Dinner* came from himself or from Hindemith. Whichever way it was, this story of a New England family, portrayed over several generations at the traditional Christmas feast, took immediate hold of his imagination. He asked Wilder to prepare a libretto.

Returning to Switzerland after successful concerts in New York, Chicago and Washington, he at once set to work on drawing up a detailed musical plan for the opera, which he sent to Wilder on 14 May 1960 as a guide for preparing the libretto. This, together with part of the subsequent correspondence between them, is reproduced in *Paul Hindemith: Die letzten Jahre.* Wilder, always a deliberate worker, found difficulty in keeping up with Hindemith's brisk pace. "I am very ashamed at the slowness with which I have forwarded these instalments," he wrote on 3 August 1960, "but the honor of working with the Maestro has enhanced a psychological difficulty I have had all my life: the inability to write *finis*, to part with material 'forever'. I am filled with the hope that if I held it longer I could 'find' some turns of phrase that would suit you better." Another letter written on 1 September emphasises his dilemma: "Hoher Herr!

How rapidly you work—but that is in the great tradition. I love that story about Schubert: 'Franzl, how is it that you are able to write so much?' 'Well—when I finish one thing, I begin another.' "

Nevertheless, at length the work was done. Hindemith completed the opera on 23 August 1960 without waiting for Wilder to write *finis* to his part of it. The author, however, gave him retrospective authority. "Of course, I concede anything you would wish," he wrote on 1 September.

The Long Christmas Dinner lasts only an hour in performance, and therefore requires a companion piece, which Hindemith asked Wilder to supply. Wilder replied: "I shall review and probe a few themes I had long in my notebooks and might furnish what we are looking for." Thus, anyway, did Gertrud quote him in her letter to Cox dated 15 January 1961. She added: "Well, we try to be serene and patient. I'm sure there is nobody today more suited to work with Paul than Wilder. But he seems to have life everlasting."

His hopes that Wilder would eventually come on a suitable idea did not prevent Hindemith from approaching other writers, among them Eugène Ionesco, Peter Ustinov and Edith Sitwell. To her he wrote from Blonay on 12 May 1961: "Would you not be interested to write a sort of one act musical comedy? I am always looking out for librettos of this kind, and it would be wonderful if an opera could be created without the usual operatic nonsense—perhaps in the spirit of your 'English (or any other) Eccentrics'."

Dame Edith responded at once with a scenario, and his comments on this (preserved, together with the previous letter, in the British Museum) is worth quoting at length for the light it throws on Hindemith's views on operatic composition. It is dated 12 June 1961:

"I considered and reconsidered your suggestions of a libretto derived from your splendid account of Carlyle's domestic sufferings, and I hope you will not be too cross with me if I voice some doubts as to the feasibility of this theme. The charming essence of your narrative is, of course, that we know: here is a great man, with whose achievements as a historian and philosopher we are acquainted, and that now we see him in incongruent and unexpectedly a[w]kward situations. This contrast can hardly be shown in a short opera—nothing can be implied;

Carlyle would, for instance, have to clear the situation by saying (singing): 'I am Th. C. who wrote about heroship etc, etc' or something to that effect, which would neither dramatically nor musically be interesting, and it would need some weighty development. So we would merely see a queer and grouchy old anonym whose peculiarities appear magnified and made disproportionally important by the music. This would probably have a rather distressing effect, the more as one would find it somewhat disrespectful towards the memory of a great man. Furthermore, music as a highly stylized and elevated form of acoustical manifestations (even if it is used as a comical means of expression) can hardly serve as a vehicle transmitting low-grade acoustical facts, as noises, crashes, crowing, and barking of dogs etc—they cannot be stylized and therefore would be in uncouth contradiction to the musical organism. Another weakness of the piece would be, that in a sequence of scenes only one single trick, e.g. the reaction of a neurotic towards external vexations, would be the contents of the piece. Although by some technical means a more convincing arrangement of this could be found and other scenes could, as you suggested, be interspersed (Mrs Carlyle's death, etc.), the question remains if that warrants the employment of singers and at least 30 musicians.

"Now you will probably think: P.H. is an old fastidious, wise-cracking bore, worse than Mr Carlyle as shown in the 'Eccentrics', with whom no collaboration is desirable—but with the same fastidiousness I have the faint hope that you will have some further suggestions. If so, please don't think of any music or of acoustical effects, but only of visual action; the musician will find out how music can be amalgamated with it, and for this some very sketchy notes only are necessary at the beginning . . ."

Since nothing was forthcoming, either from Edith Sitwell or from anyone else that fired his creative imagination, Hindemith did little composing in 1961, apart from making a few alterations in existing scores for new performances: *Neues vom Tage* in Mannheim in June and *Cardillac* in Hamburg in October. Unable, it seems, to leave any work of his untouched for long, he also added eight extra bars to *Nobilissima Visione*.

Otherwise his time was filled with conducting engagements, in England and Italy as well as in Germany, and from July to

September he was again in America, where besides conducting the Chicago Symphony Orchestra in three concerts, he directed the first American performance of *Neues vom Tage* in the open-air theatre at Santa Fé in New Mexico. It was presented in English under the title *News of the Day*. "The theater," Gertrud wrote to Cox from the La Fonda hotel in Santa Fé on 14 August 1961, "is completely exposed to weather and wind, bugs and other insects. The opening night went beautifully until a cloudburst of super-violence set an end to the show in the middle of it, drenching audience, conductor, singers, stage in an ocean of furious waters. The heroic people stood on—under hoods and umbrellas, shouting 'bravo, bravo, more, more,' etc etc. Now everybody crosses fingers until Wednesday night, second performance!"

It is noticeable to what extent Gertrud had now assumed charge of her husband's contacts with other people. She wrote virtually all his letters, and Stravinsky, who was present in Santa Fé at the time, remarks in *Dialogues and a Diary* that she "protected him from the tourists as if he were Rock Hudson". At times she also tried to protect him from his friends. The Czech violist Ladislav Cerny, to whom in the early Donaueschingen days Hindemith dedicated his second sonata for solo viola, has recalled an occasion in that same year when, after a chance meeting, he sat in an empty hall listening to the rehearsal Hindemith was conducting. Gertrud saw him sitting there and hurried up with an abrupt order that he should leave. "My husband must have undisturbed peace before a concert," she declared. This time she met her match, for Cerny remained where he was, merely remarking: "Dear lady, the peace here was wonderfully undisturbed before you came in."

This is only one of several reminiscences in circulation which depict Gertrud in the guise of a rather formidable dragon. Undoubtedly she offended many of his friends by her proprietorial manner, and with increasing frequency as time went on. But it would be unfair to compare her, for instance, with so renowned a shrew as Richard Strauss's wife Pauline. Gertrud was not self-willed: she acted always according to what she believed to be (and may indeed have been) the wishes of her husband. If her influence over him became stronger as the years went by, this need not be interpreted as the result of some long-drawn-out Strindbergian battle of wills. It was perhaps the result of living so closely together that he involuntarily tended to become what she thought him to be rather than what he was. His wish during his last years to be treated as a great man—and Stone's impression is confirmed by many passages in his later correspondence with his publishers—was almost certainly due to her persuasive influence: in this case undeniably a negative one, for it brought him nothing but discontent. However, it should not be forgotten that Gertrud had every reason, since his two major breakdowns in the past five years, to be concerned for his health.

When at the conclusion of their 1961 tour of America they went to New Haven to collect the last of their belongings from their former home in Alden Avenue (where the new owners had allowed them to be stored in the attic), Luther Noss noticed that he had lost some of his previous robustness. Thornton Wilder too, with whom during that visit Hindemith discussed the idea of making a companion piece for *The Long Christmas Dinner* out of another Wilder play, *Pullman Car Hiawatha*, was also having trouble with his health, and he did not get very far with his scenario.

On 5 November 1961, when the first production of *The Long Christmas Dinner* was already in rehearsal at Mannheim, Gertrud sent a despairing appeal to Wilder's sister Isabel in New Haven: "Have you seen the admirable beginning of a sketch for *Hiawatha*-libretto he made before going to Canada? It is perfect in style, rhythm, mood and Paul was earnestly believing that it would be a matter of days for the rest to arrive. The *Christmas Dinner* has met with great enthusiasm, all the singers and producers seem to be deliriously happy. . . . (Paul) has to surround it . . . with ballets, because tenaciously he wants to hold it until he can have a whole Wilder-night. . . . It is pathetic to see him wait for that ONE thing, which would give him so great a joy."

The Long Christmas Dinner was presented at Mannheim on 17 December 1961 (under Hindemith's musical direction and in his own German translation) together with two of his ballets, *Hérodiade* and *Nobilissima Visione*. But these and the other pieces presented with it at subsequent productions (three of Milhaud's *Opéras minutes* in Berlin in 1962 in honour of their composer's seventieth birthday, the early ballet *Der Dämon* in New York in 1963) were only temporary solutions. Not only was Hindemith determined that the companion piece must be a new work, but he also wished it to be a comedy—something, as Gertrud expressed it in a letter to Thornton Wilder on 9 April 1962, "to bring up a smile again after the handkerchiefs have been waving". This letter, written after a meeting with Wilder in Italy just before the Rome production of *The Long Christmas Dinner*, shows that Hindemith's hopes were still pinned on Wilder's play about a journey in a night train. "If, as you say, you will find time to finish *Hiawatha*," Gertrud went on, "would you consider to have some passengers in the train who are lively and happy, even funny? Paul dreams of the travelling virtuoso who practises at night on his violin . . ."

Unfortunately the libretto was never completed. The loss is twofold. *The Long Christmas Dinner*, lacking a suitable companion piece, has so far not succeeded in establishing itself firmly on the stage; while posterity has been deprived of a work of mature musical comedy which might have belied the impression that with the passing of time Hindemith lost his sense of humour.

It is true that some evidence of that valuable ingredient of his early work is contained in the *Mainzer Umzug*, a choral work written in 1962 for the two-thousandth anniversary of the founding of the city of Mainz. But this description of an imaginary procession through the ancient city, written (by Carl Zuckmayer) in local dialect, was devised for a very special occasion, and is not likely ever to achieve a very wide appeal.

Chapter 5

1963·

THE FINAL YEAR

IN A LIFE of constant struggle—against the poverty of his childhood, the hostility towards his early music, the persecution of the Nazis, the exile in America—Hindemith had always been sustained by his belief in himself, his energy and his abounding humour. These weapons, which had so successfully carried him through the years of strife, were less well adapted to cope with the problems of final acceptance, fame and old age. Self-confidence could begin to look like obstinacy. Energy is a physical thing: to make no allowances for an aging body is to invite exhaustion. Humour, which could be the sustaining factor, is unfortunately dependent to a large extent on the other two. In intention there was no diminution in Hindemith's sense of humour: in effect it could often turn sour. His reference to the Art Prize of North Rhine-Westphalia, which he was awarded in 1958, as "the Ruhr coal and pumpernickel prize" might in earlier days have sounded amusingly self-deprecating. But since he was sixty-two and an acknowledged *Meister*, it sounds rather unpleasantly arrogant, particularly when he adds to it (in the letter to Ludwig Strecker in which the above phrase occurs) the remark: "All this prize giving is becoming truly inflationary."

The truth is that Hindemith was not of a character to grow old gracefully. That side of him which with advancing age demanded to be treated with the respect due to a great master (whether due to Gertrud's influence or not) was at odds with the persistently youthful sceptic who loathed all dissembling. Among his intimate friends he remained what he had always been—cheerful, full of fun, companionable. His succession of homemade Christmas cards, most of them including the lion which was Gertrud and the little bald-headed man which was himself, shows his high spirits were basically unimpaired. And basically, one feels, he was neither unhappy nor embittered. It was simply that those other more negative qualities—the anger, the irritability, the vulnerability—could no longer as he grew older be so successfully held in check by his humour. He did not, in his final years, acquire serenity—though perhaps that is only another way of saying that he never became resigned.

Certainly he made no concessions to age in the number of conducting and recording engagements he accepted—indeed they rather increased as his urge to compose gradually died down. His last tour of America, in March and April 1963, was a strenuous one, but it happily confirmed that the reconciliation was complete, on both sides.

On 13 March he conducted the first American performance of *The Long Christmas Dinner*, sung for the first time in English, the language in which it had been composed. The première might have taken place at New Haven, where Wilder was still living and where *The Long Christmas Dinner* had indeed first been produced as a play. Luther Noss had been eager to arrange it, but owing to a letter failing at a crucial time to reach him, the Yale School of Music lost its chance, and the opera was put on at the Juilliard School of Music in New York, together with the ballet *Der Dämon*.

From New York Hindemith went to Chicago to conduct a concert and then returned to New York for two concerts (each repeated) with the New York Philharmonic Orchestra. The first programme consisted of his own Requiem, *When Lilacs Last in the Door-Yard Bloom'd* (the audience, at his request, refraining from applause at the end) and Bruckner's *Psalm 150*. The second, on 25 April, included the first performance of his new Organ Concerto. This had been commissioned by the orchestra for the opening of the Lincoln Center for the Performing Arts, and there in the Philharmonic Hall it was conducted by the composer with Anton Heiller as soloist.

There was another important award awaiting him on his return to Europe, and in May he went to Rome to receive it— the Balzan Prize. On 28 June he delivered a lecture to his fellow members of the order *Pour le mérite* in Bonn. On both occasions he clearly demonstrated in his addresses that he had lost none of his old fighting spirit. As a final summary of the beliefs which had guided him throughout his life they are worth quoting in detail, even at the cost of some repetition. Both contained a staunch reaffirmation of his belief in tonality and in the twelve

K

notes of the chromatic scale as the indivisible elements of music.

"Now that the materials of sound have been finally discovered," he said in Rome, "the musician finds himself in a similar position to the poet and novelist, who are also unable to alter or add anything significant to their working material, which is language, if they wish to remain comprehensible. For the communication of things so far unsaid the only path now left open to the musician is that leading to the other dimension of height and depth—to the heights of the spirit (whose potentialities we can grasp by comparison with religion, philosophy and the pure sciences) and to the depths of the human psyche."

Attempts to divide the basic elements of music still further or to manipulate the twelve existing notes according to mathematical formulae he described in Rome as glimpses across seas and deserts uninhabited by man. In Bonn he changed both the viewpoint and the metaphor.

Entitling his lecture "Dying Waters", he compared composers who were content to treat their twelve equal notes as elements of a tonal language with fishes swimming in a clear stream. Those who sought to add to these tones or to force them into mathematical patterns were guilty of polluting the water. Foremost among the offenders he placed the followers of the twelve-tone system. "The serial twelve-tone groups, horizontally as well as vertically arranged, are nothing more than permutations of the numbers one to twelve, equated to the notes of the chromatic scale—a mental activity scarcely superior to the invention or solution of a crossword puzzle." As for *musique concrète*, which was then at the height of its fashion in Germany, he remarked that this "at least does not disturb us by reminding us of music". Electronic music, he thought, could perhaps find its way back to real music if it were prepared to include tonal material among its sounds.

Hindemith ended his talk in Bonn with a grim, if humorously phrased, warning for the future:

"Either we let our musical organisms go on swimming around in the murky waters of an inarticulate twelve-tone soup, where —like the salmon in the rivers they grow large and fat but become inedible—or we keep within the bounds of our tonal system and its tonal possibilities. These are maybe limited in the same way that a sphere is limited, but they are just as inexhaustible as the potentialities of language, in which we also use no more than about two dozen sound symbols. The inexhaustibility of artistic creators is the inexhaustibility of human thought itself, and if a musician has received the gift of presenting his fellow mortals with an image of this inexhaustibility in his own way (and subject to the limitations of his time and material) and with each work conjures up for them a small universe, then he has fulfilled his artistic task. But not if he hides himself behind aurally incomprehensible formulae and contents himself, for his own pleasure, with the mere technical solution of sound problems."

Finally he evoked a vision of a "United Nations computer", which would work out all possible tonal combinations. "How comforting it is to think of composers who will not go near this computer or have anything to do with its combinations; who will prefer to buy themselves a few bundles of music paper and, with happy thoughts of all those people who expect from music not sensations but pleasure, write down what the spirit of the eternally youthful Orpheus suggests to them! Within our venerable tone system, with its equally venerable tonality, they will feel like merry fish in the clean, gleaming and swirling waters of a mountain stream. The others will by then scarcely know what a mountain stream is."

One might label this reactionary (and it is a word to which Hindemith would not have objected, since it placed him in the same class as Bach, who was also, he tells us, regarded by his contemporaries as reactionary). Yet his words do not support those who suggest that in his final years Hindemith became bitter. Undoubtedly he was disappointed that the new generation of composers showed few signs of heeding his advice. But bitterness is a purely subjective response which can only arise when one feels wounded in one's self-esteem. Hindemith had momentarily succumbed to it when he considered himself rejected by the Americans, but that feeling had been overcome. What grounds for bitterness could he now have when he saw his compositions maintaining and indeed gaining in popularity throughout the world, and his services as conductor in lively demand? The criterion of his musicianship had always been communication with his fellow men, and he could justifiably claim that, as far as his own activities were concerned, he had proved its validity.

A graceful tribute was paid to him in the final year of his life by William Walton, whom he had helped and encouraged when both of them were young men. Walton's *Variations on a Theme by Hindemith*, based on a passage from the Cello Concerto, was dedicated to the composer and his wife. Hindemith expressed his gratitude in a letter from Blonay dated 29 July 1963:

"Egregio Amico—Finally our criss-cross journeys came to an end and we could sit down in front of the exhaust of our gramophone and play your piece, score before us. Well, we had a half hour of sheer enjoyment. You wrote a beautiful score and we are extremely honoured to find the red carpet rolled out even on the steps to the back door of fame. I am particularly fond of the honest solidity of workmanship in this score—something that seems almost completely lost nowadays. Let us thank you for your kindness and for the wonderfully touching and artistically convincing manifestation of this kindness (even old Mathis is permitted to peep through the fence, which for a spectre like him seems to be some kind of resurrection after artificial respiration!). I am glad that George Szell had a great (and well deserved) success with the piece in the States. I also shall put it on my programs as soon as possible. I wrote to the Oxford Press people that this could only be the case during the next season, i.e., starting autumn 1964, since I received the score at a time when all programs for 63/64 were settled and could not be changed. I hope this will be all right with you, and I shall do my best to become a worthy interpreter of WW."

This letter (quoted in *The Music of William Walton* by Frank Howes) clearly shows that Hindemith in his sixty-eighth year had no thoughts of his time drawing to an end. In October he went to Rome to supervise a production of Monteverdi's *Orfeo* in his own arrangement, and in November he conducted two concerts in Vienna, at which Anton Heiller and the Philharmonic Orchestra played his Organ Concerto of the previous year. On the following day, in the Piaristenkirche, he conducted the first performance of his Mass, a setting for mixed chorus *a cappella*.

It was his last work. That this should be a Roman Catholic one does not mean that at the end he was converted to the religious beliefs which his wife so fervently held. Zermatten has described him as an agnostic, but this is as misleading as the assumption of another Swiss friend, Georges Haenni, that

Hindemith had been "converted to Catholicism" just because he once said to Haenni's daughter: "If there is a religious truth, it is the Roman church which possesses it." Neither statement means more than that Hindemith (though confirmed as a boy in the Protestant faith) exercised the artist's right not to identify himself with any one faction. He preferred to remain spiritually free, sympathetic to all speculations but committed finally to none. For this state the word agnostic is too negative. Hindemith, as both life and works show, was in the widest sense a religious man, and the Mass was written, not for any sectarian purpose, but simply *ad majoram gloriam Dei*—"for the greater glory of God". It was his own favourite expression for musicians who worked humbly and without thought of reward for the benefit of mankind, and he applied it to Furtwängler as well as to Bruckner and Bach.

The rest of the story of Hindemith's life can be told in Gertrud's own exact words. They were written from Blonay to Luther and Osea Noss on 20 April 1964, four months after his death in a hospital in Frankfurt on 28 December 1963:

"It was all too sudden. But for Paul it was a blessed, peaceful going. He just had left the Vienna Philharmonics after 2 exciting concerts there. The day after these concerts he inaugurated his new Mass almost secretly in the beautiful Piaristenkirche in Vienna, a marvel of the late Baroque. Dr [Hans] Gillesberger (Wiener Kammerchor), his old companion, had studied the highly difficult piece and at 7.30 in the evening, at a liturgical Evening-Mass it was sung under Paul's direction, without press and announcement. Naturally 'everybody' was there. The church was illuminated and the Academic Choir sang the Responses. Heiller was on the Organ. There was something in the air, you cannot fathom or describe. Everybody was deeply moved. We had no idea it was to be Paul's last 'music'-making. He was so happy, but also strangely moved.

"The next day we left for a few days here at home for his birthday. But he got very sick (I guess a kidney attack) and I managed to get him to our old doctor to Frankfurt. He made blood-tests and ordered an immediate exam in the hospital. They searched him for 5 weeks—gave him terrific amounts of antibiotics, which he hated. He got weaker and weaker, high temperature, but no pain at all, thank God. Then the strokes hit him—it was all a very progressed arterio-sclerosis. I was fortunate enough to be continuously at his side. He did not know he was going and there was no heart-breaking farewell for him. Everything sounds and seems unreal to me. Keep on thinking a bit towards me."

Gertrud survived her husband a little over three years. She remained alone, with only a daily help, in the large house at Blonay. Two months after his death she wrote to a friend in Berlin, Erika Heinisch: "I miss him terribly, but there's no cure for that." As she had lived for him during his lifetime, so she continued after his death. She kept in touch with their old friends, but did not go to visit them. Memorial concerts were held at Yale on 7 and 8 November 1964, and George Lam was appointed chairman of a Commemoration Committee to plan a Paul Hindemith Collection at the university. Gertrud wrote to Luther and Osea Noss on 29 September 1964 asking them to thank Lam for his efforts, but she added: "I'd rather have you dim his activity. Nothing would be farer away from Paul's spirit than to have a PH-Committee (!!!), PH-events, PH-collections, etc. etc. If they sing the Mass well, he will be with them. For the rest—make it as modest and unpretentious as possible." She declined Yale's invitation to attend the memorial concerts, putting off a visit to New Haven to "perhaps another year". She never went back.

On 26 January 1965 she wrote again to Luther and Osea Noss, asking them to prevent publication of any of the many greetings cards and caricatures Hindemith drew for his friends. "For years Paul refused firmly all demands for his drawings and fun-items. He hated the idea that these harmless things would get analysed and commented in some 'Life and Time' edition, as they wanted very much to do it." But she herself co-operated with Dr Martin Hürlimann in the preparation of a biographical volume similar in style and format to the volume *Zeugnis in Bildern*, which had been published to mark Hindemith's sixtieth birthday. The new volume, entitled *Paul Hindemith: Die letzten Jahre* (The Final Years) and published in 1965, does in fact contain a generous supply of his "fun-drawings". She helped too in supplying material for the memorial exhibition in Frankfurt which took place in 1965 about the date of Hindemith's seventieth birthday.

On 4 December 1966 she made a will leaving the whole

Hindemith estate to be used for the establishment of a Hindemith Foundation. The main purpose of this would be "to aid
and promote music in the spirit of Paul Hindemith, and most
particularly contemporary music".

Shortly after making her will she went into hospital for an
operation, but she told none of her friends that she was seriously
ill. Indeed, she pretended to the end that she was on the road
to recovery. She died of cancer on 16 March 1967 in her sixty-
seventh year and was buried beside her husband in the church-
yard of Saint-Légier in Waadt, within sight of their home at
Blonay.

BIBLIOGRAPHY

Briner, Andres: *Paul Hindemith* (Atlantis-Verlag, Zurich, 1971)

Busch, Fritz: *Pages from a Musician's Life* (Hogarth Press, London, 1953)

Chujoy, Anatole: *The New York City Ballet* (Knopf, New York, 1953)

Geissmar, Berta: *The Baton and the Jackboot* (Hamish Hamilton, London, 1944)

Hindemith, Paul: *A Composer's World—Horizons and Limitations* (Harvard U.P., 1952. Paperback: Anchor Books, New York, 1961)

—— *Komponist in seiner Welt* (author's own German version of above) (Atlantis-Verlag, Zurich, 1959)

—— *Johann Sebastian Bach—Ein verpflichtendes Erbe* (Insel-Verlag, Frankfurt, 1953)

—— *Johann Sebastian Bach—Heritage and Obligation* (author's own English version of above) (Yale U.P., 1952)

—— *Unterweisung im Tonsatz. Band I: Theoretischer Teil* (New extended edition: Schott, Mainz, 1940)

—— *Band II: Übungsbuch für den zweistimmigen Satz* (Schott, Mainz, 1939)

—— *Band III: Der dreistimmige Satz* (Schott, Mainz, 1970)

—— *The Craft of Musical Composition* (English translation of above): *Book I: Theoretical Part*, translated by Arthur Mendel (Schott, London, 1945)

—— *Book II: Exercises in Two-Part Writing*, translated by Otto Ortmann (Associated Music Publishers, New York, 1941)

—— *A Concentrated Course in Traditional Harmony. Book I* (revised edition, Schott, London, 1968)

—— *Book II: Exercises for Advanced Students* (translated by Arthur Mendel) (Schott, London, 1953)

—— *Aufgaben für Harmonieschüler* (author's own German version of Book I of above) (Schott, Mainz, 1949)

—— *Harmonieübungen für Fortgeschrittene* (original version of Book II of above) (Schott, Mainz, 1949)

—— *Elementary Training for Musicians* (revised edition, Schott, London, 1968)

Howes, Frank: *The Music of William Walton* (O.U.P., London, 1965)

Hürlimann, Martin (Editor): *Wilhelm Furtwängler im Urteil seiner Zeit* (Atlantis-Verlag, Zurich, 1955)

Kemp, Ian: *Hindemith* (O.U.P., London, 1970)

Lübbecke, Fried: *Der Muschelsaal* (Verlag Waldemar Kramer, Frankfurt, 1960)

Massine, Léonide: *My Life in Ballet* (Macmillan, London, 1968)

Milhaud, Darius: *Notes without Music* (Calder and Boyars, London, 1967)

Rieple, Max: *Musik in Donaueschingen* (Rosgarten-Verlag, Konstanz, 1959)

Riess, Curt: *Furtwängler: Musik und Politik* (Scherz-Verlag, Berne, 1953)

Schonberg, Harold C.: *The Great Conductors* (Gollancz, London, 1968)

Stein, Erwin (Editor): *Arnold Schoenberg Letters* (Faber, London, 1964)

Stravinsky, Igor and Craft, Robert: *Dialogues and a Diary* (Faber, London, 1968)

Strobel, Heinrich: *Paul Hindemith* (3rd revised edition, Schott, Mainz, 1948)

Thiess, Frank (Editor): *Wilhelm Furtwängler Briefe* (Brockhaus, Wiesbaden, 1964)

Thomas, Walter: *Richard Strauss und seine Zeitgenossen* (Langen-Müller, Munich, 1964)

Wulf, Joseph: *Musik im Dritten Reich* (Mohn-Verlag, Gütersloh, 1963)

Zuckmayer, Carl: *Als wär's ein Stück von mir* (Fischer-Verlag, Frankfurt, 1966)

Paul Hindemith: Zeugnis in Bildern (Testimony in Pictures) (German-English, Schott, Mainz, 1961)

Paul Hindemith: Die letzten Jahre (Schott, Mainz, 1965)

Paul Hindemith: Werkverzeichnis (Schott, Mainz, undated)

Paul Hindemith: Catalogue of Published Works and Recordings, compiled by Kurt Stone (Associated Music Publishers, New York, 1954)

Hindemith-Jahrbuch 1971/I (Paul-Hindemith-Institut) (Schott, Mainz)

Hindemith-Jahrbuch 1972/II (Paul-Hindemith-Institut) (Schott, Mainz)

Revue Musicale de Suisse Romande (Numéro spécial Paul Hindemith, June 1973)

CHRONOLOGICAL LIST OF WORKS

THIS LIST CONTAINS the main literary works and all major compositions from 1914, the year in which Hindemith for the first time dignified his work with opus numbers. The very many compositions which preceded his Opus 1 (mainly for solo instruments or chamber music combinations) have not been included: most were destroyed either by Hindemith himself or in air raids during the Second World War. Also omitted are a number of minor compositions, most of them very short occasional pieces or the outcome of class exercises, and editings of works by other composers. I have also not included separately the many piano reductions, transcriptions and arrangements which Hindemith himself made of his own works.

The dates given are those of composition, not of publication or first performances. In the majority of cases these would anyway be the same, but even a composer with the facility of a Hindemith may be assumed to have kept themes, passages or even whole movements in his drawer for use when the occasion arose. Consequently the date of composition as shown should not be regarded as entirely conclusive. The precise order in which the works were composed can also not be deduced with complete accuracy from the order in which they are here listed: very often Hindemith worked on more than one composition simultaneously. However, with the help of documentary evidence I have placed them in chronological order as far as that is possible at this stage.

Some of the works shown as unpublished were designated by the composer himself as worthy of inclusion in a complete edition of his compositions, and it is thus possible that they may subsequently be published.

The list serves simultaneously as an index. On the pages indicated details will be found concerning origins, performances, etc.

1914

Andante and Scherzo for Clarinet, Horn and Piano,
  Opus 1 (destroyed)

1915   *page*
String Quartet in C major, Opus 2 (destroyed)   41
Concerto in E flat major for Cello and Orchestra, Opus 3
    (destroyed)   49

1916
Sinfonietta, Opus 4 (unpublished)
Lieder in Aargauer Mundart, Opus 5 (unpublished)
Waltzes for piano duet, Opus 6 (unpublished)   43

1917
Quintet in E minor for Strings and Piano, Opus 7
    (destroyed)   43, 49–50, 57, 58
March in F minor, for piano duet (destroyed)
Sonata in G minor for Solo Violin (unpublished)
Two Songs, for contralto and piano (unpublished)
3 Pieces for Cello and Piano, Opus 8 (Hindemith's first
    published work)   46
Three Songs, for soprano and orchestra, Opus 9 (un-
    published)   50–1
Polonaise, for piano (unpublished)

1918
String Quartet No. 1 in F Minor, Opus 10   52–3, 57, 58, 60
Sonata in E flat for Violin and Piano, Opus 11/1   53–4, 57, 58
Sonata in D for Violin and Piano, Opus 11/2   58
Two Pieces for Organ (destroyed)
Wie es wär, wenn's anders wär, for soprano, flute, oboe,
    bassoon, 2 violins, viola, 2 cellos (unpublished)

1919
Sonata in F for Viola and Piano, Opus 11/4   57, 58
Mörder, Hoffnung der Frauen, one act opera, Opus 12   52, 62–4, 83
Sonata for Solo Viola, Opus 11/5
Sonata for Cello and Piano, Opus 11/3
Melancholie, four songs for mezzo-soprano and string
    quartet, Opus 13 (unpublished)
Three Hymns by Walt Whitman, for baritone and piano,
    Opus 14 (unpublished)   60
In einer Nacht, piano pieces, Opus 15 (unpublished)

1920   *page*

Piano Sonata, Opus 17 (unpublished)   60
Acht Lieder, 8 songs for soprano and piano, Opus 18
String Quartet No. 2 in C major, Opus 16   64–5
Das Nusch-Nuschi, one act opera, Opus 20   62–4, 65, 77, 109,
                                                    119, 120
Tanzstücke (Five Dance Pieces), for piano, Opus 19

1921

Sancta Susanna, one act opera, Opus 21   63–4, 119, 120
String Quartet No. 3, Opus 22   309

1922

Des Todes Tod, 3 songs for female voice, 2 violas, 2 cellos,
    Opus 23a   66
Die junge Magd, 6 songs for contralto with flute, clarinet
    and string quartet, Opus 23/2   66, 67, 218
Kammermusik Nr 1 (small orchestra), Opus 24/1   66, 67, 73, 309
Sonata for Solo Viola, Opus 25/1   61, 63, 66, 154, 285, 309
Kleine Kammermusik für fünf Bläser (flute, oboe, clarinet,
    horn, bassoon), Opus 24/2   66
Little Sonata for Viola d'Amore and Piano, Opus 25/2   66
Suite 1922, for piano   66, 67, 186
Sonata for Viola and Piano, Opus 25/4 (unpublished)
Sonata for Solo Cello, Opus 25/3
Der Dämon, ballet, Opus 28   66, 67, 286, 289
Tuttifäntchen, Christmas play for children   66, 67, 80

1923

Das Marienleben, song cycle for soprano and piano, Opus
    27 (begun 1922)   12, 15, 66, 67, 75, 76–7, 80, 165–6, 235
Klaviermusik mit Orchester, for orchestra and piano (left
    hand), Opus 29 (unpublished)
Quintet for Clarinet and Strings, Opus 30   74
Sonata for Solo Viola, Opus 31/4 (unpublished)
Kanonische Sonatine, for 2 flutes, Opus 31/3
String Quartet No. 4, Opus 32   76, 80
Lieder nach alten Texten (6 Songs on Old Texts), for mixed
    chorus unacc., Opus 33

1924 *page*
Sonata for Solo Violin, Opus 31/1
Sonata for Solo Violin, Opus 31/2
String Trio, Opus 34 74, 309
Die Serenaden, cantata for soprano, oboe, viola, cello,
Opus 35 80, 309
Kammermusik Nr 2 (Piano Concerto), Opus 36/1 74-5

1925
Kammermusik Nr 3 (Cello Concerto), Opus 36/2 309
Kammermusik Nr 4 (Violin Concerto), Opus 36/3
Klaviermusik (Piano Music), Opus 37: Part I (Part II
1926)
Konzert für Orchester (Concerto for Orchestra), Opus 38 309
3 Stücke für 5 Instrumente (clarinet, trumpet, violin, double
bass, piano)

1926
Cardillac, opera in 3 acts, Opus 39 75, 81-2, 83-4, 133, 233, 235,
236, 255, 274, 275, 277
Das triadische Ballett, ballet (unpublished) 82-3
Konzertmusik für Blasorchester (Concert Music for Band),
Opus 41 82
Klaviermusik (Piano Music), Opus 37: Part II (Part I
1925)
Spielmusik, for strings, flutes, oboes, Opus 43/1
Lieder für Singkreise (Songs for Group Singing), Opus 43/2

1927
Kammermusik Nr 5 (Viola Concerto), Opus 36/4 90, 98
Schulwerk für Instrumental-Zusammenspiel (Educational
Music for Instrumental Ensembles), Opus 44
Kammermusik Nr 6 (Viola d'Amore Concerto), Opus 46/1
Hin und zurück, one act opera, Opus 45a 90, 94, 134, 177
Kammermusik Nr 7 (Organ Concerto), Opus 46/2 90

1928
Music for film *Vormittagsspuk,* for player-piano (un-
published) 91
Sing- und Spielmusik für Liebhaber und Musikfreunde (Music
to Sing and Play, for Amateurs and Music Lovers),
Opus 45 92-3

page

Frau Musica, for 2 solo voices, mixed chorus and strings,
Opus 45/1   92

1929

Neues vom Tage, opera in 3 acts (begun 1928)   15, 90, 94, 120,
233-4, 236
4 pieces for *Lindberghflug* by Bertolt Brecht (unpublished)   96
Lehrstück, cantata to text by Brecht   16, 95-6, 261
Trio for Piano, Viola and Heckelphone (or Tenor
Saxophone), Opus 47

1930

Wir bauen eine Stadt, opera for children   16, 99, 110, 186
Sabinchen, radio play (unpublished)
3 Choruses, for 4 men's voices on poem by Gottfried Benn
Konzertmusik, for viola and large chamber orchestra,
Opus 48
Konzertmusik für Klavier, Blechbläser und 2 Harfen (Concert
Music for Piano, Brass and 2 Harps), Opus 49   99, 309
Konzertmusik für Streichorchester und Blechbläser (Concert
Music for String Orchestra and Brass Instruments),
Opus 50   99, 115, 309
4 Three-Part Choruses for Boys

1931

Das Unaufhörliche, oratorio   100, 274
Konzertstück, for trautonium and strings (unpublished)
14 leichte Stücke (14 Easy Duets for 2 Violins)

1932

Philharmonisches Konzert (Philharmonic Concerto)   100, 310
Plöner Musiktag (A Day of Music in Plön)   100-1, 109, 120, 128

1933

String Trio   108, 309
2 Songs, with piano, to words by Hölderlin
15 Songs to words by Claudius, Rückert, Novalis, Busch
(unpublished)

1934   *page*
Symphony *Mathis der Maler*   111–12, 116–17, 121, 123, 175,
                                       177, 220, 310
Scherzo for Viola and Cello   115, 309

1935
Mathis der Maler, opera in 7 scenes (begun 1933) 12, 15, 18, 46,
    111–13, 116–18, 120, 122, 124, 129, 130, 131, 133, 134, 143,
        157, 158–9, 160, 164, 166–7, 196, 220, 224, 232, 273, 275
Sonata in E for Violin and Piano   131, 134
Der Schwanendreher (Viola Concerto)   129–30, 134, 155, 309
4 Songs, with piano, to words by Hölderlin

1936
Trauermusik (Music of Mourning), for viola and strings   130–1,
                                       133, 240, 309
Piano Sonata No. 1 in A   134
Piano Sonata No. 2 in G   134
Piano Sonata No. 3 in B Flat
Sonata for Flute and Piano

1937
Five Songs on Old Texts, for mixed chorus unacc. (revised
    version to English texts of Nos. 1, 2, 3, 6 of *Lieder nach
    alten Texten* (1923), plus new piece *Wahre Liebe*)
Book: *Unterweisung im Tonsatz* (The Craft of Musical Com-
    position) (begun 1935)   14, 15, 17, 22, 89, 135, 140, 142–53,
            159, 164, 193, 194–5, 206, 214, 236, 246, 276
Sonata for Solo Viola (unpublished)   157
Symphonische Tänze (Symphonic Dances) 156, 158, 165, 221, 310
Organ Sonata No. 1   157
Organ Sonata No. 2   157

1938
Nobilissima Visione, ballet and orchestral suite   156, 158–60, 165,
                                       220, 224, 284, 286, 310
9 Songs for an American school song book (unpublished)
Drei leichte Stücke (3 easy pieces, for cello and piano)
Sonata for Bassoon and Piano
Quartet for Clarinet, Violin, Cello and Piano
Sonata for Oboe and Piano
Sonata for Piano (Four Hands)   309

1939 *page*

Book: *Übungsbuch für den zweistimmigen Satz* (Exercises in
Two Part Writing) (begun 1938)   153, 164, 177, 178
Sonata in C for Viola and Piano   309
Three choruses for Four Men's Voices
Concerto for Violin and Orchestra   164, 167, 174, 175, 186,
217, 218, 220, 310

Sonata in C for violin and piano
Six Chansons, for mixed chorus unacc.   162
Sonata for Clarinet and Piano   164
Sonata for Harp   164, 217
Variations on an Old Dance Song, for male voices unacc.
Sonata for Horn and Piano   164
Sonata for Trumpet and Piano   164

1940

Organ Sonata No. 3   178, 186
Concerto for Cello and Orchestra   178, 186, 201, 221, 292
The Four Temperaments, ballet and concert piece for piano
and strings   176, 217, 220, 223–4, 232, 310
Symphony in E flat   178, 186, 201, 221

1941

Motet, for soprano or tenor and piano (No. 8 of *13
Motetten*) (begun Dec. 1940)   187
Sonata for English Horn and Piano   201
Sonata for Trombone and Piano   201
A Frog He Went A-Courting, variations for cello and piano   201

1942

Little Sonata for Cello and Piano (unpublished)
La Belle Dame sans Merci (setting of Keats's poem for solo
voice and piano)
7 Songs to English texts by Blake, Lover, Moore, Oldys,
Shelley, Thompson and Wolfe, with piano acc.   205
18 Songs (German, French, Latin) for soprano and piano
(unpublished)
Sonata for Two Pianos   205, 206, 212
Ludus Tonalis: Studies in Counterpoint, Tonal Organization and Piano Playing   15, 205–6, 209, 217, 218

1943   *page*
Book, *A Concentrated Course in Traditional Harmony* (begun
    1942)   193, 195
String Quartet No. 5 in E flat   208
Symphonic Metamorphosis of Themes by Carl Maria von Weber
                                    175–6, 208, 310
In Praise of Music (revised version of *Frau Musica*, 1928)   218
Amor und Psyche (Cupid and Psyche) Overture   208, 310
Sonata for Saxophone and Piano
Sing on there in the Swamp, for voice and piano   215
Motet, for soprano or tenor and piano (No. 13 of *13
    Motetten*)

1944
Hérodiade, ballet and orchestral piece   211–12, 286
To Music, for voice and piano to words by Herrick
2 Motets, for soprano or tenor and piano (Nos. 2 and 11 of
    13 Motetten)
The Frog, for voice and piano (unpublished)   210–11

1945
String Quartet No. 6
Concerto for Piano and Orchestra   216, 226

1946
Book, *Elementary Training for Musicians* (begun 1945)   193–4
Requiem: *When Lilacs Last in the Door-Yard Bloom'd*   219–20,
                                    278, 281, 289, 310
Symphonia Serena   223, 225, 226, 310

1947
Apparebit repentina dies, for chorus and brass   225, 226, 309
Concerto for Clarinet and Orchestra   225, 309

1948
Sonata for Cello and Piano   234
Das Marienleben (revised version, begun 1936)   134, 201, 221,
                                    223, 235–6, 255, 266
Septett für Blasinstrumente (flute, oboe, clarinet, bass
    clarinet, bassoon, horn, trumpet)   242

1949
Concerto for Horn and Orchestra   239, 241, 309

page

Concerto for Woodwinds, Harp and Orchestra 239
Sonata for Double Bass and Piano 239
Concerto for Trumpet, Bassoon and String Orchestra 239

1950

Sinfonietta in E (begun 1949) 241
Book, *A Composer's World* 16, 17, 240, 246–57, 267
Lecture, *Johann Sebastian Bach—Heritage and Obligation*
257–60, 267

1951

Symphony in B flat for Concert Band 310
Symphony *Die Harmonie der Welt* 243, 267–8, 310

1952

Cardillac, revised version of opera with own libretto
(begun 1948) 235, 236–7, 255, 266, 277, 284
Sonata for Four Horns

1953

Cantique de l'espérance (Part III of cantata *Ite, angeli veloces*,
1955) 243, 245, 260, 261–2, 272
Neues vom Tage, revised version of opera 265–6, 272, 284, 285
Book, *Komponist in seiner Welt* (German version of *A
Composer's World*) 265

1954

Nil

1955

Sonata for Tuba and Piano 272
2 Songs, for voice and piano to words by Oscar Cox 272
Triumphgesang Davids (Part I of cantata *Ite, angeli veloces*) 272
Custos quid de nocte (Part II of cantata *Ite, angeli veloces*) 272

1956

Die Harmonie der Welt (libretto) 18, 19–20, 167, 239, 273–4

1957

Die Harmonie der Welt, opera in 5 acts (continuous work
begun in 1956) 12, 19–20, 100, 164, 225, 243, 260, 272,
273–6, 279

1958

Oktett (clarinet, bassoon, horn, violin, 2 violas, cello and
double bass) (begun 1957) 277, 279

page
12 Madrigale, for mixed chorus unacc.   260, 279, 282
2 Motets, for soprano or tenor and piano (Nos. 5 and 7 of
    13 Motetten)   260
Pittsburgh Symphony   259, 280

1959

5 Motets, for soprano or tenor and piano (Nos. 3, 4, 6, 9,
    10 of *13 Motteten*)   281

1960

2 Motets, for soprano or tenor and piano (Nos. 1, 12 of
    13 Motetten)
March, for orchestra
The Long Christmas Dinner, one act opera 260, 282–3, 286–7, 289

1961

Duet for *Cardillac*, Act 3 (No. 16)

1962

Mainzer Umzug, cantata   287
Concerto for Organ and Orchestra   259, 289, 292

1963

Messe (Mass), for mixed chorus unacc.   260, 292–3, 294

GRAMOPHONE RECORDINGS BY PAUL HINDEMITH

HINDEMITH'S RECORDINGS, predominantly of his own works, began in 1934 and continued throughout his life, in Great Britain, the USA and Germany. In this attempt to provide a complete list of his recordings without regard to current availability, I have been much indebted, particularly as far as the earlier recordings are concerned, to Kurt Stone's *Paul Hindemith: Catalogue of Published Works and Recordings*. Owing to pressings in other countries, reissues, etc., the number shown against each title may not be the only one under which the record has been issued.

As violist:

Scherzo for Viola and Cello: with Feuermann. Columbia History of Music DB 1305.

Schwanendreher, Der: With Fiedler Sinfonietta. RCA Victor 15922/4

Serenaden, Die: Duo: with Rudolf Hindemith (cello). Polydor 66193

Sonata for Solo Viola, Opus 25/1. Columbia 17083

Sonata in C for Viola and Piano (1939): with Sanroma. RCA Victor 10–0005/8

String Quartet No 3: Amar Quartet. Polydor 66422/4

String Trio No 1: 1st and 3rd movements: with Amar (violin), Frank (cello). Polydor 66573/4

String Trio No 2: with Goldberg (violin), Feuermann (cello). Columbia M 209

Trauermusik: with string orch. cond. Reibold. RCA Victor 15643

Serenade in D, Opus 8 (Beethoven): with Goldberg (violin), Feuermann (cello). Columbia CM 217

As pianist:

Sonata for Piano (Four Hands): with Sanroma. RCA Victor M 637

As Conductor:

Apparebit Repentina Dies: Vienna Singakademie and Symphony Orchestra. Capitol P 8134

Clarinet Concerto: De Cahuzac, Philharmonia Orchestra. Columbia 33CX 1533

Horn Concerto: Brain, Philharmonia Orchestra. Columbia 33CX 1676

Kammermusik Nr 1: Philharmonic Chamber Ensemble. Contemporary Records AP 101

Kammermusik Nr 3: Varga (cello), Philharmonic Chamber Ensemble. Contemporary Records AP 101

Konzert für Orchester, Opus 38: Berlin Philharmonic Orchestra. Deutsche Grammophon DGM 18474

Konzertmusik für Klavier, Blechbläser und zwei Harfen, Opus 49: Haas (piano), Berlin Philharmonic Orchestra. Deutsche Grammophon DGM 18474

Konzertmusik für Streichorchester und Blechbläser, Opus 50: Philharmonia Orchestra. Columbia 33CX 1512

Nobilissima Visione: Philharmonia Orchestra. Columbia 33CX 1533

Overture Cupid and Psyche: Berlin Philharmonic Orchestra. Deutsche Grammophon DGM 18474

Philharmonisches Konzert: Berlin Philharmonic Orchestra. Capitol P 8134

Requiem: When Lilacs First in the Door-Yard Bloom'd: Hoengen (mezzo-soprano), Braun (baritone), Vienna State Opera chorus, Vienna Symphony Orchestra. Vox PNL 1760

Symphonia Serena: Philharmonia Orchestra. Columbia 33CX 1676

Symphonic Dances: Berlin Philharmonic Orchestra. Deutsche Grammophon DG LPM 18507

Symphonic Metamorphosis of Themes by Carl Maria von Weber: Berlin Philharmonic Orchestra. Deutsche Grammophon DGM 18301

Symphony in B flat for Concert Band: Philharmonia Orchestra. Columbia 33CX 1512

Symphony Die Harmonie der Welt: Berlin Philharmonic Orchestra. Deutsche Grammophon DGM 18181

Symphony Mathis der Maler: Berlin Philharmonic Orchestra. Deutsche Grammophon LPM 18507

Thema mit 4 Variationen (Die vier Temperamente): Otto (piano), Berlin Philharmonic Orchestra. Deutsche Grammophon DGM 18301

Violin Concerto: David Oistrakh (violin), London Symphony Orchestra. Decca SXL 6035

Choral works by J. S. Bach, Dufay, di Lasso, Gabrieli, Gesualdo, Handl, Monteverdi, Palestrina, Perotin, Weelkes: Yale Collegium Musicum. Overtone Records 4/5

INDEX

Albert, Eugen d', 81

Amar, Licco, 65, 74, 109, 132

Amar Quartet, 65-6, 72, 73-4, 79, 90, 93, 98

American Ballet, 165, 223-4

Amsterdam Concertgebouw Orchestra, 44-5, 130

Angriff, Der, 121, 242

Aranyi, Jelly d', 157

Associated Music Publishers, New York, 154, 178, 184-5, 193, 201, 234

Augustine, St, 85, 247-8

Bach, Johann Sebastian, 11, 17, 19, 76, 101, 128, 130, 162, 205, 233, 234, 241, 244, 257-9, 269, 291, 293

Baden-Baden Festival, 21, 82-3, 90, 91-3, 94-6, 98

Baird, Cameron, 168, 173

Balanchine, George, 165, 176, 223-4

Balzan Prize, 289

Barrère, Georges, 155

Bartholomew, Marshall, 155, 206, 207

Bartók, Bela, 14, 72, 137, 184, 220, 281

Basil, Colonel de, 133, 156

Basle Chamber Orchestra, 127, 243

Bassermann, Fritz, 36, 41

Bauer, Carl, 184-5

Bauer, Mrs Phyllis, 9, 185

Bayreuth Festival, 263

Beethoven, Ludwig van, 19, 46, 61, 198, 252, 253, 254, 263, 279-80

Beggar's Opera, The, 81

Benn, Gottfried, 100

Berg, Alban, 72, 87, 210, 220, 281

Berkowitz, Leonard, 205

Berkshire Music Festival, *see* Tanglewood

Berlin Festival, 98

Berlin Philharmonic Orchestra, 87, 100, 117, 122, 220

Berlin State Opera, 83, 87, 120, 122, 166

Bernstein, Leonard, 176, 278

Biber, Heinrich, 204

Bienicke Library, New Haven, 9, 91

Biggs, E. Power, 178

Blei, Franz, 62

Boatwright, Helen, 244

Boatwright, Howard, 9, 85, 191, 195, 208, 244

Boethius, 85, 247-8

Bonaventura, Sam, *picture facing* 160

Born, Claire, 84

Borries, Siegfried, 87

Boston Chamber Music Club, 155

Boston Symphony Orchestra, 99, 186, 203

Boulanger, Nadia, 139-40

Boult, Adrian, 130-1, 170

Bozyan, Frank, 181, 182

Bozyan, **Mrs Margaret**, 182-3, 243-4

Brahms, Johannes, 42

Brain, Dennis, 241

Brecher, Gustav, 56

Brecht, Bertolt, 16, 81, 94-6, 100

Breitkopf und Härtel, 43, 46-7

Briner, Andres, 17, 261

British Broadcasting Corporation, 9, 97, 130-1, 133

Bruckner, Anton, 269, 289, 293

Brüning, Heinrich, 101, 102

Budapest String Quartet, 208

Buffalo, University of, 168, 173–4, 176
Bülow, Hans von, 45
Burg, Robert, 84
Burkard, Heinrich, 64, 70–2, 82
Busch, Fritz, 56, 61–2, 83–4, 109
Busoni, Ferruccio, 71

Cäcilienverein, Frankfurt, 41, 42
Cahn, Peter, 32, 35, 61
Cardillac, see references in Chronological List of Works (pp. 302, 307)
Carlyle, Thomas, 283–4
Casals, Pablo, 108
Casper, Walter, 65
Cazden, Norman, 152
Cerny, Ladislav, 285
Cevat Bey, 127
Chavez, Carlos, 155
Chicago Symphony Orchestra, 285
Chicago University, 210
Chujoy, Anatole, 224
Clark, Edward, 97, 130
Claudel, Paul, 243, 245, 261–2, 272
Collegium Musicum, Yale, 207–8, 226, 244
Columbia University, 234
Composer's World, A, see references in Chronological List of Works (p. 307)
Cooke, Arnold, 9, 87, 88, 280
Coolidge, Mrs Elizabeth Sprague, 64, 99, 154, 155, 211
Copland, Aaron, 13, 176
Cornell University, 168, 174
Courtauld, Mrs Elizabeth, 96–7
Cox, Oscar, 12, 244, 264–5, 266, 269, 271, 272, 273, 275, 277–9, 281, 283, 285
Craft of Musical Composition, The, see references in Chronological List of Works (p. 304)

Crocker, Joy, 195
Curtis, L. P., 210

Dali, Salvador, 175, 176
Dallas Symphony Orchestra, 223
Debussy, Claude, 33, 45, 49, 220
Delius, Frederic, 56, 72
Dent, Edward, 87
Denzler, Robert F., 159
Deutsche Allgemeine Zeitung, 120–1
Deutsche Arbeitsfront, 115
Deutsche Zeitung, 119
Deutsche Zukunft, 131
Diaghilev, Serge, 93–4
Dobrowen, Issay, 84
Donaueschingen Festival, 21, 64–5, 70–3, 82–3, 86, 244, 285
Donovan, Richard, 182, 204, 207, 244, 280
Dorati, Antal, 223, 225
Dougherty and Ruzitska (two-piano team), 206
Dreisbach, Philipp, 62, 71, 73
Drury Lane Theatre, 159
Dulles, John Foster, 278–9
Dunlap, John, 196, 197

Ebert, Carl, 157
Eisenhower, Dwight, 234
Ellington, Duke, 154
Erdmann, Eduard, 71
Evans, Edwin, 77
Ewald, Reinhold, 59

Feuermann, Emanuel, 98, 107, 108, 115
Fiedler, Arthur, 155
Flesch, Mrs Gabriele, 9, 78, 114, 214
Flesch, Hans, 78, 113–14, 134, 214
Flesch, Karl, 107
Flesch-Thebesius, Max, 9, 78

Foss, Lukas, 9, 176, 177, 190, 191, 192, 200

Fraenger, Wilhelm, 63

Fraker, Charles, 196

Francis of Assisi, St, 156, 157, 159-60

Frank, Maurits, 46, 49, 65, 74

Frankfurt Opera, 29, 38, 40-1, 45, 47, 56, 68, 69, 76, 159, 232

Frankfurt University, 234

Frankfurter Zeitung, 57, 119, 161

Free University, Berlin, 237, 242

French, Robert, 215

Funk, Walther, 119, 134-5

Fürstenberg, Max Egon Fürst zu, 70-1, 74, 82

Furtwängler, Wilhelm, 56, 87, 100, 109, 111, 112, 114, 117, 118, 120-2, 126, 140, 142, 157, 209, 231-2, 267-9, 293

Gabrieli, Giovanni, 282

Gal, Hans, 106

Gebrauchsmusik, *see under* Hindemith, Paul

Geissmar, Berta, 107, 111, 123

Gentzmer, Harald, 87

George V, King, 130-1, 240

Gershwin, George, 192

Gesellschaft für Neue Musik, Cologne, 74

Gieseking, Walter, 134, 142, 232

Gillesberger, Hans, 293

Goebbels, Joseph, 113, 114, 121-3, 126, 129, 131, 134, 159, 166, 214, 242

Goering, Hermann, 120, 122, 166

Goldberg, Symon, 108, 115

Goodman, Benny, 225

Graener, Paul, 115

Graham, Martha, 211

Grainger, Percy, 77

Grosz, Wilhelm, 72

Grumman, Ellsworth (Mr and Mrs), 182, 183, 204, 205, 215

Grünewald, Matthias, 18, 19, 46, 105, 111, 113, 118, 160, 275

Haas, Joseph, 71, 72

Hába, Alois, 72, 73, 74

Hadley, Henry, 176

Haenni, Georges, 162, 178, 292-3

Hagen, Oscar, 82

Hallé Orchestra, 277

Hamburger Nachrichten, 159

Handel, George Frideric, 82

Harmonie der Welt, Die, see references in Chronological List of Works (p. 307)

Hartmann, Rudolf, 275

Harvard University, 13, 239-40, 241, 246

Harvard University Press, 246

Hausegger, Siegmund von, 115

Havemann, Gustav, 65, 107, 111, 114, 119, 120, 125-6, 129

Hegner, Anna, 31

Hegner, Otto, 31

Heiller, Anton, 289, 292, 293

Heinisch, Erika, 294

Heinisch, Rudolf, 89

Helmann, Ferdinand, 174

Hemingway, Louis, 196, 199, 207

Heppenstall, Rayner, 280

Herzog, Friedrich, 119, 133

Hesse, Grand Duke of, 34

Hindemith, Carl Wilhelm Paul (grandfather), 26

Hindemith, Gertrud (*née* Rottenberg), *passim*. Background and education, 25, 78; marriage, 77-8; attitude to her husband, 79-80, 132-3, 140, 169, 180-5, 187-8, 265, 281, 285-6; gives first performance of *Die Serenaden*, 80; difficulties in emigrating to USA, 178-9; graduates in

Hindemith, Gertrud—*cont.*
French at Yale, 204, 216;
widowhood and death, 294–5
Hindemith, Karl (step-uncle),
26
Hindemith, Paul, birth, 27;
education, 27–8, 31–7; first
professional engagements, 40–
1, 47; marriage, 77–8; as
teacher, 13, 87–9, 143–4,
173–4, 176–7, 189–200, 202–3,
250, 251, 270; relations with
National Socialists, 18–19,
63–4, 101–2, 105–41 *passim*,
142–3, 157, 159, 160–1, 165–7,
213–14, 242, 268–72, 278; in
Great Britain, 96–8, 115, 124,
130–1, 234, 266, 277, 279–80,
284; in Turkey, 127–9, 131–3,
135–9, 158; in USA, 154–6,
158, 164–5, 173–227, 234,
238–41, 243–5, 280–2, 285–6,
289; death, 293–4
Ideas on music and composition: 12–17, 21, 50–2, 53–4,
60, 76–7, 80, 81, 85–7, 136–9,
143–53, 205–10, 225, 235–7,
246–60, 276, 283–4, 289–91;
on *Gebrauchsmusik* (Music to
Sing and Play), 16–17, 86,
92–3, 95–6, 99, 101, 129–30,
248, 256, 261; on twelve-
tone system, 89, 127, 151–2,
290
Works: *see index references in*
Chronological List of Works
(pp. 299–308); first compositions, 33, 34, 39, 46–7; uncompleted works, 105–6, 158,
165, 167, 176; juvenile plays,
30–1, 37, 38–9, 44
Hindemith, Robert Rudolph
(father), 26–30, 37, 40, 44
Hindemith, Rudolf (brother),
27, 28, 29–30, 36–7, 43, 44,
53, 59, 65, 142–3, 214, 232

Hindemith, Sophie (*née* Warnecke, mother), 27–9, 55,
59, 77, 81, 143, 166, 213, 214,
217, 226, 232, 233–4, 235,
240–1
Hindemith, Toni (sister), 27,
28, 29–30, 37, 59, 77, 81, 214,
232
Hindemith Collection, Yale
University, 9, 165, 168, 191,
195, 196, 199, 200, 205, 206,
207, 210, 294
Hindemith Institute (Foundation), Frankfurt, 9, 44, 90,
295
*Hindemith (Paul): Die letzten
Jahre*, 282, 294
*Hindemith (Paul): Zeugnis in
Bildern*, 27, 32, 33, 35, 49,
272–3, 294
Hinks, Carroll, 215
Hitler, Adolf, 101, 102, 114,
119, 120, 122, 140, 157
Hoch Conservatorium, Frank-
furt, 32–3, 37, 40, 41, 49, 51,
57, 106
Hochschule für Musik (Staat-
liche), Berlin, 85, 87, 98, 102,
107, 109, 110, 118, 122, 124,
127, 129, 132, 135, 140, 142,
157, 158, 220, 237
Hoffmann, E. T. A., 81, 236
Hoffmann-Onegin, Lilli (One-
gin, Sigrid), 42, 44
Holl, Karl, 57
Holt, David, 196
Honegger, Arthur, 262
Hubermann, Bronislav, 90, 108
Humperdinck, Engelbert, 32
Hürlimann, Martin, 294

International Society of Con-
temporary Music, Salzburg
(ISCM), 73–4, 86, 98, 99
Ionesco, Eugène, 283
Ives, Charles, 181, 182, 192

Jacobsen, George, 195–6
Jarnach, Philipp, 72
Jöde, Fritz, 86, 92, 107, 109, 129, 206
Joio, Norman del, 190, 191
Jüdischer Kulturbund, 109–10
Judson, Arthur, 269
Juilliard School of Music, New York, 218, 289
Jürgens, Helmut, 274

Kalkmann, Franz, 26–7, 28–9, 30
Kalliwoda, Johann Wenzeslaus, 70
Kampfbund, 106–8, 114
Kaye, Ulysses, 191
Keilmannsegg, Graf von, 48–9, 54
Keiser, Reinhart, 43, 46
Keller, Dr von (German Ambassador in Turkey), 133
Kemp, Ian, 17, 100
Kepler, Johannes, 18, 19–20, 224, 273, 275–6
Kestenberg, Leo, 109
Kind, Silvia, 129
Kirkpatrick, Ralph, 182, 204, 211
Kirstein, Lincoln, 223
Kleiber, Erich, 83, 87
Klein, Fritz, 120
Klemperer, Otto, 83, 84, 87, 94, 96, 100, 109, 201, 209
Knorr, Ivan, 32–3, 36
Kokoschka, Oskar, 52, 62
Korty, Sonya, 109
Koussevitzky, Serge, 90, 96, 99, 155, 167, 175, 176, 177–8, 186, 209
Kraft durch Freude, 115
Krell, Max, 67
Krenek, Ernst, 72, 184, 193, 220
Kreutzer, Konradin, 70
Kroll Opera, Berlin, 83, 87, 94
Kulenkampff, Georg, 134, 135, 142, 166

Kulturgemeinde, 114, 119, 121, 133
Kupper, Annelies, 235
Kusche, Ludwig, 75

Lam, George, 90, 196–9, 294
Landau, Victor, 152
Landes, Maria, 232
Lauer-Kottlar, Beatrice, 76, 109
Legal, Ernst, 94
Legge, Walter, 9, 115, 273
Leigh, Walter, 87
Levine, Morris, 191, 197
Lewertoff, Else (née Thalheimer), 74, 85, 91–2, 109–10
Lewertoff, Schlomo, 110
Lewin, Frank, 191, 200
Library of Congress, Washington, 154–5, 156, 211
Lincoln Center for the Performing Arts, New York, 289
Lion, Ferdinand, 81–2, 236
Lipatti, Dinu, 233
Liszt, Franz, 42, 70
Lohmann, Carl, 210
London Symphony Orchestra, 97
Louisville Symphony Orchestra, 241
Lowe, Mrs Margret (née Thalheimer), 9, 46, 74, 174–5, 178, 187–8
Lübbecke, Fried, 45–6, 59, 64, 77, 214, 240
Lübbecke-Job, Emma, 42, 45, 50, 57, 59, 64, 74–5, 76, 99, 142, 214
Luftwaffe, 133, 135

McGregor, Willard, 206
Macleod, Joseph, 157
Machaut, Guillaume de, 158
Mahler, Gustav, 45, 46
Mahlke, Elisabeth, 237–8
Mainardi, Enrico, 135

Mallarmé, Stéphane, 211–12

Marienleben, Das, see references in Chronological List of Works (pp. 301 and 306)

Martinu, Bohislav, 93, 184

Massine, Léonide, 156, 157–8, 159–60, 165, 174, 175–6, 208

Mathis der Maler, see references in Chronological List of Works (p. 304)

Mauriac, François, 157, 159–60

Mayer, Robert, 109

Mendel, Arthur, 142, 234, 246

Mendelssohn, Arnold, 34–6, 85

Mengelberg, Willem, 38, 41–2, 44, 45, 56, 130, 142, 164, 165, 174, 269

Mersmann, Hans, 86, 109

Metropolitan Museum, New York, 226, 244

Metropolitan Opera, New York, 165

Milhaud, Darius, 9, 16, 72, 91, 92, 162, 184, 202, 286

Miller, Carl S., 9, 200, 211, 226

Mitropoulos, Dimitri, 209

Monteux, Pierre, 165

Monteverdi, Claudio, 266, 292

Mozart, Wolfgang Amadeus, 17, 70, 72, 101, 233, 241, 254

Munich Opera, 274–5, 279

Museum Concerts, Frankfurt, 38, 41–2, 56

Musik, Die, 119

Mysz-Gmeiner, Lula, 42, 44

Nabokoff, Nicholas, 165, 168, 173

National Institute of Art and Letters, 226–7

Neues vom Tage, see references in Chronological List of Works (pp. 303 and 307)

Neue Zeitung, Berlin, 237

New York City Ballet, 165, 223–4

New York Philharmonic Orchestra, 208, 289

New York Times, 238, 239

Nikisch, Artur, 71

Noss, Luther, 9, 182, 190, 196, 204, 207, 210, 216, 217, 220, 244, 246, 272, 278, 279, 280–1, 282, 286, 289, 293, 294

Noss, Mrs Osea, 9, 204, 215, 217, 263, 266, 272, 279, 280–1, 293, 294

Ohms, Elisabeth, 165

O'Meara, E. J., 206

Ormandy, Eugene, 208, 209

Parker, Horatio, 181, 182

Penzoldt, Ernst, 105

Pepping, Ernst, 87

Perrin, Maurice, 162–3

Petraschke, Richard, 59

Petrassi, Goffredo, 281

Peyre, Henri, 204, 244

Pfitzner, Hans, 71, 72, 115, 119, 120

Philadelphia Musical Academy, 215–16

Philadelphia Orchestra, 208

Piatigorsky, Gregor, 186, 234

Piston, Walter, 192

Praetorius, Ernst, 132, 136

Prechter, Else Clara, 72

Preetorius, Emil, 166

Preussner, Eberhart, 29, 33, 64, 232

Promenade Concerts, London, 97

Prussian Academy of the Arts, 87, 109

Raff, Joachim, 32

Ravel, Maurice, 72, 224

Rázonyi, Lászlo, 137

Rebner, Adolf, 31–4, 37, 40, 41, 42, 43, 45–6, 50, 60–1

Rebner Quartet, 41, 46, 57, 60–1, 65
Reger, Max, 33, 71, 269
Rehberg, Willy, 71
Reichskulturkammer, 114, 121
Reichsmusikkammer, 114, 117, 119, 122, 123, 128, 165
Reinhardt, Eugen, 28
Reinhart, Werner, 74, 80, 142, 162
Reizenstein, Franz, 9, 87, 88, 108, 110
Revue Musicale de Suisse Romande, 162, 169, 178–9, 261, 263
Rexroth, Dieter, 9
Riéder, Hélène, 162–3
Rieple, Max, 64, 72, 95
Riess, Curt, 122
Rilke, Rainer Maria, 76, 162
Robert Shaw Choral, 220
Rodzinsky, Artur, 208, 209
Rolland, Romain, 81
Ronnefeldt, Emmy, 41, 43, 44, 45, 46, 48, 50, 51, 52, 53–4, 65, 76
Ronnefeldt, Herr and Frau, 44, 47, 50, 52–3, 54, 59
Roosevelt, Franklin Delano, 219
Rosbaud, Hans, 36–7, 117, 209
Rosenberg, Alfred, 108, 114, 119, 121, 122, 133, 157
Rottenberg, Gertrud, *see* Hindemith, Gertrud
Rottenberg, Ludwig, 38, 42, 44, 45, 47, 56, 62, 67, 78, 114
Rottenberg, Frau (Gertrud Hindemith's mother), 25, 45, 78, 214, 216
Royal Philharmonic Orchestra, London, 271

Sabahattin (Turkish composer), 139
Sabata, Victor de, 157
Sacher, Paul, 127, 209, 243

Sachs, Curt, 107, 109
Sanroma, Jesus, 155, 158, 216
Sargent, Malcolm, 97
Scherchen, Hermann, 56, 73, 82, 209
Schiffer, Marcellus, 94, 265, 266
Schlemmer, Oskar, 83
Schmid-Blos, Karl, 159
Schmidt, Karl, 37, 43, 46, 59
Schmidt-Isserstedt, Hans, 224
Schnabel, Artur, 90, 96, 97, 108, 142
Schneider-Schott, Günther, 9
Scholz, Bernhard, 32, 33
Schönberg, Arnold, 14, 21, 56, 71, 72–3, 87, 89, 109, 127, 150, 159, 184, 193, 198, 220
Schott und Söhne, Mainz, 9, 25, 27, 29, 57–8, 67–8, 79, 96, 154, 166, 185, 213, 272, 277
Schott and Co. Ltd., London, 167, 185, 234
Schrade, Leo, 182, 207, 208, 244
Schreker, Franz, 45, 56, 71, 72, 87, 107, 109
Schröter, Heinz, 232
Schubert, Franz, 43, 196, 277, 283
Schüler, Johannes, 123
Schulthess, Walter, 269
Schumann, Clara, 32, 45
Schumann, Robert (Violin Concerto), 157
Schünemann, Georg, 107
Seemann, Carl, 235
Sekles, Bernhard, 35–6, 41, 50, 51, 56, 57, 106
Seligmann, Kurt, 224
Sessions, Roger, 192
Shapero, Harold, 176
Sibelius Prize, 271
Simonds, Bruce, 9, 182, 190, 204, 218, 226, 244
Simonds, Mrs Rosalind, 204, 207, 218
Sitwell, Edith, 283–4

Smith, David Stanley, 158, 181-2, 189
Sonntagsblatt Staats-Zeitung und Herold, New York, 239
Sprague Hall, New Haven, 191, 207
Stege, Fritz, 119
Stein, Fritz, 107, 114, 128, 140, 142
Steinberg, William, 278, 279
Stephan, Rudi, 56
Stern, Isaac, 218
Stig, Asger, 159
Stock, Friedrich, 174
Stone, Kurt, 9, 213, 280, 286, 308
Stramm, August, 63
Straumann, Heinrich, 241
Strauss, Pauline, 285
Strauss, Richard, 33, 37-8, 42, 52, 56, 71, 72, 75, 114, 115, 117, 119, 120, 123, 128, 285
Stravinsky, Igor, 14, 15, 72, 106, 150, 158, 184, 201, 202, 220, 282, 285
Strecker, Hugo, 167, 170, 185
Strecker, Ludwig (father), 58
Strecker, Ludwig (son), 58, 81, 102, 111, 118, 133, 157, 163, 166, 232, 239, 274, 275, 277, 288
Strecker, Willy, 58-9, 167, 179, 213, 238, 277; friendship with Hindemith, 12, 58-9, 120, 134, 161, 163, 178, 240; as publisher of his works, 58, 67-8, 85-6, 96, 234; promotional activities, 75, 83-4, 90, 96-7, 131, 133-4, 220-1; relations with National Socialists, 106, 108, 111, 115-16, 117-18, 119-20, 126-7, 132-3, 140, 142, 159, 166, 214; views on Hindemith's works, 60, 77, 105, 111-13, 142, 164, 224, 274, 275

Strobel, Heinrich, 17
Strunk, Oliver, 156, 157
Sutter, Otto Ernst, 76
Svedlund, Helga, 224
Szantho, Enid, 218
Szell, George, 292
Szenkar, Eugen, 56

Tanglewood (Berkshire Music Center), 167-8, 176-8, 192, 202-3, 207
Tchaikovsky, Peter Ilyich, 42, 196
Tchelichev, Pavel, 160
Teatro San Carlo, Naples, 265
Thalheimer sisters, *see* Lewertoff, Else; Lowe, Margret
Thoburn, Crawford R., 168-9
Tietjen, Heinz, 166
Toch, Ernst, 36
Tovey, Donald, 77, 142
Trautwein, Dr (inventor of the trautonium), 108
Tristan und Isolde (Wagner), 62, 147, 150

UNESCO (United Nations Educational, Scientific and Cultural Organisation), 243, 261
Ustinov, Peter, 9, 283

Verdi, Giuseppe, 196
Verein für Theater- und Musik-kultur, Frankfurt, 57
Vienna Philharmonic Orchestra, 273, 292, 293
Vinitsky, Ruth, 191-2
Voigt, Ernest R., 154-5, 167-8, 173, 186
Volk, Arno, 9
Völkischer Beobachter, 114, 119, 122

Wagner, Richard, 57, 61, 62, 121, 147, 150, 175, 254, 274

Wagner, Wieland, 263
Wagner, Wolfgang, 263
Walter, Bruno, 56, 87
Waltershausen, Hermann, 45
Walton, William, 9, 97–8, 292
Weber, Carl Maria von, 174, 175–6
Weber, Gustav, 38
Webern, Anton, 57, 72–3
Weigel, Hans, 265
Weill, Kurt, 81, 94, 96, 184, 220
Weinheber, Josef, 279
Wells College, 165, 168, 173–4, 176
Whitman, Walt, 60, 219
Wilder, Isabel, 286
Wilder, Thornton, 9, 282–3, 286–7, 289
Winternitz, Emanuel, 9, 226, 244
Wolfsthal, Josef, 98, 108
Wood, Henry, 97, 98, 100
Woolsey Hall, New Haven, 204

Wyner, Yehudi, *picture facing* 160, 191

Yale University, New Haven (*see also* Hindemith Collection, Yale University), 13, 158, 174, 179–84, 189–227 *passim*, 239, 241–2, 243–5, 262, 271, 278, 279, 280–1, 282, 289, 294
Yale University Press, 258

Zeitschrift für Musik, 63, 119
Zermatten, Maurice, 169, 178, 263, 292
Zorina, Vera, 212
Zuckmayer, Carl, 63, 132, 163, 287
Zuckmayer, Eduard, 132, 135
Zurich Opera, 158–9, 164, 166, 224
Zurich University, 241–2, 265, 271, 273, 278